The "Stench" of Politics

The "Stench" of Politics

Polarization and Worldview on the Supreme Court

Joseph Russomanno
Foreword by Rodney A. Smolla

LEXINGTON BOOKS
Lanham • Boulder • New York • London

Published by Lexington Books
An imprint of The Rowman & Littlefield Publishing Group, Inc.
4501 Forbes Boulevard, Suite 200, Lanham, Maryland 20706

www.rowman.com

86-90 Paul Street, London EC2A 4NE

Copyright © 2023 by The Rowman & Littlefield Publishing Group, Inc.

British Library Cataloguing in Publication Information Available

Library of Congress Cataloging-in-Publication Data Available

ISBN 978-1-66692-393-3 (cloth)
ISBN 978-1-66692-395-7 (pbk.)
ISBN 978-1-66692-394-0 (electronic)

Dedicated to the scholars and journalists on whose shoulders this work stands.

"Will this institution survive the stench that this creates in the public perception that the Constitution and its reading are just political acts?"

—Justice Sonia Sotomayor
December 1, 2021
Dobbs v. Jackson Women's Health Organization, oral argument
(expressing concern that the case was brought to the
U.S. Supreme Court to achieve a political goal)

Contents

Foreword

By Rodney A. Smolla

It was for many the summer of their discontent.

In the climactic final weeks of the 2021–2022 United States Supreme Court term, the Court eliminated the constitutional right to abortion, emaciated the capacity of cities to regulate the carrying of firearms, and stripped the Environmental Protection Agency of any authority to promulgate rules calculated to mitigate the climate change crisis by shifting energy production in the United States away from sources emitting carbon dioxide.

The themes explored in this book, dealing with the role of the Supreme Court in the polarization of American politics, could not, when considered against the backdrop of the Supreme Court's decisions in the summer of 2022, be more important, or more timely.

On the surface, decisions involving abortion, guns, and clean air might seem topically disconnected. But considered more deeply for the style of their jurisprudence, they are all of a piece, and they signal a sea change in the Court's prevailing approach to constitutional and statutory interpretation.

The most dramatic exemplar was *Dobbs v. Jackson Women's Health Organization*, in which the Court overruled *Roe v. Wade*, the landmark 1973 decision establishing a woman's constitutional right to an abortion prior to fetal viability. The conservative majority in *Dobbs* grounded its opinion almost entirely in what it perceived as the lack of any textual or historic support for the recognition of an abortion right. The Court's opinion, written by Justice Samuel Alito, observed that the "Constitution makes no reference to abortion, and no such right is implicitly protected by any constitutional provision, including the one on which the defenders of *Roe* and *Casey* now chiefly rely—the Due Process Clause of the Fourteenth Amendment." Emphasizing the lack of historical support for an abortion right, the Court stated that the Due Process Clause "has been held to guarantee some rights that are not mentioned in the Constitution, but any such right must be 'deeply rooted in this Nation's history and tradition' and 'implicit in the concept of ordered liberty.'" The Court held that the right to abortion could not be fit within the category of rights deeply rooted in the nation's history, reasoning that "[u]ntil the latter part of the 20th century, such a right was entirely unknown in American law."

History also dominated the Supreme Court's analysis in its landmark 2022 decision interpreting the Second Amendment right to keep and bear arms, *New York State Rifle & Pistol Association, Inc. v. Bruen*, written by Justice Clarence Thomas. The case was the most important Second Amendment controversy to reach the Supreme Court since its landmark 2008 ruling in *District of Columbia v. Heller*, which held that the Second Amendment was not a mere collective right protecting state militias but was rather an individual right to possess firearms for self-defense. *Heller* was followed in 2010 by *McDonald v. City of Chicago*, holding that the right to bear arms was a fundamental right binding on the states through incorporation in the Fourteenth Amendment.

New York State Rifle extended the right to bear arms outside the home, into the general spaces of society, holding that New York could not prevent carrying firearms outside the home, and into the streets of New York. Critically, the Court in *New York State Rifle* held that it would not adopt the typical balancing of ends and means that is common in many areas of modern constitutional law. Tests such as the "strict scrutiny" or "intermediate scrutiny" test have emerged across the expanse of modern constitutional law to provide nuanced tools for judicial review of legislation. But in *New York State Rifle* the Court rejected application of such tests in the Second Amendment context, choosing instead to ground Second Amendment analysis entirely in history. "To justify its regulation," the Court held, "the government may not simply posit that the regulation promotes an important interest." Instead, the Court explained, "the government must demonstrate that the regulation is consistent with this Nation's historical tradition of firearm regulation." For the Court, it was all about how guns were regulated when the nation was formed after the Revolution, or reformed, after the Civil War. As the Court put it: "Only if a firearm regulation is consistent with this Nation's historical tradition may a court conclude that the individual's conduct falls outside the Second Amendment's 'unqualified command.'"

The 2022 decisions on abortion and guns evidenced a deep-seated skepticism by the Court's conservative majority of any notion that the meaning of the Constitution should in any sense evolve over time. This view stands in stark contrast with Justice Kennedy's opinion for the Court in its landmark 2015 same-sex marriage decision, *Obergefell v. Hodges*. The jurisprudential centerpiece of *Obergefell* was the insight that the "nature of injustice is that we may not always see it in our own times." Justice Kennedy's opinion in

Obergefell imagined a Constitution that was not static but dynamic. Moreover, the decision in *Obergefell* argued that this was *not* turning our modern backs on the founding generations, but rather carrying out the ongoing constitutional experiment *in the manner that the framers intended*. As the Court explained, the "generations that wrote and ratified the Bill of Rights and the Fourteenth Amendment did not presume to know the extent of freedom in all of its dimensions, and so they entrusted to future generations a charter protecting the right of all persons to enjoy liberty as we learn its meaning."

This same theme, over how the Supreme Court should contend with history, and the extent to which it should embrace a jurisprudence that anticipates evolution, was also prominent in the Court's blockbuster 2022 decision interpreting the Clean Air Act, *West Virginia v. Environmental Protection Agency*. The cased posed the question of whether the Environmental Protection Authority possessed the statutory authority to promulgate rules that would move the United States away from sources of energy production that contribute to global warming, and toward alternative energy sources that are less damaging to the global climate. Announcing what was arguably a new rule of administrative law and statutory construction, coined "the major questions doctrine," the Court held that administrative agencies could not embark on such major changes in public policy unless clearly authorized to do so by Congress.

In a dissenting opinion written by Justice Elena Kagan and joined by her then two remaining liberal colleagues, Justices Sonia Sotomayor and Stephen Breyer, Justice Kagan addressed head-on the importance of a more flexible jurisprudence that allows for dynamic evolution. Justice Kagan argued that in modern times Congress delegates major decisions to administrative agencies all the time, and all for good reason. To begin, she argued, members of Congress often know they lack the scientific or technical expertise to regulate in detail, and so intentionally delegate broad authority to agencies with greater expertise. All Congress can sensibly hope to do, Justice Kagan argued, is to express to agencies an "overall direction." Through these overall directions expressed over time, Justice Kagan argued, "the administrative delegations Congress has made have helped to build a modern Nation." Citing numerous examples, Justice Kagan argued that broad delegations were essential to augment legislation:

Congress wanted fewer workers killed in industrial accidents. It wanted to prevent plane crashes and reduce the deadliness of car wrecks. It wanted to ensure that consumer products didn't catch fire. It wanted to stop the routine adulteration of food and improve the safety and efficacy of medications. And it wanted cleaner air and water. If an American could go back in time, she might be astonished by how much progress has occurred in all those areas. It didn't happen through legislation alone. It happened because Congress gave broad-ranging powers to administrative agencies, and those agencies then filled in—rule by rule by rule—Congress's policy outlines.[1]

Yet notwithstanding the power of these arguments, Justice Kagan's position did not prevail.

As you contemplate the discussions in the chapters of this book that follow, I urge you to bear in mind, as you consider the dichotomy between static and dynamic approaches to the role of the Supreme Court, a related dichotomy, phrased in slightly different vocabulary. Call it the distinction between the "conception" and the "concept."

Those who wrote the Constitution, or those who wrote the Clean Air Act, surely had their internal mental *conceptions* of how the words they wrote would be applied. In the aftermath of the Civil War, those who wrote the Fourteenth Amendment's guarantee of "equal protection of the laws" had no *conception* that it would include equal protection for women, let alone persons identifying as LGBTQ+, elements of identity not even in their vocabulary. But the *concept* they enacted, a concept of equal protection, left room for subsequent generations to see what those original authors could not. To channel the amazing grace of *Obergefell*—we once were blind but now we see.

Conservative Justices are capable of distinguishing between the conception and the concept. Justice Neil Gorsuch, writing for the Court in 2020 in *Bostock v. Clayton County*, saw that when it prohibited discrimination on the basis of sex in enacting the Civil Rights Act of 1964, Congress necessarily prohibited discrimination on the basis of sexual orientation. It may not have been within the *conception* of legislators in 1964 that they were protecting gays, lesbians, or transgender persons from employment discrimination. But the *concept* those members of Congress enacted, a ban on discrimination on the basis of sex, automatically included a ban on discrimination on the basis of sexuality, because all sexual orientation discrimination is necessarily sex discrimination. If two employees, one who is female and the other who is male, are each married to a male, and an employer fires the male married to a male but not the female married to a male, it is by definition the male gender of the fired employee that got him fired. In 1964 members of Congress may not have seen this, but in 2020 Justice Gorsuch and a majority of the Court did. The concept trumped the conception.

As you ponder concepts and conceptions, please enjoy the constitutional history and analysis in the chapters that follow for what they reveal of the path of the Supreme Court in our increasingly partisan and perilous times.

NOTE

1. *West Virginia v. EPA*, 142 S. Ct. 2587, 2643 (2022) (Kagan, J., dissenting).

Introduction

"Let's Talk About How Truly Bizarre Our Supreme Court Is." That was the title of an episode of Ezra Klein's *New York Times* podcast in early 2022. Though the course had been previously charted, and in a sort of self-fulfilling prophesy, the U.S. Supreme Court proceeded to demonstrate just how bizarre it could be.[1] An unprecedented leak. Reinterpreting parts of the U.S. Constitution. Revoking a constitutionally based individual right and decades of precedent with a single ruling.[2] The justice who authored that opinion subsequently "gloating"[3] about it while criticizing a "growing hostility to religion."[4] A Chief Justice losing his ability to lead and sway votes.[5] And more.

If ever a historical incident peeled back the layers of the character of a nation and its institutions, it was the abortion rights case of 2022. While both a leaked Supreme Court draft opinion and the official opinion released nearly two months later thrust the nation into an upheaval of debate, analysis, and furor,[6] it also revealed and solidly confirmed much about the Court itself.[7]

Already viewed by many as no longer independent or justice-seeking,[8] the Court's majority—a supermajority,[9] according to many—clearly and firmly moved the institution into the same realm as the body of elected officials who convene across First Avenue in the nation's capital, overwhelmingly political.[10] Modeling Congress and other political institutions by adopting the blatantly political practice of the leak, the unprecedented act sealed that deal.[11] Providing the draft to achieve some political end did nothing to refute the notion that an institution once respected for its independence and ideological neutrality had now spiraled into a political abyss.[12] The Court's politicization threatens not only the institution itself, but also the nation.[13]

In his book, *On Tyranny*, Yale historian Timothy Snyder highlights the need to defend institutions as integral to preserving decency and democracy. "We tend to assume that institutions will automatically maintain themselves against even the most direct attacks," he writes.[14] The U.S. Supreme Court is under attack domestically. The conservative-led assault is designed not so much to destroy the institution, but instead to strip it of its traditional properties, including its objectivity in interpreting and applying the U.S. Constitution.[15] Rather than a balanced, fair approach, the Court's authority has become one-sided. The result is an institution where preserving "equal justice under law" is now merely pretense, little more than the inscription on its building.

As much as the Court impacts the lives of every American,[16] it is a product of the nation—a politicized, polarized, and tribalized nation. Contrary to popular belief and conventional wisdom, and as noted above, the Court is no longer an independent, apolitical institution.[17] Instead, its decisions are now fueled by the same kinds of ideological party politics found in many other government institutions. Though many have tried, including its own members, simply declaring the Court as nonpolitical—itself a political act—does not make it so. Especially given its current composition, the Court is well down the path of narrowing rights and minimizing opportunities for justice. Although its nine members have very similar kinds of education and training, they possess different perspectives, ideologies, and worldviews. The latter factor, in fact, is the key—and the key to this analysis.

As summer turned to fall in 2021, some members of the U.S. Supreme Court undertook an effort to rehabilitate their institution's image. Not unlike what occurred during the aftermath of *Bush v. Gore*[18] in late 2000—when a sharply divided Court stopped Florida's vote recount, essentially declaring George W. Bush the winner of that year's presidential election—concern permeated the nation that the credibility of its highest court had been tarnished. Justice Stephen Breyer, for example—the author of one of four separate dissenting opinions in that 2000 case—insisted then that the divisions exposed were due to neither ideology nor politics, but instead occurred simply because of competing legal views.[19]

At the dawn of a new term more than two decades later, several members of the Court again attempted to rehabilitate their institution's image. Its reputation was eroding in the eyes of many, and included their belief that the Court is politicized.[20] In part, that perception stemmed from another split decision, one that came to the Court initially on its emergency "shadow docket," the execution of which is itself a divisive process.[21] The decision upheld a Texas law that severely restricted access to abortions.[22] As occurred in the aftermath of *Bush v. Gore,* the justices insisted that they and their colleagues follow the law, not their personal beliefs.[23] They included Justice Breyer again,[24] and also Justices Clarence Thomas,[25] Samuel Alito,[26] and the Court's newest member at that time, Justice Amy Coney Barrett.[27] In effect, their pleas were made to deny that polarization, so prevalent throughout the country, had also infected the Court. The "stench" of politics referred to by Justice Sonia Sotomayor later that year was already a concern.[28]

Less than one week after Justice Sotomayor's oral argument bombshell in December 2021,[29] the Presidential Commission on the Supreme Court of the United States issued its final report.[30] While refraining from specific recommendations, the Commission—whose establishment reflected the rising concerns about the Court—thoroughly analyzed the institution within contemporary America. On multiple occasions, for example, the report cited America's polarization[31] and "how the deeply divided nature of our polity affects debates over the Court,"[32] with the Court "at the center of escalating partisanship."[33] A disconnect between citizens and the Court was reflected in polling conducted in mid-July 2022. Of all respondents, 43 percent had "hardly any" confidence in the Court, a dramatic increase from only three months beforehand.[34] As the gulf between rulings and the views of many Americans grew, Justice Elena Kagan forthrightly acknowledged the Court's predicament after the conclusion of the tumultuous 2021–2022 term: "[I]f, over time, the court loses all connection with the public and the public sentiment, that's a dangerous thing for democracy."[35]

Traditionally, the Court and its defenders have maintained that its members and procedures are above politics.[36] Different opinions about cases, they say, stem from jurisprudential differences. Adam Cohen disagrees: "This is a fairy tale America likes to tell itself."[37] If it was true, he adds—if justices were technocrats—"presidents filling a Court vacancy would appoint the best legal scholars and judges without considering their politics."[38] Instead, great pains are now taken to ensure the proper ideological fit between a nominee and a presidential administration's political viewpoint, with desired judicial outcomes—and the molding of both law and nation—being the ultimate goal.[39] Accepting the notion that those selected to serve have political opinions, Cohen asks, "Are we really to believe nominees suddenly abandon their views when they get to the Court?"[40]

Over its past half-century, the Court has opened itself to criticism. "For five decades," writes Cohen, "the Court has, with striking regularity, sided with the rich and powerful against the poor and weak, in virtually every area of law."[41] The desire to facilitate a more equal and inclusive society by the Warren Court of the 1950s and 1960s has not only ceased, but according to Cohen, "it has been sharply reversed."[42] Critics of the current Court also include two Harvard law professors. First, Charles Fried writes that the Court's handling of key issues "has undermined or overturned precedents that embodied longstanding and difficult compromise settlements of sharply opposed interests and principles."[43] Second, according to Nikolas Bowie, "the Court has wielded an antidemocratic influence on American law."[44]

It was against this backdrop in 2021 when the Court's public credibility plummeted, and when some of its members again addressed their institution's tarnished image and the public's diminished trust that was subsequently fueled by ongoing developments.[45] At that time, Americans' opinions of the Court were the most negative that Gallup public opinion polls had measured in more than twenty years, with more people than ever believing the Court is too conservative.[46] Another poll revealed that more than 60 percent of respondents believe the Supreme Court bases its decisions more on the justices' political views than on the Constitution and law.[47] It appeared that America's Supreme Court no longer reflected America.[48]

Barely into the next year, two prominent legal scholars admitted they had lost faith in the Court, writing that it is "likely to do more harm than good to democracy."[49] As the 2021–2022 term neared conclusion, the downward trajectory in public confidence in the Court reached a new low.[50] Absent confidence in its decisions and with no means to enforce them, the Court—and the nation—potentially veer into crisis mode.[51] Doubt and distrust stem largely from the perception that the current Court is politicized. That perception is now reality.

It is suggested here that the views held by Supreme Court justices—and they do have them—reflect more than politics or ideology.[52] Importantly, a primary factor is worldview—an orienting framework possessed by everyone that governs how the world and its phenomena are perceived, and how each of us reacts to them. As described in pages that follow, a specific worldview is both hardwired and learned, and profoundly explains not just how we sense the world, but also what we believe about it. Worldview influences not only our politics, but also decisions about where we live, what restaurants we frequent, the cars we buy, the TV shows we watch, the kind of coffee[53] and beer[54] we drink and much more.[55] When we sometimes offhandedly wonder if others are "living in a different world," the answer may be a resounding, "Yes!"—at least to the extent that their worldview differs so much from our own.

In this respect, Supreme Court justices are no different from other Americans, falling into one of two worldview categories, fixed or fluid.[56] Just as worldview helps to explain how people think and behave, it can also explain how and why particular justices approach their work as they do—for example, how they read and interpret the U.S. Constitution. While the justices may, in fact, get along personally and work with respect and civility, their worldviews clash. And that is at the heart of the rancorous split decisions on so many of the Court's contentious cases.

This book analyzes polarization on, and the politicization of, the Court through the lens of worldview, suggesting that the characteristics of the political divide that afflicts the nation at large can also be applied to the Court and its members. While recognizing that the Supreme Court is divided is nothing new,[57] exploring it specifically through the analytical lens of worldview is unique. To understand its rulings, understanding the Court is necessary. That is the goal of this book—viewing the Court within the context of a divided nation.

The factors at the root of the Court's split can be elusive. To consider them, part 1 examines our divided worlds, including the Supreme Court. Chapter 1 first examines the dynamics of contemporary American polarization. This includes assessments of tribalism, nature vs. nurture, how views toward science and other information contribute to polarization, and the critical component in this analysis, worldview. In chapter 2, those dynamics are applied to the Supreme Court. This includes examining the all-important issue of how justices choose to read and interpret a variety of texts, especially the U.S. Constitution. Traditionally, a choice is made between two often-polarizing schools of thought,[58] originalism and living constitutionalism—respectively, whether the Constitution should be read and applied strictly how it is believed its authors originally intended, or instead believing that contemporary circumstances should also be considered, with conclusions often reached that transcend literal interpretations of the words. As constitutional law scholar Erwin Chemerinsky writes, "There are two very different constitutional visions. . . . All [justices] are interpreting the same constitutional text. Their divergence is a result of their markedly different political ideologies and worldviews."[59]

The dichotomy between originalism and living constitutionalism remarkably parallels worldview and its two categories, fixed and fluid. By coupling constitutional approach with worldview as an analytical tool—that is, by creating the categories of "fixed-originalist" and "fluid-living constitutionalist"—the core thinking behind many of the Court's rulings is revealed, in turn demonstrating its divisions. The rubber meets the road in part 2 where these concepts are applied directly in chapters 3, 4, 5, and 6. Selected Supreme Court rulings across four politically charged issues are examined through worldview. In part 3, the political principles and polarizing processes enveloping the Court are addressed in the concluding chapter, chapter 7.

What clearly emerges is a U.S. Supreme Court that is now palpably polarized and politicized, so divided that the members of each of its factions seem to live in opposite worlds. Some tell us this is nothing new, nor is having justices who carry out agendas.[60] What *is* new, however, is an institution now broken by the execution of a political agenda by a conservative/originalist/ fixed worldview supermajority that is determined not only to limit rights and justice for all—and even, some say, to oppress[61]—but also to rescind previously granted, constitutionally based rights by overturning long-established precedents.[62]

NOTES

1. See Ezra Klein, "Dobbs Is Not the Only Reason to Question the Legitimacy of the Supreme Court," *New York Times*, June 30, 2022, https://www.nytimes.com /2022/06/30/opinion/dobbs-mcconnell-supreme-court.html ("The Supreme Court is a strange institution").

2. See Jessica Levinson, "A Bombshell Term at the Supreme Court Will Scar America for Decades," MSNBC, July, 8, 2022, https://www.msnbc.com/opinion/ msnbc-opinion/how-supreme-court-term-will-scar-america-decades-n1296909 ("It turns out that all of the hyperbolic cliches about this Supreme Court term being a 'blockbuster' that would be full of 'bombshell' decisions were actually accurate—and perhaps even understatements").

3. Laura Bassett, "Samuel Alito Gloats About Abortion Ruling, Says Boris John-son 'Paid the Price' for Condemning It," *Jezebel*, July 28, 2022, https://jezebel.com /samuel-alito-gloats-about-abortion-ruling-says-boris-j-1849345843/amp. See also Ariane de Vogue, "Samuel Alito Mocks Foreign Critics of Repealing *Roe v. Wade* in Rome Speech on Religious Liberty," CNN, July 29, 2022, https://amp.cnn.com/ cnn/2022/07/28/politics/samuel-alito-religious-liberty-notre-dame-rome/index.html.

4. Samuel Alito, "Keynote Address," 2022 Religious Liberty Summit, Rome, July 21, 2022, https://www.youtube.com/watch?v=uci4uni608E&t=826s, audio 13:40.

5. See, for example, Joan Biskupic, "The Inside Story of How John Roberts Failed to Save Abortion Rights," CNN, July 26, 2022, https://www.cnn.com/2022/07/26/ politics/supreme-court-john-roberts-abortion-dobbs/index.html ("Chief Justice John Roberts privately lobbied fellow conservatives to save the constitutional right to abor-tion down to the bitter end, but May's unprecedented leak of a draft opinion reversing Roe v. Wade made the effort all but impossible").

6. See, for example, Peter Baker, "Battle Over Abortion Threatens to Deepen America's Divide," *New York Times,* May 6, 2022, http://www.nytimes.com/2022 /05/06/us/politics/abortion-rights-supreme-court-roe-v-wade.html. See also Lillian Boyd, Stacey Barchenger, and Ray Stern, "Court Protest Boils Over in Phoenix," *Arizona Republic*, June 26, 2022, A1; Ellie Silverman, "Outside of Kavanaugh's Home, a Neighbor Rallies for Abortion Rights," *Washington Post*, May 7, 2022, https: //www.washingtonpost.com/dc-md-va/2022/05/07/wooten-holway-protest-justice -kavanaugh-neighbor/.

7. See, for example, Erwin Chemerinsky, "The Brazenly Political Supreme Court Shows It Will Strike Down Abortion Rights," *Los Angeles Times*, May 2, 2022, https: //www.latimes.com/opinion/story/2022-05-02/roe-wade-overruled-supreme-court -politico-draft-opinion (calling the leaked opinion "right-wing Republican politics masquerading as law").

8. See, for example, Adam Liptak, "A Supreme Court in Disarray an Extraordinary Breach," *New York Times,* May 3, 2022, https://www.nytimes.com/2022/05/03/us/ politics/supreme-court-leak-roe-v-wade-abortion.html (writing of the Court's reputa-tion, "much of the nation [is] persuaded that it is little different from the political branches of the government").

9. See, for example, Ariane de Vogue, "The Year Supreme Court Conservatives Made Their Mark," CNN, December 28, 2021, https://www.cnn.com/2021/12/28/politics/the-year-supreme-court-conservatives-made-their-mark/index.html (reporting on the newly solidified 6–3 conservative majority that can move forward with an agenda even when Chief Justice John Roberts is reluctant to do so). See also Jesse Wegman, "Justice Thomas Should Take a Long Look in the Mirror," *New York Times,* May 15, 2022, https://www.nytimes.com/2022/05/15/opinion/clarence-thomas-supreme-court.html (writing of "Senate Republicans' outrageous engineering of the court's current right-wing supermajority").

10. See Shawn Huber and Michael Wines, "Leak Heightens the Perception of a Politicized Supreme Court," *New York Times*, May 4, 2022, https://www.nytimes.com/2022/05/04/us/supreme-court-approval-rating-roe-v-wade.html (the leak "caused many Americans to express doubts about whether the justices are guided by the law rather than by their political beliefs"). See also Jennifer Rubin, "The Supreme Court's Religion-Driven Mission Sets Off a Firestorm," *Washington Post*, May 3, 2022, https://www.washingtonpost.com/opinions/2022/05/03/supreme-court-alito-roe-wade-ruling/:

> The leak . . . is further evidence that the court has ceased to act like a court and now conducts itself like a partisan operation seeking to manipulate public opinion . . . [W]hen a court decides to adopt a partisan agenda of one party grounded in values the majority of the country does not hold, it risks revealing itself as a theocratic, agenda-driven body.

11. See Calvin Woodward and Hannah Fingerhut, "Supreme Court Leak Further Erodes Trust in Government," Associated Press, May 8, 2022, https://www.pbs.org/newshour/amp/nation/supreme-court-leak-further-erodes-public-trust-in-government (describing the leak as "an episode that has deepened suspicions that the high court, for all its decorum, is populated by politicians in robes"). See also Christian Farias, "Samuel Alito's Roe Message Is Clear: This Supreme Court Is Ready to Burn It All Down," *Vanity Fair*, May 3, 2022, https://www.vanityfair.com/news/2022/05/samuel-alitos-roe-message-is-clear (writing that the May 2022 leak was "confirmation that the Republican-captured Supreme Court is a political institution that responds to the vicissitudes of the electorate").

12. See Adam Liptak, "A Leaky Supreme Court Starts to Resemble Other Branches," *New York Times,* May 11, 2022, https://www.nytimes.com/2022/05/11/us/supreme-court-leak-roe-wade.html. "[The Court] looks sparsely different from the other branches: Rival factions leak and spin sensitive information in the hope of gaining political advantage, at the cost of intense scrutiny of internal operations and questions about whether its decisions are the product of reason or power." See also Liptak, "A Supreme Court in Disarray After an Extraordinary Breach" ("Only a move as extraordinary as eliminating a constitutional right in place for half a century could transform the court into an institution like any other in Washington where rival factions disclose secrets in the hope of obtaining advantage").

13. See Ariana de Vogue, "Justices Worry About the Future of the Supreme Court— and Point Fingers as to Who's to Blame," CNN, July 29, 2022, https://www.cnn.com/2022/07/29/politics/supreme-court-kagan-sotomayor-barrett-roberts-thomas/index

.html (writing of justices "sending out flares expressing concern not only for the future of the Supreme Court but the country as a whole").

14. Timothy Snyder, *On Tyranny: Twenty Lessons from the Twentieth Century* (New York: Crown, 2017), 14. See also Masha Gessen, *Surviving Autocracy* (New York: Riverhead Books, 2020), 78 (noting that because of their inherent weaknesses and fallibility, institutions have not, and will not, save us).

15. See Adam Serwer, "The Constitution Is Whatever the Right Wing Says It Is," *Atlantic*, June 25, 2022, https://www.theatlantic.com/ideas/archive/2022/06/roe-overturned-supreme-court-samuel-alito-opinion/661386/ ("the Supreme Court has become an institution whose primary role is to force a right-wing vision of American society on the rest of the country").

16. See, for example, Tierney Sneed and Lauren Fox, "Takeaways from Ketanji Brown Jackson's First Day of Supreme Court Confirmation Hearings," CNN, March 21, 2022, https://www.cnn.com/2022/03/21/politics/ketanji-brown-jackson-hearing-monday-takeaways/index.html (quoting Sen. Patrick Leahy: "The decisions made in our courts—and ultimately in the Supreme Court—affect the daily lives of each one of us").

17. See, for example, Henry Olson, "Republicans Are Right to Oppose Ketanji Brown Jackson," *Washington Post*, March 21, 2022, https://www.washingtonpost.com/opinions/2022/03/21/republicans-are-right-to-oppose-ketanji-brown-jackson-supreme-court-nominee-confirmation-hearings/ ("It's simply a matter of fact that the Supreme Court is a political football . . . It should be clear that this politicization is bad for the court and the country. But this is simply another fault line in our divisive and corrosive political wars").

18. 531 U.S. 98 (2000).

19. Tony Mauro, "High Court Justices Take Bush v. Gore for a Spin," *Recorder*, February 21, 2001, http://academic.brooklyn.cuny.edu/history/johnson/mauro.htm.

20. See, for example, Jeffrey M. Jones, "Approval of U.S. Supreme Court Down to 40%, a New Low," Gallup.com, September 23, 2021, https://news.gallup.com/poll/354908/approval-supreme-court-down-new-low.aspx.

21. See, for example, Stephen I. Vladeck, "Roberts Has Lost Control of the Supreme Court," *New York Times*, April 13, 2022, https://www.nytimes.com/2022/04/13/opinion/john-roberts-supreme-court.html (writing that the unsigned, unexplained shadow docket decisions lack principle and thus call the Court's credibility into question).

22. *Whole Woman's Health v. Jackson*, 141 S. Ct. 2494, 2498 (2021). See also *Whole Woman's Health v. Jackson*, 632 S.W. 3d 569 (Tex. S. Ct. 2022) (Texas Supreme Court effectively shutting down any federal challenge to the state's law restricting abortions after six weeks of pregnancy).

23. See Jill Abramson, "This Justice Is Taking Over the Supreme Court, and He Won't Be Alone," *New York Times*, October 15, 2021, https://www.nytimes.com/2021/10/15/opinion/clarence-thomas-supreme-court.amp.html.

24. See Ariane de Vogue, "Breyer Defends State of Supreme Court in Interview with CNN's Fareed Zakaria," CNN, September 19, 2021, https://www.cnn.com/2021/09/19/politics/breyer-fareed-zakaria-gps/index.html ("There are many jurisprudential

differences," Breyer said. "It isn't really right to say that it's political in the ordinary sense of politics"). See also Stephen Breyer, *The Authority of the Court and the Peril of Politics* (Cambridge: Harvard University Press, 2021), 54 ("[A] judge naturally decides a case in the way that he or she believes the law demands. It is a judge's sworn duty to be impartial").

25. Mike Berardino and Ann E. Marimow, "Justice Thomas Defends the Supreme Court's Independence and Warns of 'Destroying Our Institutions,'" *Washington Post*, September 16, 2021, https://www.washingtonpost.com/politics/courts_law/justice -clarence-thomas/2021/09/16/d2ddc1ba-1714-11ec-a5e5-ceecb895922f_story.html. See also Martin Pengelly, "Clarence Thomas: Supreme Court Could Be 'Compromised' by Politics," *Guardian*, March 12, 2022, https://www.theguardian.com/us -news/2022/mar/12/clarence-thomas-supreme-court-conservative-politics (illustrating that Thomas's image building was ongoing).

26. Josh Gerstein, "Alito Speaks Out on Texas Abortion Case and 'Shadow Docket,'" *Politico*, September 30, 2021, https://www.politico.com/news/2021/09/30/ alito-on-texas-abortion-case-shadow-docket-514828.

27. Chandelis Dunster, "Justice Amy Coney Barrett Says Supreme Court Is 'Not a Bunch of Partisan Hacks,'" CNN, September 13, 2021, https://www.cnn.com/2021 /09/13/politics/amy-coney-barrett-supreme-court-not-partisan/index.html ("'My goal today is to convince you that the court is not comprised of a bunch of partisan hacks,' Justice Barrett said at the McConnell Center, named after the U.S. Senator who engineered her confirmation process"). See also Adam Liptak, "Justices Sotomayor and Barrett Say the Supreme Court Remains Collegial," *New York Times*, July 28, 2022, https://www.nytimes.com/2022/07/28/us/supreme-court-sotomayor-barrett. html (reporting on a joint interview recorded in May 2022).

28. Transcript of Oral Argument, 15:3–6, *Dobbs v. Jackson Women's Health Organization*, 142 S. Ct. 2228 (2022), December 1, 2021 ("Will this institution survive the stench that this creates in the public perception that the Constitution and its reading are just political acts?").

29. Ibid.

30. Presidential Commission on the Supreme Court of the United States, December 7, 2021, https://www.whitehouse.gov/wp-content/uploads/2021/12/SCOTUS-Report -Final-12.8.21-1.pdf.

31. See, for example, Ibid., 19 ("acute polarization is likely to continue to affect the debate over the Court's role in the constitutional system, and to perpetuate partisan conflict over nominees to the Court").

32. Ibid.

33. Ibid.

34. Jessica Gresko and Emily Swanson, "AP-NORC Poll: Two-Thirds in US Favor Term Limits for Justices," AP, July 25, 2022, https://apnews.com/article/abortion -ketanji-brown-jackson-us-supreme-court-government-and-politics-only-on-ap-8adc 9a08c9e8001c8ef0455906542a60.

35. Nick Ehli and Robert Barnes, "Kagan Says Questions of Legitimacy Risky for Supreme Court," *Washington Post*, July 21, 2022, https://www.washingtonpost .com/politics/2022/07/21/elena-kagan-supreme-court-legitimacy/. See also Charles

Franklin, "New Marquette Law School Poll National Survey Finds Approval of the Supreme Court at New Lows, with Strong Partisan Differences Over Abortion and Gun Rights," Marquette University Law, July 20, 2022, https://law.marquette.edu/poll/2022/07/20/mlspsc09-court-press-release (showing that in less than two years, Americans' approval of the Court fell from 66 to 38 percent).

36. See, for example, Pete Williams, "Supreme Court Chief Justice Roberts Stresses Need for Judicial Independence," NBC News, December 31, 2021, https://www.nbcnews.com/politics/supreme-court/supreme-court-chief-justice-roberts-stresses-need-judicial-independence-n1286813 (reporting on Chief Justice Roberts' annual end-of-the-year report, including his view that federal courts are doing what is needed to achieve independence).

37. Adam Cohen, "Justice Breyer's Legacy-Defining Decision," *Atlantic*, June 12, 2021, https://www.theatlantic.com/ideas/archive/2021/06/stephen-breyer-legacy-retirement/619168/.

38. Ibid. See also Ilya Shapiro, "The Politics of Supreme Court Confirmations and Recommendations for Reform," Cato Institute, July 20, 2021, https://www.cato.org/testimony/perspectives-supreme-court-practitioners-views-confirmation-process ("Politics has always been part of the process of selecting judicial nominees, and even more part of the process of confirming them"). See also Carl Hulse, "Cloud of Supreme Court Confirmation Bitterness Hangs Over Coming Fight," *New York Times* January 29, 2022, https://www.nytimes.com/2022/01/29/us/politics/supreme-court-confirmation-battles.amp.html (describing the politics likely to influence the selection and confirmation of Justice Breyer's successor).

39. This may be especially relevant when considering the notion of a conservative judicial revolution. See, for example, Jackie Calmes, *Dissent: The Radicalization of the Republican Party and Its Capture of the Court* (New York: Twelve, 2021); Erwin Chemerinsky, *The Conservative Assault on the Constitution* (New York: Simon & Schuster, 2010); Jefferson Decker, *The Other Rights Revolution: Conservative Lawyers and the Remaking of American Government* (New York: Oxford University Press, 2016); Linda Greenhouse, *Justice on the Brink: The Death of Ruth Bader Ginsburg, the Rise of Amy Coney Barrett, and Twelve Months That Transformed the Supreme Court* (New York: Random House, 2021), xii (writing that the nomination of Amy Coney Barrett to the Supreme Court in 2020 "was the culmination of a project launched years before [by conservatives] . . . to take back the Supreme Court"); Amanda Hollis-Brusky, *Ideas with Consequences: The Federalist Society and the Conservative Counterrevolution* (New York: Oxford University Press, 2015); Stephen M. Teles, *The Rise of the Conservative Legal Movement: The Battle for Control of the Law* (Princeton, NJ: Princeton University Press, 2010).

40. Cohen, "Justice Breyer's Legacy-Defining Decision." See also Adam Serwer, "The Lie About the Supreme Court Everyone Pretends to Believe," *Atlantic*, September 28, 2021, https://www.theatlantic.com/ideas/archive/2021/09/lie-about-supreme-court-everyone-pretends-believe/620198/:

> I take exception to . . . the demand from judges and justices that the public acquiesce to their self-delusion that they are wise sages who hold themselves above the vulgarities of

partisan politics, even as they deliver sweeping victories to a conservative movement and Republican Party that have worked for half a century to achieve those victories.

See also David Orentlicher, "Politics and the Supreme Court: The Need for Ideological Balance," *University of Pittsburgh Law Review* 79 (Spring 2018): 413 (noting "of course, a Justice's political philosophy does matter. Otherwise, Republican Senators would have considered Merrick Garland's nomination to the Supreme Court in 2016, and other nominations also would not fail because of partisan opposition") (footnotes omitted).

41. Adam Cohen, *Supreme Inequality: The Supreme Court's Fifty-Year Battle for a More Unjust America* (New York: Penguin Press: 2020), xv.

42. Ibid., xxix.

43. Charles Fried, "Not Conservative," *Harvard Law Review Blog*, July 3, 2018, https://blog.harvardlawreview.org/not-conservative.

44. Nikolas Bowie, "Presidential Commission on the Supreme Court of the United States: The Contemporary Debate Over Supreme Court Reform: Origins and Perspectives," written testimony, June 30, 2021, https://www.whitehouse.gov/wp-content/uploads/2021/06/Bowie-SCOTUS-Testimony-1.pdf.

45. See, for example, Bob Woodward and Robert Costa, "Virginia Thomas Urged White House Chief to Pursue Unrelenting Efforts to Overturn the 2020 Election, Texts Show," *Washington Post*, March 24, 2022, https://www.washingtonpost.com/politics/2022/03/24/virginia-thomas-mark-meadows-texts/. See also Matt Ford, "Ginni Thomas Is Giving the Supreme Court a Bleeding Ulcer It Can't Cure," *New Republic*, March 25, 2022, https://newrepublic.com/article/165858/ginni-thomas-january-6-texts (reporting on regular activism in conservative politics by the wife of Justice Clarence Thomas: "After years of tiptoeing up to the ethical lines, it is now clear that she will be a serious problem for the Supreme Court's legitimacy and credibility for the foreseeable future").

46. Jeffrey M. Jones, "Approval of U.S. Supreme Court Down to 40%, a New Low," Gallup.com, September 23, 2021, https://news.gallup.com/poll/354908/approval-supreme-court-down-new-low.aspx. See also Devan Cole, "New Poll: 54% of Americans Disapprove of Supreme Court Following Roe Draft Opinion Leak," CNN, May 25, 2022, https://www.cnn.com/2022/05/25/politics/supreme-court-approval-rating-drop-roe-leak/index.html.

47. John Kruzel, "Solid Majority Believes Supreme Court Rulings Based More on Politics Than Law," *The Hill*, October 20, 2021, https://thehill.com/regulation/court-battles/577444-solid-majority-believes-supreme-court-rulings-based-more-on-politics.

48. See Senator Richard Blumenthal, "The Nomination of Ketanji Brown Jackson to be an Associate Justice on the Supreme Court of the United States," Senate Judiciary Committee, March 21, 2022, https://www.judiciary.senate.gov/meetings/the-nomination-of-ketanji-brown-jackson-to-be-an-associate-justice-of-the-supreme-court-of-the-united-states, audio 2:26:48 ("I'm deeply concerned that this court is careening toward a precipice that will gravely threaten its role in our history, that it is out of step with America and that it is losing the trust and respect of the American

people that are essential to its authority. Trust in the United States Supreme Court is at a new low").

49. Erwin Chemerinsky and Jeffrey Abramson, "What Do We Teach Law Students When We Have No Faith in the Supreme Court?" *Los Angeles Times*, January 16, 2022, https://www.latimes.com/opinion/story/2022-01-16/supreme-court-conservatives-ideology-precedent-law-schools ("It is now clear that the court, with six conservatives—three appointed by Donald Trump—has a different attitude toward interpreting the Constitution and preserving fundamental rights").

50. Jeffrey M. Jones, "Confidence in U.S. Supreme Court Sinks to Historic Low," Gallup.com, June 23, 2022, https://news.gallup.com/poll/394103/confidence-supreme-court-sinks-historic-low.aspx (showing 25 percent of Americans have "a great deal" or "quite a lot" of confidence in the U.S. Supreme Court, down from 36 percent the previous year and five percentage points lower than the previous low recorded in 2014).

51. Jessica Levinson, "Justice Elena Kagan Has a Prescription for an Ailing Court," MSNBC, August 2, 2022, https://www.msnbc.com/opinion/msnbc-opinion/kagan-roberts-know-supreme-court-burning-n1297556 ("We are no longer nearing a crisis in confidence in the Supreme Court—we are already there").

52. See Wegman, "Justice Thomas Should Take a Long Look in the Mirror" ("The Supreme Court has always operated within and not outside politics; like the rest of our government, it consists of human beings"). See also Lee Epstein, Andrew D. Martin, Kevin M. Quinn, and Jeffrey A. Segal, "Ideological Drift Among Supreme Court Justices: Who, When, and How Important?" *Northwestern University Law Review* 101 (Fall 2007): 1483 (noting that justices' views can change, including while on the Court).

53. Marc J. Hetherington and Jonathan Weiler, *Prius or Pickup? How the Answers to Four Simple Questions Explain America's Great Divide* (Boston: Houghton Mifflin Harcourt, 2018), 99–100 (noting that coffee is among the most polarizing of products).

54. Ibid., 102.

55. Ibid., xi ("Worldview can encompass all sorts of cultural considerations, such as ideas about philosophy and morality. It is also, and even more significantly, shaped by psychological influences such as your emotions and the imprint left by past experiences").

56. Though it is acknowledged that nuance and "gray areas" exist, this work—like much of the literature utilized herein—relies on general categories such as liberal-conservative and fluid-fixed.

57. See, for example, Jeffrey Segal, "Why We Have the Most Polarized Supreme Court in History," *The Conversation*, March 14, 2016, https://perma.cc/QCJ5-4SY8. See also Eric Hamilton, "Politicizing the Supreme Court," *Stanford Law Review Online*, 65 (August 2012): 36; Geoffrey R. Stone, "Our Politically Polarized Supreme Court?" *Huffington Post*, November 25, 2014, http://www.huffingtonpost.com/geoffrey-r-stone/our-politically-polarized_b_5879346.html; Adam Liptak, "Adding Gorsuch, a Polarized Supreme Court Is Likely to Grow Even More So," *New York Times*, April 10, 2017, A9; Miriam Galston, "Polarization at the Supreme Court?

Substantive Due Process Through the Prism of Legal Theory," *Washington University Jurisprudence Review* 11 (2019): 255.

58. But see Jack M. Balkin, *Living Originalism* (Cambridge University Press, 2011) (arguing that originalism and living constitutionalism are compatible rather than opposed).

59. Chemerinsky, *The Conservative Assault on the Constitution*, 33.

60. See, for example, Stephen L. Carter, "The Supreme Court Has Always Been Political," *Washington Post*, May 10, 2022, https://www.washingtonpost.com/business/the-supreme-court-has-always-been-political/2022/05/05/6d85e418-cc91-11ec-b7ee-74f09d827ca6_story.html.

61. Charles M. Blow, "The Supreme Court as an Instrument of Oppression," *New York Times*, May 8, 2022, https://www.nytimes.com/2022/05/08/opinion/supreme-court-oppression.html ("originalists, those who believe that judgments by the court must conform to how the founders understood the Constitution when it was written, are so dangerous").

62. See Mary Ziegler, "The Conservatives Aren't Just Ending Roe—They're Delighting in It," *Atlantic*, May 3, 2022, https://www.theatlantic.com/ideas/archive/2022/05/supreme-court-leak-overturn-roe-polarization/629743/ ("Something fundamental about the Supreme Court has changed in recent months. It is not simply that the Court has a conservative supermajority . . . What is really striking is just how emboldened that conservative supermajority is—how willing to take on a number of deeply divisive culture-war issues").

PART 1

Divided Worlds

Chapter 1

The Nation

Polarized and Politicized

The United States is divided, and at levels rarely seen.[1] The possibility of civil war is seriously contemplated by some.[2] The U.S. Capitol insurrection on January 6, 2021—perceived by some as a prelude to civil war[3]—in many ways reflected the polarization that had been growing in the preceding years while at the same time signaling that much worse may be simmering just below the surface.[4] "Americans are angrier, more fearful, less trusting of one another and more polarized than at any time in generations and perhaps since the 1850s," wrote Peter Wehner shortly after the insurrection. "Families, friendships, churches and communities are being ripped apart by the savagery of our politics."[5] One year later, according to Jonathan Stevenson and Steven Simon, little had improved: "A year after the Jan. 6 storming of the Capitol, the United States seems perhaps even more alarmingly fractious and divided . . . The United States as we know it could come apart at the seams."[6]

A virtual cottage industry of books and other literature addressing polarization emerged.[7] Behavior once considered as being on the extreme fringes is more common and confrontational. People embrace—and even seek—conflict. "Social scientists who study conflict say the only way to understand it—and to begin to get out of it," reports Sabrina Tavernise, "is to look at the powerful currents of human emotions that are the real drivers. They include the fear of not belonging, the sting of humiliation, a sense of threat—real or perceived—and the strong pull of group behavior."[8] All of these are factors in polarized America.

While there are phenomena unique to the United States,[9] the nation and its institutions are not immune from various global developments, including the growth of populism. As Yascha Mounk wrote in 2018, "authoritarian populists are on the rise around the world, from America to Europe, and from Asia to Australia. Voters have long disliked particular parties, politicians or governments; now, many of them have become fed up with liberal democracy

17

itself."[10] Populism appeals to those who feel abandoned by established elites and their systems.[11] "These obstructions," writes George Packer, "crush the individuality that freedom lovers cherish, making them conformist, submissive, a group of people all shouting the same thing—easy marks for a demagogue."[12] Scapegoats, xenophobia, and fear are often utilized by authoritarian populists to appeal to potential followers.[13] Rather than offering solutions, they mobilize anger and fear.[14] Political strongmen inherently appeal to those with fears, then further capitalize by exacerbating that emotion to enhance their allure as the only person who can keep them safe.[15]

Fear as a motivator of beliefs permeates America's past and present.[16] Fear also dovetails with the formation of a specific worldview. While many factors contribute to determining to which worldview a person gravitates, the most fundamental, according to political scientists Marc Hetherington and Jonathan Weiler, is one's perception of how dangerous the world is: "Fear is perhaps the most primal instinct, after all, so it's only logical that people's level of fearfulness informs their outlook on life."[17] In the United States, that includes a wariness of a changing demographic landscape and an attraction to strong, uncompromising leadership that could make possible the rise of a figure who not only challenges democratic norms,[18] in part by suppressing its institutions to seize and maintain power, but also who would erect barriers—that is, walls—between themselves and their changing, "dangerous" environments.[19]

Populism, like any political approach, withers absent opportunity—both the presence of those who champion the movement and followers who possess significant buy-in. Timing can be critical, as when large segments develop the belief and become convinced that they were misled and left behind while others moved to the head of the line.[20] In turn, this can lead to the acceptance of misinformation[21] and the creation of false realities.[22] "We are witnessing a reversion to tribalism around the world, away from nation states," wrote Robert Reich in 2014. "The same pattern can be seen even in America—especially in American politics."[23] Thus, while the seeds of ideas must initially exist, their distribution, acceptance, and cultivation are facilitated by, and develop in tandem with, tribalism.

TRIBALISM

After Arizona congressman Paul Gosar posted an animated video depicting him attacking political opponents in November 2021, he was censured by the U.S. House of Representatives. All but two of his fellow Republicans voted against the censure. That vote, wrote Michael Cohen, demonstrated "the primal urge to defend a member of one's own tribe."[24] This occurs not just in government institutions, but also across a society in the throes of tribalism.[25]

Imagine that in that same society in which divisions are so intense that passionate disagreements are triggered by these decisions: the publisher of Dr. Seuss books choosing not to print more of some editions;[26] a toy manufacturer making Mr. Potato Head in a more gender-neutral way;[27] and Sesame Street's Big Bird getting a COVID vaccine.[28] All these events sent some groups of Americans into a frenzy, with the latter development called "government propaganda" and Mr. Bird being accused of "brainwashing children."[29] The COVID pandemic, in fact, became a primary source of divisions where many people preferred to risk infection and death rather than admit either error in judgment or, even worse in their view, that political opponents were right.[30] Noting that Americans were polarized according to whether they chose to be vaccinated, Kavita Patel concluded near the end of 2021 that the nation was in "a pandemic of our partisan divide . . . [O]ur country is on life support and may soon succumb to a different diagnosis: death by politics."[31] A few months earlier, Charles Blow observed, "Nothing better exemplifies the gaping political divide in this country than our embarrassing and asinine vaccine response."[32]

That response was tribal. An antiscience movement had gained a foothold, but there was more to it than that. Like minded individuals coalesced, with trust largely occurring only within groups—that is, tribes—not across them. Frequently, those groups are defined not by facts, but by what is believed.[33] Those beliefs all too often are anything but factual and become the basis of a self-defined reality.[34] Officials in a rural Arizona county, for example, rejected nearly $2 billion in federal COVID relief in early 2022 solely to make a political point, disregarding the funds' benefits.[35] According to Blow, "The public had been poisoned by partisanship."[36] Because many people believed that masking, social distancing, and receiving vaccines were political acts, they responded not with behavior to serve a greater good, but with political statements of narcissism: defiance.[37]

The group dynamic is key to tribalism. While we are all tribal to some extent,[38] scholars such as Amy Chua claim it is more than that: "Humans aren't just a little tribal. We're *very* tribal, and it distorts the way we think and feel,"[39] ultimately shaping behavior and decision making.[40] Belonging to groups fulfills a need, satisfying a craving for bonds and attachments.[41] Tribalism also contains an instinct to exclude.[42] Once people belong to a group, Chua writes, they "will penalize outsiders, seemingly gratuitously."[43] The most important goal is often to establish that another person or group is wrong.[44] This hostility toward outsiders is especially problematic when those outside the group can contribute to solutions.

When "outside the group" also means outside the borders, a sort of "exclusionary nationalism" can emerge that undermines prospects for global cooperation.[45] According to Greg Lukianoff and Jonathan Haidt, "In tribal mode, we seem to go blind to arguments and information that challenge our team's narrative."[46] Ideas are measured not by their quality, but according to *who* proposes them, in-group or out-group members.[47] Often, a negative polarization surfaces: "I hate their side more than I like my side."[48] Loyalty to the tribe and its members is paramount.[49]

Among the pioneers in recognizing and reporting on this sort of self-segregation was Bill Bishop.[50] The roles played by tribal psychology, conformity and the politics of migration were but a few of his insights. "As people seek out the social settings they prefer—as they choose the group that makes them feel the most comfortable—the nation grows more politically segregated."[51] The result, according to Bishop: "[B]alkanized communities whose inhabitants find other Americans to be incomprehensible; a growing intolerance for political differences that has made a national consensus impossible; and politics so polarized that Congress is stymied and elections are no longer just contests over policies, but bitter choices between ways of life."[52] Bishop's prescient book, *The Big Sort*, was published in 2008.

People organize themselves into groups, according to Bruce Rozenblit, where common activities and/or beliefs are shared. "The result of these groupings is a differentiation between the 'in group' and the 'out group.' The grouping creates a sense of exclusivity, which often results in feelings of superiority."[53] Chua calls this "the darkest side to the tribal instinct: the ease with which we dehumanize outsiders and the satisfaction we derive from doing so."[54] Identifying a common enemy, Lukianoff and Haidt write, is an effective way to enlarge and motivate a tribe.[55] Indeed, devaluing outsiders is common, thereby comparatively assigning greater value to one's own group.[56] "Nothing brings a group together like a common enemy," according to Ezra Klein.[57] Even political parties, writes David Brooks, "are no longer bound together by creeds but by enemies."[58] Within the worldview context, write Hetherington and Weiler, people on both sides "have come to see their opponents not simply as strangers, but as a collective menace."[59] This division by tribe is directly linked to polarization in America. In turn, both can be better explained by worldview politics.

WORLDVIEW: FIXED OR FLUID

Political conservatives and liberals are very different at the level of psychology and personality, influencing the way members of the two groups argue and process information.[60] "What if we're not all the same kind of molecule?"

asks Chris Mooney. "What if we respond to political or factual collisions in different ways, with different spins or velocities?"[61] The answers lie within the paradigm of worldview that contributes to explaining these differences. As the label "worldview" suggests, when comparing people across these categories, they view the world and its dynamics very differently.

Worldview is "a catchall for someone's deeply ingrained beliefs about the nature of the world and the priorities of a good society,"[62] as described by Hetherington and Weiler. To whichever worldview category people belong, fixed or fluid, it affects their behavior across a wide spectrum of issues, including their politics. Though probed in some depth in the pages that follow, as a foundational cornerstone for the moment, those with a fixed worldview favor the status quo or turning back the clock to bygone eras; fluid worldview holders are flexible and willing (and even desire) to risk trying new things. It is not surprising, then, that conservatives tend to align with the fixed worldview, progressives with fluid.

The worldview divide is of particular importance, largely because of its linkage to polarization.[63] Hetherington and Weiler claim it has the potential to imperil American democracy due to its intractable nature.[64] For the last fifty years, what they call an "insidious trend"[65] has surfaced: Americans' voting behavior being shaped less by their views about government and its proper role than by their feelings about racial, cultural, and security-related issues.[66] The two primary political parties have provided people with ready-made political identities. "People embrace one party or the other because it represents their core preferences and values—that is, because it caters to their particular worldview."[67] Because worldview and party identity are aligned as never before, we are polarized in ways previously unseen,[68] including the weaponization of both political partisanship[69] and the media, particularly online platforms. According to Yale historian Timothy Snyder, "Within the two-dimensional internet world, new collectivities have arisen, invisible by the light of day—tribes with distinct worldviews, beholden to manipulations."[70]

Worldview and beliefs are intertwined. Having a particular worldview drives very specific perceptions and, in turn, behaviors. To be sure, people have always seen the world in ways they want to see it, but according to Hetherington and Weiler, this phenomenon has intensified in conjunction with contemporary politics.[71] Worldview and party politics have aligned to the extent that it is now appropriate to draw the following associations: fixed = conservative/Republican; fluid = progressive/Democratic. As previously noted, nuance surfaces,[72] but these shorthand links are viable and useful.

Whether an individual falls into the fixed or fluid category depends on numerous factors. It is suggested here that fixed and fluid are groups that conform to the "laws" of tribalism. Each category is a tribe, assuming the various dynamics of tribalism including having its own sets of beliefs and perceptions, and with members who largely insulate themselves from their adversaries. These "others" are often viewed with wariness, sometimes as enemies, with the desire to exclude them.[73] Because they see the world differently, they see its problems and solutions differently.[74] In fact, they often fail to agree on what the problems are.[75] What leads to these differences between tribes, parties, and worldview categories? It's complicated.

Nature and Nurture

Worldview politics are often viewed as surfacing in response to one's environment and its various influences. Indeed, that is an important factor, but there are also physiological roots.[76] Both nurture and nature combine to develop worldview.[77] That is, in addition to environmental influences, people are predisposed to adopt traits and beliefs that lead them in specific directions throughout their lives.[78] This includes the formation of their worldview. A field of study referred to as political neuroscience has revealed that differences in brain development between people are important in how worldview develops.[79]

It should not be surprising that brain development affects how we process information. What may be not so obvious, however, is how that development creates a predilection that often drives us into one of the two worldview categories, fluid or fixed. In describing the nature/nurture duality of political view formation, Mooney writes, "[P]eople are partly making their political brains, partly inheriting them, but the sum total of the process is measurable divergences in brain structure or in brain functioning."[80]

The human brain evolved from humble beginnings. The newer brain was built on and around the older brain which contains the flight-or-fight mechanisms necessary for survival. Though perhaps needed less frequently now than when our ancestors wandered the Serengeti plains, that older brain remains and can override higher brain functions, including when danger occurs.[81] When there is no time for abstract reasoning or examining nuance in certain situations, these rapid-fire reactions are prioritized.[82] Thus, according to Mooney, "while the newer parts of the brain may be responsible for our species' greatest innovations and insights, it isn't like they always get to run the show."[83]

Though all human brains evolved, not all did so identically. According to Hetherington and Weiler, "the size of the amygdala, which is the part of the brain that governs survival instincts, tends to be larger among conservatives than liberals."[84] The larger the amygdala, the more dominant the survival instinct that it houses. In those people, the binary flight-or-fight response to various stimuli is more likely to be triggered, overriding other possible reactions with potentially dangerous situations on the radar of consciousness.[85] In turn, it is more likely that danger is perceived as perpetually present, resulting in actions and precautions being taken to maintain safety. A belief system—or worldview—is structured accordingly,[86] with the safety consciousness of the fixed worldview being especially dependent on the tribe.[87] A predictable world that establishes and maintains a status quo is viewed as a better, safer world. Change is seen as threatening.[88] Thus, eliminating variability is preferred—unless it is the change of returning to what was. For those sensitive to danger and chaos, an unambiguous and unwavering style of communication, leadership and overall existence is favored—"This is the way it is"—because it satisfies a need for order and cognitive closure, relieving dissonance. According to Hetherington and Weiler, the stronger the desire for closure, the more someone seeks answers that eliminate ambiguity and uncertainty.[89] Certainty is safe. Therefore, people often seek the comfort of safety and closure even when certainty is unwarranted. "Certainty and similar states of 'knowing what we know,'" writes neurologist Robert Burton, "function independently of reason."[90]

Because of the amygdala, all humans are disadvantaged when it comes to reasoned deliberation. Our brains are wired to react viscerally and emotionally to many stimuli. However, due to inequity in brain evolution—specifically, the amygdala—some humans are particularly disadvantaged.[91] Their brains are especially "emotional," with the default position viewing the world in blacks or whites, not in shades of gray. That is, in these people the survival instinct is prioritized. When threats are presented, the fight-or-flight reaction is triggered. A response is necessary—now!—to deal with the threat.[92] Avoid it or remove it. Fear is prominent, not only for those who are directly threatened, but also for those who need to be convinced of the danger.

To be sure, being safe has its place. A key evolutionary period was dominated by the ability to survive. That is, it is not surprising that the brain evolved in a way that prioritizes survival, including the avoidance or elimination of threats and danger. Yet as discussed above, differences in brain evolution account for differences in what we believe and how we behave in response to those beliefs. Not every situation is a legitimate threat or poses danger, but some people are predisposed to believe that threats exist when others do not. Completing the loop, these beliefs—and the behaviors that follow—are often consistent not only with one another, but also to those that conform to the principles and expectations of specific groups, tribes, and political parties.

Each of the worldview categories, fixed and fluid, has specific attributes. As noted above, each group has become synonymous with specific political equivalents: fixed, Republican and conservative; fluid, Democratic and liberal/progressive. Fear is at the heart of determining to which category a person is drawn.[93] Because people on the political right are generally more attuned to danger—and thus more safety-oriented—than their liberal counterparts, responses to various stimuli differ.[94] It is not coincidental, for example, that conservatives have been advocates of gun rights much more so than liberals. Guns, many believe, are instruments of safety.[95] The more guns, the better and safer we are, they believe (see chapter 4).

Also within the safety realm, according to Hetherington and Weiler, "conservatives erect more barriers—more defense mechanisms—between themselves and their environment."[96] Those with a fixed worldview, they say, seek protection because they are less inclined to trust others.[97] Picture, for example, a politician appealing to members of his base by promising to build a border wall to keep them safe from others who would pose danger by crossing the border. Those with fixed worldviews are much more likely to be supportive.[98] Banning travel to the United States from nations whose populations are largely dominated by "others" is rooted in the same thinking.[99] At best, outsiders are viewed as unhelpful and, more likely, threatening.[100]

There is a straight line from brain evolution to worldview. When we were in the caves, there was a natural suspicion of those who looked different.[101] For some today, their brains remain in the cave. Consistent with their safety orientation, conservatives tend to be cautious—wary, wanting to "play it safe, to avoid the unfamiliar, and to react more quickly to potential uncertainty."[102] Engaging in routines to increase predictability are prioritized, adding order to environments thought to be replete with danger.[103] By contrast, people with more fluid worldviews "are less innately fearful of difference, a quality that gives them leeway to embrace variety"[104] across many contexts.

Worldview permeates beliefs and behaviors outside of politics, with these other fixed-fluid divides illustrating the safety-caution dynamic. For example, Republicans are more likely to go to tried-and-true chain restaurants (that serve American food), whereas liberals—who are more open to new experiences—are more apt to go to "hole-in-the-wall" establishments that serve ethnic cuisine.[105] "Americans make these decisions," write Hetherington and Weiler, "not *because* they are Democrats or Republicans but because the same worldview that influences their political views also shapes their lifestyle choices."[106] As noted above, choices of coffee, beer, and automobiles also reflect worldview. Where to live is yet another dimension: Those with fluid worldviews tend to favor cities;[107] those with a fixed worldview are more inclined to choose suburbs and rural areas.[108] A significant factor is space, which is often viewed as a precondition for safety. In addition—and illustrating the link with tribalism—as more people of one worldview inhabit certain areas, they become less hospitable to members of the other worldview.

Science and the Pursuit of Truth

> During Adlai E. Stevenson's 1956 presidential campaign, a woman
> called out to him: "Senator, you have the vote of every thinking person!"
> Stevenson called back, "That's not enough, madam, we need a majority."[109]

Like much of what is discussed in these pages, human differences in the
acceptance or rejection of general facts and science are rooted in worldview.
How people see the world and their place in it governs a variety of beliefs
and behaviors including whether someone is open-minded to new ideas or
tends to reject them. While there may be no better contemporary example of
how beliefs can divide Americans than COVID-19 responses,[110] the role of
disparate views toward science, knowledge, and truth in polarized America
extends beyond a single issue or period.[111]

Long before COVID, the United States became splintered according to
knowledge—that is, acceptance or rejection of fact-based, scientifically
verified information rather than belief in anything less. Beliefs are often
developed as matters of convenience, confirming already-held biases.[112] To
combat these biases and lapses in objectivity, the scientific method began
to take root during the seventeenth century's Scientific Revolution.[113] Not
unlike the checks and balances incorporated into some forms of government
as well as defenses of speech freedom,[114] this method instituted checks and
balances on human bias to help ensure that the most reliable information
emerged.[115] However, when that information fails to conform to preconcep-
tions, rather than reconsidering their disproven views, some people choose
to reject the science—not merely specific findings, but science overall.[116] A
better approach lies in accepting the limits of our ability to know and that contrary evidence may appear to "overthrow a cherished theory."[117] According to
Burton, "Faith-driven arguments, by invoking irrefutable divine authority that
will always be right, do not have to make this concession."[118]

Just as blind, unfounded acceptance of information is problematic, the
same applies to baseless rejection of data. This led to a growing segment of
Americans who practice what has been referred to as willful ignorance.[119]
Their rejection of facts and science is reinforced and rewarded within their
tribes.[120] As Tom Nichols writes, "ignorance has become hip, with some
Americans now wearing their rejection of expert advice as a badge of cultural
sophistication."[121] This position is echoed by Timothy Snyder: "Generic cynicism makes us feel hip and alternative even as we slip along with our fellow
citizens into a morass of indifference."[122] This issue includes the rejection of
both science and fallibility—that is, the acknowledgment of the possibility
of our own error in judgment.[123] Adam Grant maintains that thinking like a

scientist "requires searching for reasons why we might be wrong—not for reasons why we must be right—and revising our views based on what we learn."[124] Certitude is the enemy of reason, learning and growth.[125] "If we're certain that we know something," according to Grant, "we have no reason to look for gaps and flaws in our knowledge—let alone fill or correct them."[126] Many people lack both the necessary humility, as Grant describes it,[127] and the recognition of their own fallibility to acknowledge the validity of science.[128]

Because belief in or rejection of science is often linked to politics and party, it can be especially divisive. That is, when one party and its leaders— that is, tribe leaders—repeatedly criticize the pursuit of knowledge and truth through scientific inquiry, members of that tribe tend not only to embrace that message, but also demand that fellow members accept it or risk being ostracized.[129] The pressure to conform is significant,[130] a sort of peer pressure that varies according to the peers (i.e., tribe) that one chooses. As revealed by scientific polling, within the context of science, this occurs in the Republican party at far higher rates than it does with their Democratic counterparts.[131]

Viewing this phenomenon through the lens of worldview brings it further into focus. As Mooney bluntly describes this, "change-friendly liberals have a built-in reason to be more pro-science, and change-resistant conservatives more anti-science—at least on the most disruptive of issues."[132] While hesitancy to accept the results of scientific research historically cut across both parties, Naomi Oreskes reports that "Republican hesitancy . . . seems to have different and deeper roots."[133] That is, Republican Party-inspired doubt about government-reported science is not a new phenomenon.[134] "[T]his is what the party's spokespeople have been saying for 40 years, from the early days of acid rain to our ongoing debates about climate change."[135]

The history of American anti-intellectualism is well documented. Historian Richard Hofstadter, for example, called it older than our national identity.[136] He described it as "a pure and unalloyed dislike of intellect or intellectuals . . . a resentment and suspicion of the life of the mind and of those who are considered to represent it."[137] He added that this disposition "constantly minimize[s] the value of that life."[138] Ironically, opposition to science and ideas accelerated during a period in which findings and discoveries benefited everyone, in part through advancements in technology. Perhaps not so ironically, that technology—for example, social media—was an instrument in the spread of the cynical mindset, what some psychologists now refer to as anti-enlightenment.[139] "America is now ill," writes Susan Jacoby, "with a stream of intertwined ignorance, anti-rationalism, and anti-intellectualism that has mutated, as a result of technology, into something more dangerous than the cyclical strains of the past."[140] That danger includes the transformation of skepticism[141] to the more extreme cynicism.[142]

Granted, a healthy skepticism toward any information is useful, if not vital. Ironically, skepticism is at the heart of the scientific method whose underlying mantra is "Prove it."[143] As nineteenth-century philosopher John Stuart Mill advocated, ideas—not just new ones, but also accepted concepts—need to be challenged to ensure their continued validity.[144] Rather than systematic skepticism, however, a tendency to reject information out of hand—particularly in opposition to supportive evidence—is healthy neither for individuals nor for the society they inhabit. That happens for a variety of reasons including the information's source—for example, dismissing government recommendations due to a general distrust—and/or that it conflicts with preexisting beliefs, a prioritization of beliefs over facts.[145] Rejecting the advice of experts asserts autonomy.[146]

This denial of evidence-based information is often directly tied to the fixed worldview. As noted, the fixed approach favors the status quo and predictability—and even returning to previous eras (e.g., "Make America Great Again") when life is thought to have been simpler and straightforward.[147] Scientific research, on the other hand, is characterized by uncertainty. Science is an engine of change that challenges beliefs, accompanied by a self-awareness that knowledge is not static. Within that context, change is a given, and a positive one. According to Mooney, science "fuels innovation, uncovers uncomfortable realities about our species and our world."[148] On those issues where the political right is dubious of science, Yuval Levin suggests that "it usually arises when science poses some kind of threat to what conservatives see as the imperative of cultural continuity."[149] This is wholly consistent with fixed worldview doctrine.

The fixed worldview is especially predisposed to seeking and accepting information that confirms beliefs and, in turn, rejecting data that challenges those beliefs.[150] Inconsistency between preexisting beliefs and newly encountered information leads to cognitive dissonance, a widely accepted concept in psychology describing a state of discomfort when someone simultaneously holds two or more conflicting thoughts.[151] How one deals with that dissonance is often governed by worldview. Those with a fixed worldview are more likely to rationalize in favor of their preexisting beliefs by seeking information that confirms them—what might be regarded as selective exposure. It sometimes takes the form of blind loyalty to views and those who advocate them—what resembles tribal allegiance.[152] It is not merely coincidental that the increase in these phenomena parallels the shift in the media environment, specifically the rise of outlets such as the Fox News Channel, Breitbart News, and the utilization of social media platforms where (mis)information to confirm fixed worldview perspectives is readily available.

A convergence of tribalism and misinformation was on display, for example, in June 2022 when the Fox News Channel was the only major American television news organization that did not offer live coverage of the first public hearing of the congressional committee investigating the attack on the U.S Capitol the previous January.[153] To do so, according to one analyst, "would have been to present information that was unwelcome to many core Fox News viewers."[154] In a twisted approach to counter programming, however, rather than simply ignoring the hearings, the network fed its viewers a steady diet of misinformation about the events of January 6, 2021.[155]

The tendency to seek, accept, and in some cases present only information that conforms to already-held beliefs contains elements of confirmation bias[156] and motivated reasoning.[157] Each has escalated in the era of worldview politics.[158] Even in the face of contrary evidence, people cling to and justify their preexisting views. Moreover, the more committed people are to a belief, the harder it is for them to relinquish it, even in the face of overwhelming contrary evidence. Rather than acknowledging an error in judgment and abandoning the opinion, they tend to develop a new attitude or belief that will justify retaining it.[159] Consistent with political neuroscience findings, Mooney reports that "when engaged in biased political reasoning, partisans were not using parts of the brain associated with 'cold,' logical thinking. Rather, they were using a variety of regions associated with emotional processing and psychological defense."[160] When that bias is particularly strong, according to Hannah Nam, "that can lead to things like simply rationalizing or accepting long-standing inequalities or injustices."[161] Thus, while science is at the center of the issue, a steadfastness against change extends to political and cultural matters, as well.[162] This process of justification creates information silos that, given group (i.e., tribal) dynamics, become echo chambers. According to Grant, "Our convictions can lock us in prisons of our own making."[163]

Because so many people—especially those with fixed worldviews[164]—prioritize loyalty to beliefs and tribe over facts, some wonder whether people really want accurate information.[165] Given that discovering truth is the goal of inquiry,[166] this suggests another reason that some are hostile to science: they may be motivated to avoid truth in order to maintain the illusions of their preferred "reality." A world structured according to their beliefs is somehow more comfortable, predictable, safer—and fixed. Information can be framed, and beliefs formulated, to be consistent with already-held beliefs. According to Burton, this can especially occur when data surprises people: "We have an innate tendency to characterize the unexpected and unlikely according to our worldview."[167]

Safety and personal security aside, however—and because they are instruments in the pursuit of truth—the rejection of science and fact-based knowledge should serve as a social alarm. That is, truth avoidance ought to be a red flag warning. "Authoritarians don't want to control just the government, the economy and the military," Rebecca Solnit writes. "They want to control the truth. Truth has its own authority, an authority a strongman must defeat at least in the minds of his followers, convincing them to abandon fact, standards of verification, critical thinking and all the rest. Such people become a standing army awaiting their next command."[168]

Truth is elusive when large portions of the information universe are excluded, whether by personal choice or through various forms of censorship implemented by domineering authorities. "All too often," writes Blackburn, "people who think they have been denied trustworthy sources of information take refuge in believing whatever they would like to be true."[169] False realities result, and those who would disrupt them are reviled outsiders. These include not only those who advocate science- and evidence-based knowledge, but also those who seek truth. Because scientists and researchers are often based in America's colleges and universities, institutions of higher education have become not merely another source of political divide, but also "one of the higher-profile battlegrounds in the worldview conflict."[170] Members of the fixed worldview often have animosity toward higher education and those who produce knowledge that conflicts with their worldview.[171] Though many holders of the fixed worldview attended college, others see college education as an opportunity they were denied, and degree-holders as another "other" to resent. Hetherington and Weiler refer to the fluid-fixed views on institutions of higher education as "remarkably different" and among the most "bracing partisan differences"[172] across all issues.

The aversion to change by fixed worldview members is relevant here. Change is resisted, in part, because the cultural transformation it may summon is unwanted and viewed as contributing to the regression of the nation's institutions. Life is seen as a zero-sum game in which, for example, rights granted to others reduces *their* rights and opportunities. This includes beliefs about higher education and who attends.[173] As Chua writes, "Every group feels attacked, pitted against other groups . . . In these conditions, democracy devolves into zero-sum group competition—pure political tribalism."[174]

Too often, information is not viewed as a tool for deeper understanding—that is, a path to truth. Instead, it is used as a weapon to defend and argue for beliefs. The phenomenon is accelerated when people are granted permission, even encouraged, to do so by sources they trust.[175] The distinction between beliefs and fact is difficult for some to grasp.[176] One can interpret a situation, but as Blackburn points out, to do so "is just to have a *belief* about it."[177] An interpretation may be flawed, particularly when it strays from fact-based evidence. Any conclusions stemming from such a scenario are unlikely to be true or lead to the truth. Thus, the danger in trivializing the truth is not only that it is rejected, but that falsehoods are so readily accepted in lieu of fact. As Solnit writes of such people, "Without the yoke of truthfulness around their necks, they can choose beliefs that flatter their worldview or justify their aggression."[178]

The value of truth occurs on multiple levels. Among them, according to Blackburn, "Once we have it, truth radiates benefits such as knowledge and, perhaps most notably, success in coping with the world."[179] Conversely, however, coping with the world by *rejecting* truth has become a way of life for some.[180]

Another aspect of truth's multidimensional value lies in its role in achieving justice. Truth is a perquisite for justice.[181] Without knowing the facts of a case, it is impossible to determine whether justice has been achieved.[182] Many have argued that the purpose of a trial is to search for truth.[183] As demonstrated above, however, the perception of truth and fact can be less than objective. As is the case elsewhere within the judiciary—and across the nation—the truth and how it is interpreted are not viewed identically across the political and worldview spectrums.

NOTES

1. See, for example, David Brooks, "America Is Falling Apart at the Seams*,*" *New York Times*, January 13, 2022, https://www.nytimes.com/2022/01/13/opinion/america -falling-apart.html (writing of America's "long-term loss of solidarity, a long-term rise in estrangement and hostility. This is what it feels like to live in a society that is dissolving from the bottom up as much as from the top down"). See also Ross Douthat, "Let's Not Invent a Civil War," *New York Times*, January 12, 2022, https:// www.nytimes.com/2022/01/12/opinion/civil-war-america.html:

> The country is definitely more ideologically polarized than it was 20 or 40 years ago . . . We are more likely to hate and fear members of the rival party, more likely to sort ourselves into ideologically homogeneous communities, more likely to be deeply skeptical about public institutions and more likely to hold conspiratorial beliefs . . . that undercut the basic legitimacy of the opposition party's governance.

See also Aidan Connaughton, "Americans See Stronger Societal Conflicts Than People in Other Advanced Economies," *Pew Research Center*, October 13, 2021, https://www.pewresearch.org/fact-tank/2021/10/13/americans-see-stronger-societal -conflicts-than-people-in-other-advanced-economies ("The United States stands out among 17 advanced economies as one of the most conflicted when it comes to questions of social unity. A large majority of Americans say there are strong political and strong racial and ethnic conflicts in the U.S. and that most people disagree on basic facts").

2. See, for example, Michelle Goldberg, "Are We Really Facing a Second Civil War?" *New York Times*, January 6, 2022, https://www.nytimes.com/2022/01/06/ opinion/america-civil-war/html; Barbara Walter, *How Civil Wars Start,* xvi (2022),

xvi ("I've seen how civil wars start . . . And I can see those signs emerging here at a surprisingly fast rate"); *How Close is the US to Civil War? Closer Than You Think, Study Says*, CNN, December 20, 2021, https://www.cnn.com/videos/politics/2021/12 /20/us-civil-war-study-barbara-walter-intvu-intl-ovn-vpx.cnn; Paul D. Eaton, Antonio M. Taguba, and Steven M. Anderson, "3 Retired Generals: The Military Must Prepare Now for a 2024 Insurrection," *Washington Post*, December 17, 2021, https: //www.washingtonpost.com/opinions/2021/12/17/eaton-taguba-anderson-generals -military (expressing concern over split loyalties in the military surfacing, under which "it is not outlandish to say a military breakdown could lead to civil war"); William G. Gale and Darrell M. West, "Is the U.S. Headed for Another Civil War?" *Brookings*, September 16, 2021, https://www.brookings.edu/blog/fixgov/2021/09/16/ is-the-us-headed-for-another-civil-war/ ("Is it really possible that America could face the possibility of civil war in the near future? It may seem unthinkable, and yet there's much to worry about"); Monica Duffy Toft, "How Civil Wars Start" *Foreign Policy*, February 18, 2021, https://foreignpolicy.com/2021/02/18/how-civil-wars-start ("Until quite recently, a civil war seemed all but impossible in the United States—something of the past, for most citizens, not of the future. But the Capitol insurrection on January 6 and the rise of violent domestic extremism have set off alarm bells about the potential for another descent into internal war"). But see Jamelle Bouie, "Why We Are Not Facing the Prospect of a Second Civil War," *New York Times*, February 15, 2022, https://www.nytimes.com/2022/02/15/opinion/second-civil-war.html.

3. See "Here's Every Word from the Seventh Jan. 6 Committee Hearing on its Investigation," NPR, July 12, 2022, https://www.npr.org/2022/07/12/1111123258/jan -6-committee-hearing-transcript (statements and testimony including several references to the insurrection being the beginning of a "civil war").

4. See, for example, James A. Piazza, "Politician Hate Speech and Domestic Terrorism*,*" *International Interactions* 46, no. 3 (2020): 431 (theorizing that hate speech by politicians deepens political polarization and, in turn, produces conditions under which domestic terrorism increases). See also David Remnick, "Is a Civil War Ahead?" *New Yorker*, January 5, 2022, https://www.newyorker.com/news/daily -comment/is-a-civil-war-ahead ("A year after the attack on the Capitol, America is suspended between democracy and autocracy").

5. Peter Wehner, "The End of Trump Can Be the Beginning of America," *New York Times*, January 22, 2021, https://www.nytimes.com/2021/01/22/opinion/trump-legacy .html. See also Damien Cave, "How Australia Saved Thousands of Lives While Covid Killed a Million Americans," *New York Times*, May 15, 2022, https://www .nytimes.com/2022/05/15/world/australia/covid-deaths.html (suggesting that citizen trust in science and institutions accounts for the wide discrepancy in COVID-related deaths in Australia and the U.S.).

6. Jonathan Stevenson and Steven Simon, "We Need to Think the Unthinkable About Our Country," *New York Times*, January 13, 2022, https://www.nytimes. com/2022/01/13/opinion/january-6-civil-war.html.

7. See, for example, Ezra Klein, *Why We're Polarized* (New York: Avid Reader Press, 2020); Sam Rosenfeld, *The Polarizers* (Chicago: University of Chicago Press, 2018).

8. Sabrina Tavernise, "First They Fought About Masks. Then Over the Soul of the City," *New York Times*, December 26, 2021, https://www.nytimes.com/2021/12/26/us/oklahoma-masks.html.

9. See Jennifer McCoy and Benjamin Press, "What Happens When Democracies Become Perniciously Polarized," Carnegie Endowment for International Peace, January 22, 2022, https://carnegieendowment.org/2022/01/18/what-happens-when-democracies-become-perniciously-polarized (writing that there are "a number of features that make the United States both especially susceptible to polarization and especially impervious to efforts to reduce it. One such feature is the durability of identity politics in a racially and ethnically diverse democracy").

10. Yascha Mounk, *The People vs. Democracy: Why Our Freedom Is in Danger & How to Save It* (Cambridge: Harvard University Press, 2018), 2.

11. See Richard Hofstadter, *The Paranoid Style in American Politics, and Other Essays* (New York: Knopf, 1952), 39 (describing these people as believing that "America has been taken away from them . . . [and feeling] they have no sense to political bargaining or the making of decisions").

12. George Packer, "How America Fractured Into Four Parts," *Atlantic*, July/August 2021, https://www.theatlantic.com/magazine/archive/2021/07/george-packer-four-americas/619012/.

13. See Ibid.
A character in Jonathan Franzen's 2010 novel, *Freedom*, puts it this way: "If you don't have money, you cling to your freedoms all the more angrily. Even if smoking kills you, even if you can't afford to feed your kids, even if your kids are getting shot down by maniacs with assault rifles. You may be poor, but the one thing nobody can take away from you is the freedom to fuck up your life."
See also George Washington, "Farewell Address," National Archives, September 17, 1796, https://founders.archives.gov/documents/Washington/05-20-02-0440-0002 (warning that political parties "are likely . . . to become potent engines, by which cunning, ambitious, and unprincipled men will be enabled to subvert the power of the people and to usurp for themselves the reins of government, destroying afterwards the very engines which have lifted them to unjust dominion").

14. Packer, "How America Fractured into Four Parts."

15. See Katherine Stewart, "Eighty-One Percent of White Evangelicals Voted for Donald Trump. Why?" *Nation*, November 17, 2016, https://www.thenation.com/article/archive/eighty-one-percent-of-white-evangelicals-voted-for-donald-trump-why/ (including fear as a factor that motivated Trump voters).

16. See, for example, Charles Slack, *Liberty's First Crisis: Adams, Jefferson, and the Misfits Who Saved Free Speech* (New York: Atlantic Monthly Press, 2015), 9 ("The greatest enemy of liberty is fear. When people feel comfortable and well protected, they are naturally expansive and tolerant of one another's opinions and rights. When they feel threatened, their tolerance shrinks"); Justin Townley, "The Great Recession and the Politics of Economics: Is the Color of the Economic Crisis the Color of Presidential Fear?" *Berkeley La Raza Law Journal* 22 (2012): 51 ("Many former Presidents created fear of the unknown in the American people to advance their political agendas based on their insecurities about those different racially or

culturally"); Anthony Lewis, *Make No Law: The Sullivan Case and the First Amendment* (New York: Random House, 1991), 59 ("The Federalists of 1798 were hardly unique in practicing the politics of fear"); David L. Altheide, *Terrorism and the Politics of Fear* (Lanham, MD: Rowman & Littlefield), 2006, 2 ("[A]uthorities promote fear among citizens because they know that concerns for personal safety will tempt even the most cynical observer to hand over their lives for protection"); Al Gore, *The Assault on Reason* (New York: Penguin Books, 2007), 23 ("Fear is the most powerful enemy of reason . . . Reason may sometimes dissipate fear, but fear frequently shuts down reason"); *Whitney v. California*, 274 U.S. 357, 375 (1927) (Brandeis, J., concurring) ("[The Founders recognized] that fear breeds repression; that repression breeds hate; that hate menaces stable government").

17. Marc J. Hetherington and Jonathan Weiler, *Prius or Pickup? How the Answers to Four Simple Questions Explain America's Great Divide* (Boston: Houghton Mifflin Harcourt, 2018), xi.

18. Ibid., 41 ("When people are wired for wariness, trust comes less easily").

19. Ibid., 4. See also Myah Ward, "Trump, in Return to D.C., Hints at 2024 While Rehashing 2020," *Politico*, July 26, 2022, https://www.politico.com/news/2022/07/26/trump-dc-2024-capitol-riot-00048052 (quoting Donald Trump: "If we don't have safety, we don't have freedom. We don't have a country. America First must mean safety first"); Tara Trower Doolittle, "Don't Let Trump, Others Who Hate, Speak for You," *Austin American-Statesman*, December 13, 2015, E4 ("And then there are the crowds who cheer Trump's incendiary diatribes encouraging Americans to sort themselves by religion and race, commit war crimes by killing innocent civilians and rekindle failed, inhumane policies from past eras"); Michael Bond, "Trump's Volatile Crowds Not An Accident," *USA Today*, March 23, 2016, 7A ("Trump himself has laid the groundwork with a rhetorical strategy designed to tap into people's basic fears and most partisan inclinations"); Khosrow Semnani, "Trump's Fear-Mongering Threatens GOP," *Deseret News*, December 15, 2015, https://www.deseret.com/2015/12/17/20578932/trump-s-fear-mongering-threatens-republican-party ("[W]hat [Trump] is selling is fear"); Richard Cohen, "Trump Has Taught Me to Fear My Fellow Americans," *Washington Post*, May 31, 2016, A15; Nick Corasaniti, "Donald Trump, in First Ad, Plays to Fears on Immigration and ISIS," *New York Times*, January 5, 2016, www.nytimes.com/2016/01/05/us/politics/in-first-ad-donald-trump-plays-to-fears-on-immigration-and-isis.html.

20. See generally Michael J. Sandel, *The Tyranny of Merit: What's Become of the Common Good?* (New York: Farrar Strauss Giroux, 2020), 5 (criticizing the American meritocracy in which "those who land on top come to believe that they deserve their success. And, if opportunities are truly equal, it means that those who are left behind deserve their fate as well"). See also David Brooks, "Joe Biden Is Succeeding," *New York Times*, November 18, 2021, https://www.nytimes.com/2021/11/18/opinion/biden-infrastructure-stimulus-bill.html (writing that in early 2021, "We had become a country dividing into two nations, one highly educated and affluent and the other left behind. The economic gaps further inflamed cultural and social gaps, creating an atmosphere of intense polarization, cultural hostility, alienation, bitterness and resentment").

21. While this work does not focus on misinformation, its link to polarization is acknowledged. People who are angry and seeking relief are susceptible to information that targets the source of their anger, including untruthful information. They seek affirmation and are willing to cling to what they perceive as a way out. The in-group reinforces beliefs that are appealing and enhance the ability to both designate and blame others. See Elizabeth Williamson and Emily Steel, "Conspiracy Theories Made Alex Jones Very Rich. They May Bring Him Down," *New York Times*, September 7, 2018, https://www.nytimes.com/2018/09/07/us/politics/alex-jones-business-infowars-conspiracy.amp.html. Referring to Alex Jones's steaming website "Infowars":

> [He] has built a substantial following appealing to an angry, largely white, majority male audience that can choose simply to be entertained or to internalize his rendering of their worst fears: that the government and other big institutions are out to get them, that some form of apocalypse is frighteningly close and that they must become more virile, and better-armed, to survive.

22. See Simon Blackburn, *On Truth* (Oxford: Oxford University Press, 2018), 8:

> [A]ll too often people who think they have been denied trustworthy sources of information take refuge in believing whatever they would like to be true . . . The danger is then people lock themselves into sealed silos, refusing any information or evidence that contradicts whatever comfortable view of things they have hit upon.

See also Tom Nichols, *The Death of Expertise: The Campaign Against Established Knowledge and Why It Matters* (New York: Oxford University Press, 2017), 14 ("misinformation pushes aside knowledge").

23. Robert Reich, "The New Tribalism and the Decline of the Nation State," *Huffington Post*, March 24, 2014, https://www.huffingtonpost.com/robert-reich/the-new-tribalism-and-the_b_5020469.html.

24. Michael A. Cohen, "House Censure Vote Shows How the GOP Rarely Breaks Ranks," MSNBC, November 18, 2021, https://www.msnbc.com/opinion/house-censure-vote-paul-gosar-shows-how-rarely-gop-breaks-n1284070.

25. See Jennifer Medina and Reid J. Epstein, "Republican Celebrations and Democratic Anger Reveal a Widening Political Divide," *New York Times*, November 19, 2021, https://www.nytimes.com/live/2021/11/19/us/kyle-rittenhouse-trial/rittenhouse-verdict-conservatives-liberals ("Like so much else in modern America, Friday's acquittal of Kyle Rittenhouse both revealed and widened the split between the country's hostile political factions").

26. Alexandra Alter and Elizabeth A. Harris, "Dr. Seuss Books Are Pulled, and a 'Cancel Culture' Controversy Erupts," *New York Times*, March 4, 2021, https://www.nytimes.com/2021/03/04/books/dr-seuss-books.html.

27. Joseph Pisani, "Mr. Potato Head Drops the Mister—Sort Of," Associated Press, February 25, 2021, https://apnews.com/article/mr-potato-head-goes-gender-neutral-d3c178f2b9b0c424ed814657be41a9d8.

28. Ben Kessen, "Big Bird's Vaccination Announcement Sparks Backlash from Conservatives, GOP," NBC News, November 7, 2021, https://www.nbcnews.com

/news/us-news/big-bird-vaccine-announcement-sparks-backlash-conservatives-gop-n1283425.

29. Rachel Treisman, "Big Bird Got 'Vaccinated' Against COVID-19, Drawing Outrage from Republicans," NPR, November 8, 2021, https://www.npr.org/2021/11/08/1053548074/big-bird-covid-19-vaccine-conservative-backlash-ted-cruz.

30. See Farhad Manjoo, "What If Humans Just Can't Get Along Anymore?" *New York Times*, August 4, 2021, https://www.nytimes.com/2021/08/04/opinion/technology-internet-cooperation.html. See also Thomas B. Edsall, "This Is What Made Covid the 'Almost Ideal Polarizing Crisis,'" *New York Times*, January 26, 2022, https://www.nytimes.com/2022/01/26/opinion/covid-biden-trump-polarization.html (quoting Princeton political scientist Nolan McCarty: "Covid seems to be the almost ideal polarizing crisis. It was conducive to creating strong identities and mapping on to existing ones").

31. Kavita Patel, "Republicans Losing Faith in Their Doctors Makes the Covid Pandemic Worse," MSNBC, December 27, 2021, https://www.msnbc.com/opinion/republicans-losing-faith-their-doctors-makes-covid-pandemic-worse-n1286560. See also Vera Bergengruen, "The Antivax Movement Is Taking Over the Right," *Time*, February 14/21, 2022, at 16–17.

32. Charles M. Blow, "Anti-Vax Insanity," *New York Times*, August 8, 2021, https://www.nytimes.com/2021/08/08/opinion/anti-vaccine-america.html. See also Derek Thompson, "Millions Are Saying No to the Vaccines. What Are They Thinking?" Atlantic, May 3, 2021, https://www.theatlantic.com/ideas/archive/2021/05/the-people-who-wont-get-the-vaccine/618765/; and Brooke Harrington, "The Anti-Vaccine Con Job Is Becoming Untenable," Atlantic, August 1, 2021, https://www.theatlantic.com/ideas/archive/2021/08/vaccine-refusers-dont-want-blue-americas-respect/619627/.

33. See Steven Pinker, *Enlightenment Now: The Case for Reason, Science, Humanism, and Progress* (New York: Viking, 2018), 357 ("[C]ertain beliefs become symbols of cultural allegiance. People affirm or deny these beliefs to express not what they *know* but who they *are*") (emphasis in original).

34. See Bruce Rozenblit, *Us Against Them: How Tribalism Affects the Way We Think* (Kansas City: Transcendent Publications, 2008), 116 ("The belief must prevail, and we can't let a little thing like reality get in the way"). The concept of "truthiness," coined by satirist Stephen Colbert in 2005, is applicable: "[A] truthful or seemingly truthful quality that is claimed for something not because of supporting facts or evidence but because of a feeling that it is true or a desire for it to be true." See Merriam-Webster, https://www.merriam-webster.com/dictionary/truthiness.

35. Jack Healy, "Why an Arizona County Turned Down $1.9 Million in Covid Relief," *New York Times*, February 11, 2022, https://www.nytimes.com/2022/02/11/us/covid-relief-funds.html ("To conservatives, rejecting the money felt like a high-desert declaration of independence").

36. Blow, "Anti-Vax Insanity."

37. See Christopher Lasch, *The Culture of Narcissism: American Life in an Age of Diminishing Expectations* (New York: W.W. Norton & Company, 1979) (describing narcissism as a defensive reaction to social change and instability, a cynical "ethic of self-preservation and psychic survival" that afflicted America).

38. See, for example, Pinker, *Enlightenment Now*, 357 ("We all identify with particular tribes or subcultures, each of which embraces a creed on what makes for a good life and how society should run its affairs").

39. Amy Chua, *Political Tribes: Group Instinct and the Fate of Nations* (New York: Penguin Books, 2018), 41 (emphasis in original).

40. Rozenblit, *Us Against Them*, 7.

41. Chua, *Political Tribes*, 1.

42. Ibid.

43. Ibid. See also Hetherington and Weiler, *Prius or Pickup?* xviii ("People on both sides of the worldview/party divide, in short, have come to see their opponents not simply as strangers, but as a collective menace").

44. Nichols, *The Death of Expertise*, 41.

45. See Thomas B. Edsall, "Trumpism Without Borders," *New York Times*, June 16, 2021, https://www.nytimes.com/2021/06/16/opinion/trump-global-populism.html (quoting Daniel Esty).

46. Greg Lukianoff and Jonathan Haidt, *The Coddling of the American Mind: How Good Intentions and Bad Ideas Are Setting Up a Generation for Failure* (New York: Penguin Press, 2018), 58.

47. See Alexandra Flores, Jennifer C. Cole, Stephan Dickert, and Leaf Van Boven, "Politicians Polarize and Experts Depolarize Public Support for COVID-19 Management Policies Across Countries," *Proceedings of the National Academy of the United States of America*, January 18, 2022, https://www.pnas.org/content/119/3/e2117543119:

> We reason that polarized public opinion in response to political elites reflects a widespread human tendency to categorize people into political ingroups and outgroups and to respond to cues from those groups. This political categorization engenders social, affective, and cognitive processes that divide public opinion when proposals are associated with political identities.

See also Bruce Finley, "People Side With Political Tribe Even When COVID Survival Plan Is Same, CU Experiment Finds," *Denver Post*, January 20, 2022, https://www.denverpost.com/2022/01/20/covid-19-psychology-experiment-university-colorado/ (reporting on the same study and quoting psychologist Leaf Van Boven, "People essentially ask: 'Well, is that my side, or the other side, that proposed this policy?' . . . Almost any issue we want to deal with has this problem. Solutions tend to be proposed by one side or the other side. And, when that happens, ordinary people toe their party line"). See also Ibid. ("Across all countries, liberal and conservative respondents were significantly more likely to support a policy when told elites from their own party endorsed it. When a policy was presented as backed by a bipartisan coalition or neutral experts, it earned the most support").

48. Charles Homans, "Where Does American Democracy Go From Here?" *New York Times Magazine*, March 20, 2022, 33 (quoting Sarah Longwell). See also Chua, *Political Tribes*, 1 (writing that tribe members "seek to benefit their group mates even when they personally gain nothing").

49. See Jonathan Haidt, "After Babel: How Social Media Dissolved the Mortar of Society and Made America Stupid," *Atlantic* (May 2022), 59 (writing that social media has become a platform to "broadcast" one's own tribal loyalties).

50. Bill Bishop, *The Big Sort: Why the Clustering of Like-Minded America is Tearing Us Apart* (Boston: Houghton Mifflin Harcourt, 2008).

51. Ibid., 14.

52. Ibid.

53. Rozenblit, *Us Against Them*, 76. "My tribe is superior to your tribe because we do 'this' and you do 'that,' and the 'this' is always superior to the 'that,' no matter what 'this' and 'that' represent." Ibid., 75. See also Rosabeth Moss Kanter, "Is Tribalism Inevitable?" *Huffington Post*, July 26, 2013, https://www.huffingtonpost.com/rosabeth-moss-kanter/is-tribalism-inevitable_b_3661436.html ("Groups of strangers are quick to find reasons that they are superior to the others").

54. Chua, *Political Tribes*, 105.

55. Lukianoff and Haidt, *The Coddling of the American Mind*, 63.

56. See Elizabeth Crouch Zelman, *Our Beleaguered Species: Beyond Tribalism* (Scotts Valley, CA: CreateSpace Publishing, 2015), 226 (writing that tribalism's "underlying assumption is that members of one's own group are of greater value than those from other groups").

57. Klein, *Why We're Polarized*, 63.

58. David Brooks, "The Retreat to Tribalism," *New York Times*, January 1, 2018, https://www.nytimes.com/2018/01/01/opinion/the-retreat-to-tribalism.html.

59. Hetherington and Weiler, *Prius or Pickup?* xviii.

60. See, for example, Chris Mooney, *The Republican Brain: The Science of Why They Deny Science—and Reality* (Hoboken, NJ: John Wiley & Sons, Inc., 2012), 10. See also Hetherington and Weiler, *Prius or Pickup?* 4 ("the average liberal and the average conservative respond differently to the same experiences").

61. Mooney, *The Republican Brain*, 9.

62. Hetherington and Weiler, *Prius or Pickup?* x–xi.

63. See Jimmy Carter, "I Fear for Our Democracy," *New York Times*, January 9, 2022, SR4 (referring to "the toxic polarization that threatens our democracy" and "the polarization that is reshaping our identities around politics").

64. Hetherington and Weiler, *Prius or Pickup?* xx.

65. Ibid., 20.

66. See Rozenblit, *Us Against Them*, 97 (explaining what seems to be illogical voting behavior by many Americans: "They are *not* voting against their economic interests. They are voting *for* their belief system, their tribe") (emphases in original).

67. Hetherington and Weiler, *Prius or Pickup?* 22. See also Ibid., 61 (describing partisanship as being about more than about politics, including basics of life).

68. Ibid., 90 (noting that when worldview did not polarize, American society was more integrated—for example, Democrats and Republicans living among one another much more so than now). See also Ibid., 144–46 (citing the rise of media bubbles and their protective cocoons that "tend to reinforce their audience's existing beliefs about the [negative] motives and character of the other side, while reaffirming the essential goodness of the home team").

69. Ibid., 23.

70. Timothy D. Snyder, *On Tyranny: Twenty Lessons from the Twentieth Century* (New York: Crown, 2017), 74. See also Haidt, "After Babel," 56 (writing that social media has weakened the pillars of successful democracies, including the need for strong institutions).

71. Hetherington and Weiler, *Prius or Pickup?* xx.

72. See Ibid., 18 (describing worldview on a spectrum, with most Americans falling in the middle).

73. Ibid., xviii (writing that people in both worldview categories see those on the other side as a collective menace). See also Ibid., xx (as dislike for those in the opposite category has deepened, people see the world in ways that favor themselves).

74. See Ibid., xviii. See also Ibid., 55 ("[T]he Democratic and Republican parties have unwittingly turned themselves from regular political organizations to super-charged in-groups whose members' loyalty is determined as much by outlook as by politics").

75. Ibid., xvii.

76. See Ibid., xix (writing that worldview politics is rooted in in human psychology). See also Mooney, *The Republican Brain*, 37 ("Beliefs are *physical*. To attack them is like attacking one part of a person's anatomy") (emphasis in original).

77. See Robert A. Burton, *On Being Certain: Believing You Are Right Even When You're Not* (New York: St. Martin's Griffin, 2008), 195 ("Different genetics, temperaments, and experience led to contrasting worldviews").

78. See John R. Hibbing, Kevin B. Smith, and John R. Alford, *Predisposed: Liberals, Conservatives, and the Biology of Political Differences* (New York: Routledge, 2013).

79. See, for example, Chris Mooney, "Scientists Are Beginning to Figure Out Why Conservatives Are . . . Conservative," *Mother Jones*, July 15, 2014, https://www.motherjones.com/politics/2014/07/biology-ideology-john-hibbing-negativity-bias. See also Ryota Kanai, Tom Feilden, Colin Firth and Geraint Rees, "Political Orientations Are Correlated with Brain Structure in Young Adults," *Current Biology* 26, no. 8 (2011): 677–80.

80. Mooney, *The Republican Brain,* 122.

81. See Michael Shermer, *The Believing Brain: From Ghosts and Gods to Politics and Conspiracies—How We Construct Beliefs and Reinforce Them as Truths* (New York: Times Books, 2011), 59–60 (writing that it is better to overestimate danger and remain alive than it is to underestimate it and be killed).

82. See Burton, *On Being Certain*, 8 ("An immediate reflexive action has clear evolutionary benefits over more time-consuming conscious perception and deliberation").

83. Mooney, *The Republican Brain,* 31.

84. Hetherington and Weiler, *Prius or Pickup?* 7.

85. Kanai, Feilden, Firth, and Rees, "Political Orientations Are Correlated with Brain Structure in Young Adults," 677 (finding "that greater liberalism was associated with increased gray matter volume in the anterior cingulate cortex, whereas greater conservatism was associated with increased volume of the right amygdala").

86. Lukianoff and Haidt, *The Coddling of the American Mind*, 35 (a culture of "safetyism" has surfaced—"an obsession with eliminating threats (both real and imagined) to the point at which people become unwilling to make reasonable trade-offs demanded by other practical and moral concerns").

87. See David Ropeik, "How Tribalism Overrules Reason, and Makes Risky Times More Dangerous," BigThink.com, May 14, 2012, https://bigthink.com/risk-reason -and-reality/how-tribalism-overrules-reason-and-makes-risky-times-more-dangerous ("We have evolved to depend on our tribes, literally, for our safety and survival").

88. See Rebecca Solnit, "An Assault on the Truth," *New York Times*, January 9, 2022, SR4 (addressing change-averse people: "The world is moving on; those who'd rather it stand still are eager to push narratives depicting these shifts as degeneration and white Christian heterosexual America as profoundly imperiled").

89. Hetherington and Weiler, *Prius or Pickup?* 31. See also Harriet Hall, "On Being Certain," *Science-Based Medicine*, May 6, 2008, https://sciencebasedmedicine.org/on -being-certain: ("A 'feeling of knowing' probably had an evolutionary advantage. If we are certain, we can act on that certainty rather than hesitating . . . Certainty makes us feel good: it rewards learning, and it keeps us from wasting time thinking too much; but it impairs flexibility").

90. Burton, *On Being Certain*, xi.

91. See Ibid., 28 (citing research demonstrating the role of the amygdala, "long known to be crucial to the recognizing, processing, and remembering of emotional reactions, including the fear response").

92. See Ibid., 8 ("An immediate reflexive action has clear evolutionary benefits over more time-consuming conscious perception and deliberation").

93. Lydia Denworth, "Conservative and Liberal Brains Might Have Some Real Differences," *Scientific American*, October 26, 2020, https://www.scientificamerican .com/article/conservative-and-liberal-brains-might-have-some-real-differences/ ("On the whole, the research shows, conservatives desire security, predictability and authority more than liberals do, and liberals are more comfortable with novelty, nuance and complexity"). This caveat is acknowledged:

> While these findings are remarkably consistent, they are probabilities, not certainties— meaning there is plenty of individual variability. The political landscape includes lefties who own guns, right-wingers who drive Priuses and everything in between. There is also an unresolved chicken-and-egg problem: Do brains start out processing the world differ- ently or do they become increasingly different as our politics evolve? Furthermore, it is still not entirely clear how useful it is to know that a Republican's brain lights up over X while a Democrat's responds to Y. Ibid.

94. Hetherington and Weiler, *Prius or Pickup?* xvii (to those with a fixed world- view, "You can never let down your guard; you can never be too careful. Anyone who disagrees is a threat to the country's security").

95. See Charles M. Blow, "The American Killing Fields," *New York Times*, May 25, 2022, https://www.nytimes.com/2022/05/25/opinion/uvalde-shooting-republicans .html:

[C]onservatives on the Supreme Court . . . have upheld a corrupt and bastardized interpretation of the Second Amendment. But Republicans have also done so by promoting fear and paranoia. They tell people that criminals are coming to menace you, immigrants are coming to menace you, a race war (or racial replacement) is coming to menace you and the government itself may one day come to menace you.

96. Hetherington and Weiler, *Prius or Pickup?* 4.

97. Ibid., 40.

98. See Ibid., 48 (writing that of those who support building a wall on the U.S.-Mexico border, less than one-third have a fluid worldview while more than three-fourths have a fixed worldview).

99. See Ibid., 50 (more than three-quarters of fixed people favor the ban while one-quarter of fluid people do).

100. See Ibid., 12.

101. Ibid., 41 (writing that people tend to trust those who look like them, and to be wary of people who do not).

102. Ibid., 10.

103. Ibid. (writing that for those who perceive danger in the world, increasing predictability is an important psychological function, adding order to their environment). See also Ibid., 15 (writing that for those who perceive danger, making life orderly and predictable is essential).

104. Ibid., 42. See also Ibid., 44 (noting a significant different in attitudes about race between fixed and fluid people).

105. Ibid., 61.

106. Ibid. (emphasis added).

107. Ibid., 65.

108. Ibid.

109. Lawrence Dorfman, *The Snark Handbook: A Guide to Verbal Sparring* (New York: Skyhorse Illustrated, 2009), 67.

110. This is described in the introduction.

111. But see Michiko Kakutani, *The Death of Truth* (New York: Tim Duggan Books, 2018), 13 (describing the recent era of "truth decay"—the "diminishing role of facts and analysis in American public life that has joined the post-truth lexicon that includes such now familiar phrases as 'fake news' and 'alternative facts'").

112. See Nichols, *The Death of Expertise*, 47 (describing confirmation bias as "the tendency to look for information that only confirms what we believe, to accept facts that only strengthen our preferred explanations, and to dismiss data that challenge what we already accept as truth").

113. See John H. Calvert, "Kitzmiller's Error: Defining 'Religion' Exclusively Rather Than Inclusively," *Liberty University Law Review* 3 (Spring 2009): 281 (referring to Francis Bacon as the inventor of scientific method as well as quoting the seventeenth-century philosopher: "[T]he philosophy which I bring forward . . . does not flatter the understanding by conformity with preconceived notions").

114. See Vincent Blasi, "Holmes and the Marketplace of Ideas," *Supreme Court Review* (2004): 1 (describing the scientific method and its relationship with speech freedom). See also Ibid., 19:

A key tenet of that tradition is that all propositions are subject to perpetual testing. And that process of testing . . . must always hold out at least the possibility that prior under-standings will be displaced. Time, after all, has upset many scientific laws. In short, no matter how elegant and coherent the explanation and supportive the current data, we might be wrong.

See also Irene M. Ten Cate, "Speech, Truth, and Freedom: An Examination of John Stuart Mill's and Justice Oliver Wendell Holmes's Free Speech Defenses," *Yale Journal of Law and the Humanities* 22 (Winter 2010), 35 (comparing the methods advocated by Mill and Holmes including how they parallel scientific inquiry).

115. See, for example, John Stuart Mill, *On Liberty, Utilitarianism and Other Essays, ed.* Mark Philip and Frederick Rosen (Oxford: Oxford University Press, 2015), 45–46 (1859) (arguing that what is believed to be true may be false; that "con-flicting doctrines, instead of being one true and the other false, [may] share the truth between them" and both doctrines may be needed to progress; and knowing both the right and wrong view may build confidence and a deeper understanding of the truth). See also *Abrams v. United States*, 250 U.S. 616, 630 (1919) (Holmes, J., dissenting) ("[T]he ultimate good desired is better reached by free trade in ideas—that the best test of truth is the power of the thought to get itself accepted in the competition of the market").

116. See Nichols, *The Death of Expertise*, 23 ("[T]he public constantly searches for the loopholes in expert knowledge that will allow them to disregard all expert advice they don't like").

117. Burton, *On Being Certain*, 195.

118. Ibid.

119. See Mark Alicke, "Willful Ignorance and Self-Dece*ption*," *Psychology Today*, September 10, 2017, https://www.psychologytoday.com/us/blog/why-we-blame /201709/willful-ignorance-and-self-deception ("Willful ignorance occurs when indi-viduals realize at some level of consciousness that their beliefs are probably false, or when they refuse to attend to information that would establish their falsity"). See also Nichols, *The Death of Expertise*, 1 ("The United States is now a country obsessed with the worship of its own ignorance . . . [W]e're proud of not knowing things").

120. See Rozenblit, *Us Against Them*, 101 (explaining how the power of the tribe over its members is strong enough to lead them to reject beliefs they once held sacred). *See also* Andrew Sullivan, "America Wasn't Built For Humans," *New York Magazine*, September 18, 2017, http://nymag.com/daily/intelligencer/2017/09/can -democracy-survive-tribalism.html ("One of the great attractions of tribalism is that you don't actually have to think very much. All you need to know on any given sub-ject is which side you're on").

121. Nichols, *The Death of Expertise*, 21. See also Ibid., 1:

The foundational knowledge of the average American is now so low that it has crashed through the floor of "uninformed," passed "misinformed" on the way down, and is now plummeting to "aggressively wrong." People don't just believe dumb things; they actively resist further learning rather than let go of those beliefs.

See also Hetherington and Weiler, *Prius or Pickup?* 143 (stating that many Americans are "much more likely to encounter information that confirms their beliefs—or that makes them more extreme, and they can pass it along, whether it is true or not, like a virus to others").

122. Snyder, *On Tyranny*, 73.

123. See Hetherington and Weiler, *Prius or Pickup?* 139–40 ("Acknowledging inconvenient truths also requires people to consider that they made a mistake . . . [N]ot only will well-intentioned efforts to correct a person's misperceptions be unlikely to make much headway, such attempts might actually make him or her defensive about—and more resolute in—their mistaken beliefs").

124. Adam Grant, *Think Again* (New York: Viking, 2021), 25.

125. See Oliver Wendell Holmes, "Natural Law," *Harvard Law Review* 32, no. 1 (1918): 40 ("Certitude is not the test of certainty. We have been cocksure of many things that were not so. Men to a great extent believe what they want to").

126. Grant, *Think Again,* 42. See also Ezra Klein, "David Shor Is Telling Democrats What They Don't Want to Hear," *New York Times*, October 8, 2021, https://www.nytimes.com/2021/10/08/opinion/democrats-david-shor-education-polarization.amp.html (describing "educational polarization"—how varying levels of education serve as a primary driver of divisions in America).

127. Grant, *Think Again,* 46. "Humility is often misunderstood. It's not a matter of having low self-confidence. One of the Latin roots of *humility* means 'from the earth.' It's about being grounded—recognizing that we're flawed and fallible" (emphasis in original).

128. See Thomas L. Friedman, "Make America Immune Again," *New York Times*, May 5, 2020, https://www.nytimes.com/2020/05/05/opinion/coronavirus-us-immunity.html ("we've let ourselves be dumb-as-we-wanna-be for so many years—devaluing science and reading, bashing public servants for political sport, turning politics into entertainment").

129. See Solnit, "An Assault on the Truth" ("The Republicans remain committed to punishing and casting out dissenters—such as Representative Liz Cheney, who has been ostracized since she accurately recognized the criminality of January 6"). See also Nicholas Fandos and Jesse McKinley, "N.Y. Republican Drops Re-Election Bid After Bucking Party on Guns," *New York Times*, June 3, 2022, https://www.nytimes.com/2022/06/03/nyregion/chris-jacobs-congress-guns.html (reporting on GOP candidate Chris Jacobs who suffered political backlash in 2022 after suggesting support for assault weapons regulation. "If you stray from a party position, you are annihilated," Jacobs said).

130. See, for example, Steven Pinker, *Enlightenment Now*, 357 ("certain beliefs become symbols of cultural allegiance. People affirm or deny these beliefs to express not what they *know* but who they *are*") (emphases in original).

131. Jeffrey M. Jones, "Democratic, Republican Confidence in Science Diverges," Gallup, July 16, 2021, https://news.gallup.com/poll/352397/democratic-republican-confidence-science-diverges.aspx (showing 79 percent of Democrats have confidence in science compared to 45 percent of Republicans).

132. Mooney, *The Republican Brain*, 85.

133. See, for example, Naomi Oreskes, "The Reason Some Republicans Mistrust Science: Their Leaders Tell Them To," *Scientific American*, June 1, 2021, https://www.scientificamerican.com/article/the-reason-some-republicans-mistrust-science-their-leaders-tell-them-to/. See also Jack Brewster, "Republican Confidence In Science Drops Nearly 30 Points Since 1975, Poll Finds," *Forbes*, July 16, 2021, https://www.forbes.com/sites/jackbrewster/2021/07/16/republican-confidence-in-science-drops-nearly-30-points-since-1975-poll-finds; Jeffrey M. Jones, "Democratic, Republican Confidence in Science Diverges," Gallup, July 16, 2021, https://news.gallup.com/poll/352397/democratic-republican-confidence-science-diverges.aspx (showing 79 percent of Democrats have confidence in science compared to 45 percent of Republicans).

134. Jones, "Democratic, Republican Confidence in Science Diverges":

[M]any Republican political leaders' statements and policies have been critical of COVID-19 guidance put forth by health experts, and GOP leaders have often resisted requiring citizens to follow mitigation strategies. In contrast, Democratic leaders have generally pursued policies to prevent the spread of the coronavirus but imposed restrictions on social and economic activity . . . Republican mistrust may stem from conservative thought leaders' allegations of liberal bias in the scientific community, perhaps because colleges and universities employ many scientists. Republicans also mistrust colleges and universities and cite a liberal political agenda as the reason for that lack of trust.

135. Oreskes, "The Reason Some Republicans Mistrust Science."

136. Richard Hofstadter, *Anti-Intellectualism in American Life* (New York: Vintage Books, 1962), 6. See also Michael J. Thompson and Gregory R. Smulewicz-Zucker (eds.), *Anti-Science and the Assault on Democracy* (Amherst, NY: Prometheus Books, 2018), 7:

From religiously motivated arguments against the teaching of evolution in public schools to the denial of climate change, new-ageist espousals of alternative medicine, the regular distortion or dismissal of social-scientific data, outlandish claims about the effects of vaccinations or the fluoridation of water, and widespread basic ignorance about concepts such as "theory" or "evidence," antiscience viewpoints are becoming more and more manifest in our daily lives.

See also Sarah Longwell, quoted in "Where Does American Democracy Go From Here?" *New York Times Magazine*, March 20, 2022, 49: "Republicans have decided that it's no longer important to be tethered to the truth."

137. Hofstadter, *Anti-Intellectualism in American Life*, 7.

138. Ibid.

139. See Melissa Healy, "Psychologists Ask: What Makes Some Smart People So Skeptical of Science?" *Los Angeles Times*, January 21, 2017, https://www.latimes.com/science/sciencenow/la-sci-sn-science-skepticism-psychology-20170120-story.html (quoting social psychologist Matthew Hornsey: "We grew up in an era when it was just presumed that reason and evidence were the ways to understand important issues; not fear, vested interests, tradition or faith. But the rise of climate skepticism and the antivaccination movement made us realize that these enlightenment values

are under attack"). See also Haidt, "After Babel," 60 ("by giving everyone a dart gun, social media deputizes everyone to administer justice with no due process").

140. Susan Jacoby, *The Age of American Unreason in a Culture of Lies* (New York: Vintage Books), 2018, xxviii. See also Lyrissa Barnett Lidsky, "Nobody's Fools: The Rational Audience as First Amendment Ideal," *University of Illinois Law Review* (2010): 828–29 ("faith in human reason is misplaced," with people using "mental shortcuts" that "can cause decision making to depart from what strict rationality would dictate").

141. See Merrill Perlman, "How Is Skepticism Different Than Cynicism? Find the Answer in Ancient Greece," *Columbia Journalism Review,* October 15, 2015, https://www.cjr.org/language_corner/skepticism-cynicism.php ("A seeker after truth; an inquirer who has not yet arrived at definite convictions").

142. Perlman, "How Is Skepticism Different Than Cynicism?" ("One who shows a disposition to disbelieve in the sincerity or goodness of human motives and actions, and is wont to express this by sneers and sarcasms; a sneering fault-finder").

143. See Michael Shermer, "What Skepticism Reveals About Science," *Scientific American*, July 1, 2009, https://www.scientificamerican.com/article/what-skepticism -reveals/ (in part, describing science's null hypothesis—the burden of proof is on the person asserting a positive claim, not on the skeptics to disprove it). See also Nichols, *The Death of Expertise*, 53 (describing the scientific method as "the set of steps that lead from a general question, to a hypothesis, testing, and analysis").

144. John Stuart Mill, "On Liberty" in *The Basic Writings of John Stuart Mill* (New York: The Modern Library, 2002), 44 (1859) ("Both teachers and learners go to sleep at their post as soon as there is no enemy in the field").

145. See Shermer, "What Skepticism Reveals About Science":

I conclude that I'm a skeptic not because I do not want to believe but because I want to *know*. I believe that the truth is out there. But how can we tell the difference between what we would like to be true and what is actually true? The answer is science (emphasis in original).

146. Nichols, *The Death of Expertise*, 1.

147. See Hetherington and Weiler, *Prius or Pickup?* 37 (writing of the importance of tradition for those with a fixed worldview, and why a slogan like "Make America Great Again" especially resonated with them, recalling an era of school prayer and fixed gender roles).

148. Mooney, *The Republican Brain*, 85.

149. Ibid., 86 (quoting Yuval Levin).

150. Ibid., 263 ("We know that conservatives tend to be more intense in their loyalty and dedication to their group . . . and helps to explain their willingness to double down on certain wrong beliefs that are politically vital to their party. They're defending their 'band of brothers,' so to speak").

151. "Cognitive Dissonance*,*" *Psychology Today*, accessed June 21, 2022, https://www.psychologytoday.com/us/basics/cognitive-dissonance. See also Leon Festinger, *A Theory of Cognitive Dissonance* (Stanford, CA: Stanford University Press, 1957), 3

("When dissonance is present, in addition to trying to reduce it, the person will actively avoid situations and information which would likely increase the dissonance").

152. See Julie Beck, "This Article Won't Change Your Mind," *Atlantic*, March 13, 2017, https://www.theatlantic.com/science/archive/2017/03/this-article-wont-change-your-mind/519093/ ("[I]f the thing you might be wrong about is a belief that's deeply tied to your identity or worldview—the guru you've dedicated your life to is accused of some terrible things, the cigarettes you're addicted to can kill you—well, people . . . do[] all the mental gymnastics it takes to remain convinced that they're right"). See also Solnit, "An Assault on the Truth," ("[G]ullibility means you believe something because someone else wants you to").

153. U.S. House Select Committee to Investigate the January 6th Attack on the United States Capitol, https://january6th.house.gov.

154. David Folkenflik, "Only One Major Cable News Channel Did Not Carry the Jan. 6 Hearing Live: Fox News," NPR, June 11, 2022, https://www.npr.org/2022/06/10/1104116455/fox-news-jan-6-hearing.

155. Philip Bump, "Fox News Didn't Just Ignore the Jan. 6 Hearing. It Did Something Worse," *Washington Post*, June 10, 2022, https://www.washingtonpost.com/politics/2022/06/10/fox-news-didnt-just-ignore-jan-6-hearing-it-did-something-worse/.

156. See Nichols, *The Death of Expertise*, 47 (defining confirmation bias as "the tendency to look for information that only confirms what we believe, to accept facts that only strengthen our preferred explanations, and to dismiss data that challenge what we already accept as truth").

157. See, for example, "Motivated Reasoning," *Psychology Today*, accessed June 21, 2022, https://www.psychologytoday.com/us/basics/motivated-reasoning ("One of the most significant ways information processing and decision making becomes warped is through motivated reasoning, when biased reasoning leads to a particular conclusion or decision, a process that often occurs outside of conscious awareness"). See also Beck, "This Article Won't Change Your Mind" ("Motivated reasoning is how people convince themselves or remain convinced of what they want to believe—they seek out agreeable information and learn it more easily; and they avoid, ignore, devalue, forget, or argue against information that contradicts their beliefs").

158. Hetherington and Weiler, *Prius or Pickup?* 136 (writing that the rise of worldview politics has resulted in Americans being more resistant to information unless it confirms their preexisting ideas about the world).

159. 159. See generally Festinger, *A Theory of Cognitive Dissonance*.

160. Mooney, *The Republican Brain*, 41.

161. Hannah Nam, political neuroscientist, Stony Brook University, quoted in Denworth, "Conservative and Liberal Brains Might Have Some Real Differences."

162. See Hetherington and Weiler, *Prius or Pickup?* 26 ("Being conservative . . . also means believing you can't be too careful when you encounter other people, especially strangers with newfangled ideas").

163. Grant, *Think Again,* 29. See also Blackburn, *On Truth,* 8 ("people lock themselves into sealed silos, refusing any information or evidence that contradicts whatever comfortable view of things they have hit upon").

164. See Hetherington and Weiler, *Prius or Pickup?* 141 (writing of evidence that conservatives are more likely to take steps to reinforce their worldview than those on the political left). See also Ibid., 143 (writing that the results of several studies suggest that, when confronted with information that challenges preexisting beliefs, conservatives may have a particularly strong propensity to reason with bias).

165. See, for example, Ibid., 141. See also Jemele Hill, "Chris Paul Bears the Brunt of Pro Sports' Vaccination Problem," *Atlantic*, June 18, 2021, https://www.theatlantic .com/ideas/archive/2021/06/chris-paul-pro-sports-vaccination-problem/619250/ ("too many people . . . are prone to stay rooted in whatever viewpoint validates their fears, however unfounded and unlikely").

166. Blackburn, *On Truth,* 13 ("Truth is the goal of inquiry, the aim of experiment, the standard signaling the difference between it being right to believe something, and wrong to do so. We must court it, for in its absence we are bewildered or lost or may even be facing the wrong way, on the wrong track altogether").

167. Burton, *On Being Certain*, 186. See also Blackburn, *On Truth,* 42 ("Reality indeed presses us to believe what is true, but sad to say, when we want to believe what is in fact false, we have defenses against the pressure. People dislike admitting that they have been taken in").

168. Solnit, "An Assault on the Truth."

169. Blackburn, *On Truth,* 8 (people believing what they want to "is abetted by the balkanization of news sources").

170. Hetherington and Weiler, *Prius or Pickup?* 78.

171. See Ibid., 76 ("Seventy-two percent of Democrats regarded the impact of these institutions as positive, while only 36 percent of Republicans felt the same").

172. Ibid., 76 (writing that even among Republicans who attended college, there is a wariness that institutions of higher education "are increasingly infested with intolerant liberalism").

173. See Jennifer Finney Boylan, "The Radical Normalcy of a Trans 'Jeopardy!' Winner," *New York Times*, January 7, 2022, https://www.nytimes.com/2022/01/07/ opinion/culture/jeopardy-trans-amy-schneider.html (writing of a game show champion who is transgender, "It's about how terrifying some Americans find any shift toward inclusivity and tolerance. It's about their unwillingness to accept the reality that it's actually not very radical to be trans anymore").

174. Chua, *Political Tribes*, 177.

175. See Farhad Manjoo, "What If Humans Just Can't Get Along Anymore?" *New York Times*, August 4, 2021, https://www.nytimes.com/2021/08/04/opinion /technology-internet-cooperation.html ("The internet didn't start the fire, but it's undeniable that it has fostered a sour and fragmented global polity—an atmosphere of pervasive mistrust, corroding institutions and a collective retreat into the comforting bosom of confirmation bias").

176. See Nichols, *The Death of Expertise*, 25 (lamenting the "disturbing characteristic" of a "thin-skinned insistence that opinion be treated as truth").

177. Blackburn, *On Truth,* 19 (emphasis in original). See also Steven R. Wiesman, "Introduction," in *Daniel Patrick Moynihan: A Portrait in Letters of an American*

Visionary, ed. Steven R. Wiseman (New York: Public Affairs, 2010), 1–2 (quoting Moynihan: "Everyone is entitled to his own opinion, but not his own facts").

178. Solnit, "An Assault on the Truth" ("Too many Americans now feel entitled to their won facts. In this too-free marketplace of ideas, they can select facts or histories to match their goals, because meaning has become transactional").

179. Blackburn, *On Truth,* 13.

180. See Mooney, *The Republican Brain*, 33 ("we sometimes have other important goals besides accuracy—including identity affirmation and protecting our sense of self. These can make us highly resistant to changing our beliefs when, by all rights, we probably should").

181. See, for example, Eric Blumenson, "The Challenge of a Global Standard of Justice: Peace, Pluralism, and Punishment at the International Criminal Court," *Columbia Journal of Transnational Law* 44 (2006): 865.

182. Tom R. Tyler, "Viewing CSI and the Threshold of Guilt: Managing Truth and Justice in Reality and Fiction," *Yale Law Journal* 115 (March 2006): 1065.

183. See, for example, John Noonan, "The Purposes of Advocacy and the Limits of Confidentiality," *Michigan Law Review* 64, no. 8 (1966): 1491; Andrew R. Herron, "Collegiality, Justice, and the Public Image: Why One Lawyer's Pleasure Is Another's Poison," *University of Miami Law Review* 44 (January 1990), 812 ("In the classic scenario, truth is a prerequisite for justice. In such a world, the goal of judicial proceedings is to produce the most accurate depiction of the dispute that is possible, the foundation of wise and informed decisionmaking").

Chapter 2

The Court

Politicized and Polarized

In 2018, Chief Justice John Roberts declared, "We do not have Obama judges or Trump judges, Bush judges or Clinton judges. What we have is an extraordinary group of dedicated judges doing their level best to do equal right to those appearing before them. That independent judiciary is something we should all be thankful for."[1] By asserting the importance of an independent judiciary, Roberts reiterated a longstanding belief, a foundation of any free and democratic nation. Subsequent to his statement, however, questions surfaced about whether his declaration remains accurate. Some of those questions—and denials—were expressed by justices themselves.[2] Particularly as it applies to justices of the U.S. Supreme Court, there are doubts about judicial independence—and at the same time, growing belief about polarization on the Court[3]—especially when it comes to allegiance to the ideology of the president who nominated them.

That the Supreme Court is polarized is not news bulletin–worthy. It does warrant analysis, however, in large part because just like the nation whose laws it judges, the Court is polarized in ways previously unseen. Neal Devins and Lawrence Baum, for example, note that in the twenty-first century, there is a linkage on the Court between party and ideology as never before:

> Since 2010, when Elena Kagan replaced John Paul Stevens, all of the Republican-nominated Justices on the Supreme Court have been to the right of all of its Democratic-nominated Justices. This pattern is widely recognized, but it is not well recognized that it is unique in the Court's history. Before 2010, the Court never had clear ideological blocs that coincided with party lines.[4]

That clear alignment with party-driven ideology worries many today. In her 2021 book *Justice on the Brink*, for example, Linda Greenhouse expresses not only her apprehension, but also lays out how this division manifested itself.

"Of course, not every Supreme Court case turns on ideology," she writes. "But when ideology matters, it matters greatly."[5] She cites specific issues that, when brought to the Court, illustrate not only ideological motivations, but also the Court's polarization. These include rights surrounding voting, guns, religion, and abortion.

At issue is more than disagreement; that has always been at the heart of the business of both the nation and the Court. Debate that sometimes results in differences of opinion is necessary in democracies and their deliberative institutions.[6] Now, however, the disagreement is over what to disagree about. It is more than basic. Seeing eye-to-eye is no longer the most significant challenge; it has been superseded by trying to exist on the same plane(t).[7]

Too often it seems that the members of the Court's opposing factions live in different worlds. There's a good reason for that: they do. That is, they have conflicting worldviews.[8] The presidential commission established in 2021 to examine reform of the Court was rooted, in part, in this polarization—both its causes and its results.[9] When we wonder how even people who, on at least one level seem to be so similar, but can think so differently, especially about basic issues regarding their shared mission, the answer lies in worldview. As the label suggests, they see the world differently.

Basic, different worldviews occur despite similarities that bring people together. A small, exclusive group like the justices of the Supreme Court can divide significantly notwithstanding similarities that include foundational traits such as background, education, and an allegiance to both the rule of law and their institution. Granted, comparable backgrounds and educations assure neither similar methods of decision making, nor similar kinds of decisions. Conversely, significant space in the literature has been devoted to how lawyers and judges think, and how it differs from how nonlawyers reason.[10] Moreover, the argument that similarity in thinking by Supreme Court justices is derived from law school education is supported not merely by the fact that all Supreme Court justices are lawyers subject to unique training, but even more so based on the specific law schools each attended. For example, eight of the nine justices of the Court's 2022–2023 term graduated not only from Ivy League law schools, but did so from one of only two, Yale or Harvard. Of the six justices who most recently left the Court, five attended Harvard.[11] If, as the literature indicates, law school is key in shaping a jurist's thought processes,[12] it would not be unreasonable to hypothesize that a substantial degree of homogeneity in reasoning and decision making would surface. One might even suspect that most Court decisions would be unanimous or close to it.[13]

Instead, as of 2022—and as it has been for much of the twenty-first century—the Court's decisions are often sharply divided. Rulings are rarely unanimous and are commonly 6–3 or 5–4.[14] Among the reasons: The lives of its members are not defined solely by background and education. They are also based on worldview and politics. Though it was still developing, each Supreme Court justice possessed a worldview upon entering law school, with further evolution of ideas and perspectives occurring subsequently. Those ideas that were learned, however, were often accepted or rejected by each person consistent with his or her worldview.[15] As discussed in chapter 1, one's worldview is hardwired to some extent, with both nature and nurture contributing to its character.[16] Thus, while law school may create a "think like a lawyer" mentality, it neither erases nor supersedes all that came before, nor does it mask all that follows.

A comparison of Justices Sonia Sotomayor and Brett Kavanaugh serves as an example. Though both graduated from Yale Law School, they will not be mistaken for ideological doppelgängers. Each is more than his/her law school influences. It is well documented, for example, that Justice Sotomayor's upbringing in New York's South Bronx by an alcoholic father and a mother considered socially distant[17] was markedly different than how Justice Kavanaugh grew up in suburban Washington, D.C., raised by affluent, law degree–holding parents and that included attendance at an esteemed prep school.[18] These and other circumstances contributed to the development of very different worldviews.

Though their agreement rates are not quite the lowest on the Court,[19] it is clear that these two justices are not ideological allies.[20] In critical 5–4 decisions, Kavanaugh and Sotomayor agree in 5.6 percent of them, nearly the lowest when comparing two justices.[21] *Jones v. Mississippi*[22] serves as an example. Kavanaugh wrote the Court's opinion that significantly rolled back the rights of juvenile criminal offenders. In a dissent called "brutal"[23] and "searing,"[24] Sotomayor referred to the reasoning in the Kavanaugh-penned opinion as shocking, an unjustified and abrupt break from precedent, and one that distorts precedent "beyond recognition" by twisting it in a way that cannot be reconciled. "It seems the Court is willing to overrule precedent without even acknowledging it is doing so," she wrote, foretelling future approaches by the Court's majority, "much less providing any special justification."[25] One observer noted that it appeared that Sotomayor "is fed up with Kavanaugh's habit of posturing as a moderate, then voting like a reactionary. When the stakes are low, Kavanaugh knows how to sound like a reasonable, empathetic centrist. But when an actual person's rights are on the line, Kavanaugh's vote is nowhere to be found."[26]

In addition to illustrating that two graduates of the same law school can have opposing (world)views, *Jones v. Mississippi* also embodies other phenomena relevant in the present context. First, because this 2021 ruling was divided precisely along ideological lines, it represents what might be referred to as "the new 5–4"—a 6–3 split in which all of the majority justices were nominated by Republican presidents, with all of the dissenters nominated by Democrats. This supermajority is particularly pertinent in that there are now five reliable conservative votes *in addition to* Chief Justice Roberts who sometimes lacks the perceived requisite loyalty to conservative causes,[27] instead assuming a role as principal mediator. Second, this ruling is among those that demand a recontextualization and reconsideration of a phenomenon explored in chapter 1—confirmation bias.

By way of reminder, confirmation bias is a "tendency to look for information that only confirms what we believe, to accept facts that only strengthen our preferred explanations, and to dismiss data that challenge what we already accept as truth."[28] In colloquial terms, it is sometimes referred to as "cherry picking."[29] Particularly when Supreme Court rulings occur along ideological lines, it is not unreasonable to consider whether and to what extent the outcome was preordained.[30] That is, a skeptic—a *healthy* skeptic, in fact—could view the outcome of a case like *Jones v. Mississippi* as entirely predictable. In an era in which jurists cling to ideology, in too many cases an observer simply needs to determine the side of a case that appeals to those who are politically conservative and hold a fixed worldview to conclude that it will have five-to-six votes.

To be sure, there are exceptions to this formula. There are many decisive, largely (or completely) unified rulings on the Court—unanimous or 8–1. In the 2020–2021 term, for example, there were more 9–0 rulings—46 percent when all nine justices participated—than any of the other vote split possibilities.[31] On what might be called the Court's politically infused cases, however, clear worldview-based divisions emerge—since 2010 in particular, when the Court crossed the Rubicon of political polarization noted by Devins and Baum.[32]

Another qualifier: This is not necessarily to suggest that in every case before the Court, each justice consciously forms a final opinion prior to analyzing the facts and hearing arguments, though it happens.[33] In some instances, it may be that during the process of evaluation, one set of briefs and arguments appeals to a justice because it corresponds to his/her worldview. For example, embedded in a case may be perceived issues of security and safety, where a specific ruling would help to alleviate the fear that is often present for some. A similar tactic can be implemented by a justice with a fluid worldview, of course, consistent with that perspective's attributes. Granted, the purpose of the judicial process includes determining results, that is, outcomes. Criticism surfaces, however, when those outcomes appear to be predetermined, either consciously or unconsciously.

Confirmation bias is uncannily similar to a phenomenon that is sometimes linked to the judiciary: Result orientation indicates a predisposition to ruling in a particular way. These inclinations or sympathies may stem from any of a variety of factors, some of which are what make anyone human. On the other hand, the presence of result orientation/confirmation bias on the bench is antithetical to the independence that members of the Supreme Court have endeavored to establish and maintain in the court of public opinion. With result orientation, a jurist may have an allegiance, conscious or unconscious, to specific values. Often, those values align with worldview. Cases are observed and the Constitution is interpreted through the lens of that same worldview. Some of the values brought to bear may be characterized as political or ideological.

Although the reality of result orientation in the judiciary is recognized, scholars are often critical.[34] Its elements: inconsistency between the issue as defined by the Court and the facts presented; disregard of stare decisis; and an unreasonable textual interpretation.[35] The problematic nature of any one of these is apparent; in combination, they are nothing less than egregious.

Result orientation also tends to summon yet another phenomenon, judicial activism. This particularly occurs, according to Louis Fisher, when "there is a transparent effort to reach a decision that squares with the policy preferences of the justices."[36] To be sure, "judicial activism" is a slippery term that carries with it multiple meanings and multiple opinions—a quintessential Pandora's Box.[37] Nevertheless, while activism is justified according to some, it often carries with it negative connotations.[38] If not a polar opposite to the generally revered standard of judicial restraint,[39] it stands in stark contrast. Over history, there have been different varieties of judicial activism—progressive activism of the 1960s,[40] for example, and a conservative effort in the 1980s, to the present effort to move the Court and the nation's law to the right.[41] Critics of judicial activism tend to coalesce along political and worldview lines. That is, some observers become critical of judicial behavior when it is perceived as activism in support of issues that conflict with *their* ideologies. Conversely, a brand of activism consistent with views tends to be embraced.[42]

CONSTITUTIONAL APPROACHES

It is not uncommon, as noted previously, for U.S. Supreme Court justices to remind the public of their commitment to independence. Indeed, historically it has been accepted that if a justice has any predilections regarding a given case, those notions are set aside to provide the necessary independent evaluation. Yet, scholars such as Jeffrey Addicott claim the evidence to the contrary is "obvious,"[43] with Court opinions consistently falling along an ideological spectrum ranging from conservative "originalist" to the liberal "living constitutionalist." Addicott poses a revealing question: "[I]f judges were supposed to follow the 'law' in rendering neutral decisions from the bench, why do so many Supreme Court opinions not only fail to achieve unanimity but seem to easily fall into fixed ideological camps?"[44] Various labels may be applied to those camps, including the fixed and fluid worldviews.

Those worldview categories and their properties can be applied on both macro and micro levels. That is, worldview can explain how someone sees the world. In addition, it illustrates how someone approaches their work—for example, how a Supreme Court justice reads and interprets the U.S. Constitution in a specific case. That interpretation is governed by worldview.

Each of the two widely accepted methods of constitutional interpretation, originalism and living constitutionalism, is accompanied by controversy. This occurs primarily because of the strong views held by those who are adherents to each and, perhaps more importantly, because of those who oppose the other. Largely speaking, these approaches to the Constitution are mutually exclusive, and to the extent that the methods and their champions may be viewed as being polarized.[45]

For the moment, a brief description of each: An originalist views the Constitution's text as sacrosanct, a fixed document that leaves little if any room for nuance, and to be read and interpreted as the Founders intended. A living constitutionalist, on the other hand, adopts an approach that begins with that same text, but also embraces the notion that its meaning and application are adaptable—that is, fluid—according to developments since the Constitution and its amendments were written. The link to worldview and its categories is apparent: originalism is a fixed approach, while living constitutionalism is a fluid approach.[46] Accordingly, the labels "fixed-originalist" and "fluid-living constitutionalist" will be adopted and utilized herein.

Originalism

Originalism's major premise, according to Princeton professor Keith Whittington, is to regard "the discoverable meaning of the Constitution at the time of its initial adoption as authoritative for purposes of constitutional interpretation in the present."[47] It arose as a response by political conservatives to the transformative, liberal rulings by the Supreme Court of the 1950s and 1960s led by Chief Justice Earl Warren—the Warren Court. Some of these rulings discerned and applied previously unacknowledged meanings to the Constitution.[48] Perhaps the most prominent of many notable rulings of that era, the *Brown v. Board of Education*[49] ruling that limited school desegregation according to race, has been recognized as being a significant catalyst of the originalist movement.[50] Subsequently, originalism evolved in accordance with conservative politics,[51] developing into a tool to help legitimize and justify conservative policies.[52] Moreover, originalism linked itself with the Republican Party,[53] appearing in all but one party platform since 1992.[54]

As the analysis of originalism developed, it was suggested that it has two histories, one as approached in the academy, the other in a political context.[55] The mere fact of the latter demonstrates a significant aspect of its nature: it has become part of a political/judicial movement, adopted by conservatives and woven into an effort to sway not merely the law, but also the nation, and armed with a purported justification that following the doctrine is done in accordance with the Founders' original intent,[56] thus deferring to a higher authority. This approach, however, is met with several challenges. First, there is evidence leading many to conclude that those same Founders purposefully structured and worded the Constitution with nuance and ambiguity to allow for—and even compel—adaptations over time.[57] Second, even *if* absolute fidelity to the original text is the best approach, the Founders' relevant intent may be largely undiscoverable.[58] Third, the premise of originalism begs a fundamental question: How can any text be viewed neutrally or objectively given the unique prisms, filters and life experiences—not to mention world-views—possessed by the readers?

The imperfections of the Constitution, written by select, land-owning white males, are generally recognized today. As Jesse Wegman writes, "the nation has rejected the worst of the founders' beliefs and values and sought to respond to the needs of a growing and changing society, either through constitutional amendments or modern interpretations of the text they cre-ated"[59]—that is, living constitutionalism. Originalism not only rejects such an approach, but by doing so, it confines the nation to the past, whether intentionally or by happenstance—another demonstration how originalism is aligned with the fixed worldview.

Though originalism demands the U.S. Constitution to be interpreted according to its original meaning as the founders intended[60]—what is some-times regarded as strict textualism—its tenets may not be so strict. First, there are issues regarding its advocates' sometimes wobbly allegiance to the doctrine. As distinguished constitutional law scholar Erwin Chemerinsky writes, "Conservatives who espouse a need to be true to the framers' intent are willing to abandon it when it does not support the results they want."[61] It seems reasonable to suggest, then, that wavering loyalty to what is typically a venerated approach in conservative circles discredits claims of the doctrine's universal applicability and its overall value. Chemerinsky, whose criticism of originalism runs deep, again weighs in here, writing that it "only allows conservative justices and judges to pretend that they are following a neutral theory when in reality they are imposing their own values."[62]

Second, within originalism's "gray areas"—typically pointed out not by its champions, but by its critics[63]—lies what has been labeled as "soft original-ism."[64] In addition, several variations to originalism's basic theory emerged over time,[65] suggesting that originalism in its earliest form was wanting. (This is supported by the circumstantial willingness to abandon the approach, as described immediately above.) Among originalism's deficiencies that critics have targeted include the uncertainty that this creates within the doctrine.[66]

Practitioners of originalism seem to be more than comfortable with any ambiguity it presents—or perhaps more accurately, they reject the reality of that uncertainty. No one was more at ease with the imprecision than Antonin Scalia. "Justice Scalia was the face of modern originalism."[67] No truer words were ever written. In this case, the words were written by now-justice and Scalia protégé Amy Coney Barrett.[68] Scalia's penchant for originalism—a "lesser evil" compared to any other method, according to the title of an essay he wrote[69]—lies in the danger that with other approaches, "judges will mistake their own predilections for the law."[70] The inference and perception that originalism is objective becomes part of its appeal. Moreover, by binding judges to texts, it is perceived by its advocates as a way to impose restraint.[71]

Originalism has achieved its footing in part by its supporters explaining its legal merits—its neutrality and legitimacy. That is, it is praised as a politically impartial approach that prevents judges from substituting their personal preferences for the law. "In reality," according to Ian Millhiser, "this method rarely lives up to such lofty promises. Many legal texts (including much of the Constitution) are ambiguous and can be fairly read in many ways."[72] Rather than recognize the nuance, however, fixed-originalists champion the comfort and safety of a singular reading that better fits within a binary worldview.[73] One either reads the text as written and intended, according to this view, or he/she reads it incorrectly. "The problem with a judge cloaking herself in 'originalism,'" writes Kaiya Arroyo, "is that she can then argue that she is being entirely rational and disinterested, when in fact she is deciding cases that best fit with her ideological views."[74] The dominance of originalism on the current Court thus casts doubt on the institution's ability to make nuanced judgments. Columbia law professor Jamal Greene is among those who have voiced this concern, and attributes it to polarization and partisanship on the Court.[75]

As much as some are enticed by originalism due to the neutrality it ostensibly brings to the bench, its advocates have gained at least as much traction by aligning themselves with social and political conservatives.[76] Relationships were forged by using originalism as a method to achieve their goals.[77] Changing the law, and thus the nation, can be accomplished in multiple ways. One method is with legislation; another, and arguably an easier way, is through the courts. Particularly as Congress has grown more dysfunctional due to obstructionist stalemate, "the Supreme Court is increasingly the locus of policymaking within the United States."[78] Liberal activism, many concluded—especially evidenced by politically charged rulings such as *Roe v. Wade*[79]—is most efficiently confronted in the courts, particularly the Supreme Court. After all, it takes only five votes there—and by people not subject to elections[80]—not the 60 senators, 268 members of the House, and one president needed for legislation to become law. Better yet in the eyes of some, through the Supreme Court, the Constitution is effectively changed, not through the nearly impossible task of amending it,[81] but instead by reinterpreting it from the bench.[82] Particularly with the goal being a return to pre-Warren-Court-era law[83]—and consistent with a fixed worldview—an antiprecedent movement, and control of the Court, was key.[84] It still is. "[T]he court's conservative majority," according to Jeff Shesol, "is both a product and a sponsor of partisan conflict."[85] As Mark Joseph Stern writes, one political party in particular—the GOP—"outsourced large chunks of its agenda to the courts which . . . are eager to oblige."[86]

A twenty-first-century view of originalism links it to—indeed, sees it as part of—a political movement. "[T]he politics of originalism," writes Mary Ziegler, "have been conducted from the bottom up as well as from the top down."[87] Originalism's contemporary popularity in some circles—an arguably paradoxical popularity given its devotion to the past[88]—stems directly from its ability to facilitate and justify certain political outcomes. According to Robert Post and Reva Siegel, "originalism connects constitutional law to a living political culture and provides its proponents a compelling language in which to seek constitutional change through adjudication and politics."[89] In short, originalism is a political instrument, at times a sharp scalpel, at other times a blunt cudgel. Rather than being any sort of neutral principle meant to preserve a fixed and unchanging Constitution,[90] and instead of focusing on process and not outcomes, adherence to originalism has become a political practice that, according to Post and Siegel, "seeks instead to forge a vibrant connection between the Constitution and contemporary conservative values."[91] Siegel is even more emphatic in describing the method used by originalism's advocates:

> [They] regularly employ the language of originalism to exhort Americans to mobilize against the Court and seek constitutional change without the intermediation of constitutional lawmaking. Originalism, in other words, is not merely a jurisprudence. It is a discourse employed in politics to mount an attack on courts. Since the 1970s, originalism's proponents have deployed the law/politics distinction and the language of constitutional restoration in the service of constitutional change.[92]

While originalism has roots in the law and has ascended as an instrument of politics, its ultimate power has been realized at the intersection of the two fields. "Since the 1980s, originalism has primarily served as an ideology that inspires political mobilization and engagement," write Post and Siegel. "Its success and influence is [*sic*] due chiefly to its uncanny capacity to facilitate passionate political participation."[93] If nothing else, originalism in its current form—a method that "forge[s] a vibrant connection between the Constitution and contemporary conservative values"[94]—illustrates the extent to which law and politics have merged. Rather than achieving the ideal of independence that it claims to embody and preserve, the judiciary, with the Supreme Court at the summit, is now clearly a political institution, due in part to its majority's allegiance to originalism.[95]

Regardless of one's view of originalism, there is no disputing that it has played a central role in American law and politics for decades.[96] At the core of the originalist creed of strict textual interpretation is the goal of restricting the reach of constitutional protections to narrow circumstances and to limited (that is, preferred) segments of the population.[97] The result appeals to many, particularly those who view America as a zero-sum enterprise with a fixed quantity of resources and rights to be allocated to a relative few. As part of that view—and taking a page from tribalism's playbook—those who possess privilege seek not merely to keep it, but also to prevent what they view as a limited resource from spilling into "undeserving" population pools.[98] Originalism's goal of reverting to previous eras—for example, the pre–Warren Court years prior and the expansion of Constitutionally based rights[99]—is thus consistent with a fixed worldview.[100] Originalism is a constitutional cover that provides conservatives a self-proclaimed legitimacy to roll back rights. According to David Kaplan, because originalists "favor a status quo forever fixed in the 18th century, they tend to favor the 'haves' of that time—and to disfavor all others, including minorities and unpopular litigants."[101]

The development of originalism and living constitutionalism are, in part, responses to one another. Originalism's critics objected that giving past generations control over the living subverts the Constitution's democratic authority. Proponents of originalism, on the other hand, counter by claiming that judicial review lacks democratic authority when judges depart from the original understanding of those who ratified the Constitution. As noted, the challenge becomes determining just what that original meaning is, and recognizing that however that is determined, it is viewed through a contemporary lens.[102] In addition, a stated refusal to apply contemporary values to the Constitution adds to doubts about the Court's legitimacy. Jamal Greene is among those who believe it is problematic when interpretational flexibility is lacking, evidenced by the difficulty in declaring the exact meaning and boundaries of a given passage in the Constitution, and unwaveringly stating that it will *always* carry an unwavering and precise meaning.[103]

Living Constitutionalism

Distinguished from originalism, living constitutionalism does not view the Constitution rigidly—that is, in a fixed manner[104]—to be read only as it was intended at the time of its ratification in 1789. Instead, as noted above, because it recognizes that the nation has evolved organically, living constitutionalism believes that the interpretation of the text should also be adaptable—that is, fluid.[105] The Constitution provides Americans an important and common reference point, to be sure, but not the only one. While the words of the Constitution are static (aside from its amendments), the nation and world are not. Advocates of living constitutionalism believe that those facts should be considered.

Although its roots are generally traced to the mid-1920s,[106] living constitutionalism especially gained traction in the aftermath of the New Deal. Rather than viewing the onset of extreme economic circumstances as requiring a flexible interpretation of the Constitution, courts remained attached to its literal meaning. Critics pushed back, demanding a more fluid approach. Then, as now, it is common to link this methodological approach to those on the political left. "Liberals and progressives," writes Mark Hendrickson, "believe that the Constitution is a living, breathing document that should evolve with the times. They want Supreme Court justices to be flexible in interpreting the Constitution and adapting 18th-century language to 21st-century applications."[107]

In one of his earliest works, and before becoming a Supreme Court justice, Oliver Wendell Holmes Jr. wrote, "The life of the law has not been logic, it has been experience."[108] Since then, scholars have analyzed these words, with many viewing them as constituting the classic testament to modern legal pragmatism.[109] It is not uncommon, in fact, to link or equate pragmatism and living constitutionalism.[110] "The felt necessities of the time," Holmes continued, "have much more to do with determining governing rules than by drawing conclusions from abstract reasoning." It is suggested here that the "experience" and "necessities of the time" that Holmes prioritized are fundamental to living constitutionalism and its recognition that the lived experiences of a nation and its people are essential in understanding and applying the law and the Constitution.[111]

It is commonly—though not universally—accepted that the Constitution is more than the sum of its parts. For example, though privacy is never once mentioned specifically in the text, it is now widely accepted as a constitutionally based right, implicit in the words.[112] Though it took several decades to be fully recognized as a matter of law, the idea of protecting privacy through the law began in the late nineteenth and early twentieth centuries, long after the ink had dried on the Constitution and Bill of Rights, triggered by and in response to cultural developments.[113] Repeated incidents catalyzed the movement. Had the Constitution's text been relied on exclusively, privacy would not be viewed as a constitutionally protected right today. As Bruce Ackerman writes in support of living constitutionalism, "Rather than focusing myopically on the great texts of the eighteenth and nineteenth centuries, we must redefine the canon to permit a deeper understanding of what Americans did, and did not, accomplish over all of our history, including the part that is closest to us."[114]

Not so ironically, the authority of the Supreme Court itself stems from an approach—that is, living constitutionalism—that views the Constitution as more than its words. While the existence of the Court is specifically stipulated in the Constitution,[115] its authority is not. That originates with the foundational 1803 ruling, *Marbury v. Madison*,[116] and the unquestioned doctrine it established, as pointed out by Justice Sonia Sotomayor: "There is not anything in the Constitution that says that the Court, the Supreme Court, is the last word on what the Constitution means. It was totally novel at that time. And yet, what the Court did was *reason from the structure of the Constitution* that that's what was intended."[117]

Therein lies a key element: reason. Looking beyond the surface to discover meaning is often anathema to the nuance-averse, fixed-originalist. To do so disturbs the comfort and safety of certainty provided by a view that typically requires consideration of only the Constitution's literal meaning.

Since its founding, the United States, and the world, has changed in incalculable ways—in the areas of technology, economics, politics and social mores, among others—ways that no one could have foreseen when the Constitution was drafted.[118] Moreover, various changes have occurred even since the last time the Constitution was amended in 1992.[119] "So it seems inevitable that the Constitution will change, too," David Strauss writes. "It is also a good thing, because an unchanging Constitution would fit our society very badly. Either it would be ignored or, worse, it would be a hindrance, a relic that keeps us from making progress and prevents our society from working in the way it should."[120] The cumbersome and lengthy nature of amending the Constitution[121] arguably prevents it from being adequately responsive to this changing world, even as cases continue to be submitted to, heard, and decided by the courts. Living constitutionalism bridges that chasm.

The development of First Amendment law serves as an example. Up to the early twentieth century, speech freedom was viewed very narrowly—almost as if the First Amendment was never ratified—in comparison to its twenty-first century interpretation.[122] As circumstances changed, however, the understanding of the speech clause also evolved. Led by many including Judge Learned Hand[123] and Justices Oliver Wendell Holmes[124] and Louis Brandeis[125]—and with influence by the developing social sciences—the judiciary began to recognize not only that "bad" speech did not always create dangerous, unsafe circumstances as was believed, but also that the First Amendment should stand against the government's ability to punish the expression of political views even when they conflict with state interests.[126] In short, though it did not carry the label at the time, living constitutionalism was materializing.

The emergence of living constitutionalism may be seen as parallel to what also occurs outside the law—in religion, for example. In Christianity, fundamentalism—which requires a strict, literal reading of the Bible—evolved in response to an era that some viewed as overly permissive.[127] Some biblical scholars, however, while revering the Bible's text as foundational, embrace its study and reinterpretation, not to mention other texts that illuminate the original work. Perhaps not so ironically, one postmodern theological approach is called Progressive Christianity. To obtain a complete and accurate picture, its followers are willing to question tradition. Moreover, it accepts human diversity, strongly emphasizes social justice and care for the poor and oppressed, and advocates for environmental stewardship of the Earth.[128] In other words, while enthusiastically accepting the Bible as an underpinning, there is also a recognition that viewing its text through the lens of contemporary society produces greater relevance and application.

As a reminder of how intertwined the originalism/living constitutionalism debate is with the Supreme Court and the tasks of its members—and an illustration of the infusion of politics in the process—the issue was invoked several times during the March 2022 Senate confirmation hearings of Ketanji Brown Jackson. Specifically, conservative members of the Senate's judiciary committee mentioned the virtues of originalism's fixed meaning on multiple occasions:

Sen. John Cornyn: "The wisdom of the founders who wrote a constitution that made sure that our rights would be fixed."[129]

Sen. Thom Tillis: "In my opinion, a justices' job is to interpret the text and words of the Constitution as written and give them their original meaning."[130]

Sen. Chuck Grassley: "I'll be looking to see whether Judge Jackson is committed to the Constitution as originally understood."[131]

Sen. Marsha Blackburn: "The American people deserve a Supreme Court justice with a documented commitment to the text of the Constitution and the rule of law, not a judicial activist who will attempt to make policy from the bench."[132]

By contrast, a senator on the other side of the aisle, Jon Ossoff, spoke of the challenge of dealing with unsettled law by "apply[ing] the Constitution faithfully over the long arc of history, as the world changes in profound ways and the text of faithful constitutional interpretation meets new facts, new contexts, and new technologies."[133]

In sum, while originalism and living constitutionalism expectedly differ in many ways, they share some traits. Rather than providing objective neutrality—and instead of contrasting with the subjectivity inherent in living constitutionalism—originalism is arguably no different from its methodological counterpart in its failure to remove the human element from the process of legal analysis. Both originalism and living constitutionalism can be, and have been, used as instruments for change—legal, political, and social. Each seeks legitimacy through what its devotees call a sound method. The difference lies in living constitutionalism's acknowledgment that discretionary judgment is present, just as it is in any human endeavor. Both approaches are, in effect, shortcuts to "amending" the Constitution. Both seek change—again, legal, political, and social. The distinction lies in direction: Consistent with not only the politics with which each approach has aligned itself, but also with the worldview inherent in each, the fluidity of living constitutionalism invites progressive change by expanding justice. Conversely, the fixed rigidity of originalism seeks to turn back the clock either by rescinding previously granted rights or by denying them to people altogether.[134] This has occurred particularly within the politically charged and contentious issues of voting rights, guns,[135] religion, and abortion. Not coincidentally, these are the same topics at the center of Supreme Court cases in which the worldview divide especially reveals itself.

NOTES

1. William Cummings, "'US Does Have Obama Judges': Trump Responds to Supreme Court Justice John Roberts' Rebuke," *USA Today*, November 21, 2018, https://www.usatoday.com/story/news/politics/2018/11/21/john-roberts-trump-statement/2080266002/ (quoting Chief Justice John Roberts).

2. See, for example, Mike Berardino and Ann E. Marimow, "Justice Thomas Defends the Supreme Court's Independence and Warns of 'Destroying Our Institutions,'" *Washington Post*, September 16, 2021, https://www.washingtonpost.com/politics/courts_law/justice-clarence-thomas/2021/09/16/d2ddc1ba-1714-11ec-a5e5-ceecb895922f_story.html. See also Ariane de Vogue, "Breyer Defends State of Supreme Court in Interview with CNN's Fareed Zakaria," CNN, September 19, 2021, https://www.cnn.com/2021/09/19/politics/breyer-fareed-zakaria-gps/index.html.

3. See, for example, Jeffrey Segal, "Why We Have the Most Polarized Supreme Court in History," *The Conversation*, March 14, 2016, https://perma.cc/QCJ5-4SY8; Eric Hamilton, "Politicizing the Supreme Court," *Stanford Law Review Online* 65 (August 2012); Geoffrey R. Stone, "Our Politically Polarized Supreme Court?"

Huffington Post, November 25, 2014, http://www.huffingtonpost.com/geoffrey-r
-stone/our-politically-polarized_b_5879346.html;

Adam Liptak, "Adding Gorsuch, a Polarized Supreme Court Is Likely to Grow
Even More So," *New York Times*, April 10, 2017, A9; Miriam Galston, "Polarization
at the Supreme Court? Substantive Due Process Through the Prism of Legal Theory,"
Washington University Jurisprudence Review 11 (2019): 255.

4. See Neal Devins and Lawrence Baum, "Split Definitive: How Party Polarization
Turned the Supreme Court into a Partisan Court," *Supreme Court Review* (2016): 301.
See also Ibid., 303: ("[This] is based on the growth in polarization among political
elites—polarization that has shaped the Court in multiple ways and that is likely to
continue. One key element of polarization is partisan sorting, in which conservatives
increasingly migrate to the Republican Party and liberals to the Democratic Party").

5. Linda Greenhouse, *Justice on the Brink: The Death of Ruth Bader Ginsburg, the
Rise of Amy Coney Barrett, and Twelve Months That Transformed the Supreme Court*
(New York: Random House, 2021), 4.

6. See, for example, *New York Times v. Sullivan*, 376 U.S. 254, 269–70 (1964)
(stating the importance of communication and debate in a democracy). See also Sandra Day O'Connor, "Remarks at the Inaugural Sandra Day O'Connor Distinguished
Lecture Series: Lubbock, Texas, November 16, 2007," *Texas Tech Law Review* 41
(Summer 2009): 1170 ("[D]emocracy elevates the importance of debate").

7. See Anne Applebaum and Peter Pomerantsev, "How To Put Out Democracy's
Dumpster Fire," *Atlantic*, April 2021, https://www.theatlantic.com/magazine/archive
/2021/04/the-internet-doesnt-have-to-be-awful/618079/:

> In this new wilderness, democracy is becoming impossible. If one half of the country
> can't hear the other, then Americans can no longer have shared institutions, apolitical
> courts, a professional civil service, or a bipartisan foreign policy. We can't compromise.
> We can't make collective decisions—we can't even agree on what we're deciding. No
> wonder millions of Americans refuse to accept the results of the most recent presidential
> election, despite the verdicts of state electoral committees, elected Republican officials,
> courts, and Congress.

8. See Evan Gerstmann, "Public Confidence in the Supreme Court Is at a Low
Point," *Forbes*, July 29, 2021, https://www.forbes.com/sites/evangerstmann/2021/07
/29/public-confidence-in-the-supreme-court-is-at-a-low-point/ ("It is certainly true
that a Justice's political world view is an important factor in how he or she interprets
the Constitution").

9. See Exec. Order No. 14,023, 86 Fed. Reg. 19,569 (April 9, 2021). In part, the
commission responded to those calling for expanding the Court's membership and
limiting justices' term length. See, for example, Elizabeth Warren, "Expand the
Supreme Court," *Boston Globe*, December 15, 2021, https://www.bostonglobe.com
/2021/12/15/opinion/expand-supreme-court/; Rosiland Dixon, "Why the Supreme
Court Needs (Short) Term Limits," *New York Times*, December 31, 2021, https://
www.nytimes.com/2021/12/31/opinion/supreme-court-term-limits.amp.html; Seung
Min Kim and Robert Barnes, "Supreme Court Term Limits Seem to Be Popular—
and Appear to Be Going Nowhere," *Washington Post*, December 28, 2021, https://

www.washingtonpost.com/nation/2021/12/28/supreme-court-term-limits; and Aaron Blake, "The Supreme Court Reform Whose Time Has Come?" *Washington Post*, December 20, 2021, https://www.washingtonpost.com/politics/2021/10/20/supreme -court-reform-whose-time-has-come ("The liberal push to 'pack' the Supreme Court with more justices was always much more likely to be an exercise in catharsis than actual reform").

10. See, for example, Frederick Schauer, "Is There a Psychology of Judging?" John F. Kennedy School of Government/Harvard University, KSG Faculty Research Working Paper Series RWP07–049, October 2007, http://ksgnotes1.harvard.edu/ Research/wpaper.nsf/rwp/RWP07-049; Jerome Frank, *Law and the Modern Mind* (New York: Brentano's, 1930); Charles Fried, "The Artificial Reason of the Law or: What Lawyers Know," *Texas Law Review* 60, no. 1 (1981): 35; Martin P. Golding, "Principled Decision-Making and the Supreme Court," *Columbia Law Review* 63 (1963): 35; Chris Guthrie, Jeffrey J. Rachlinski, and Andrew J. Wistrich, "Inside the Judicial Mind," *Cornell Law Review* 86 (2001): 777; Edward H. Levi, *An Introduction to Legal Reasoning* (Chicago: University of Chicago Press, 1948); Richard Posner, "Reasoning by Analogy," review of *Legal Reason: The Use of Analogy in Legal Argument*, by Lloyd L. Weinreb, *Cornell Law Review* 91 (March 2006): 761–74; Max Radin, "The Theory of Judicial Decision: Or How Judges Think," *American Bar Association Journal* 11 (1925): 357; Frederick Schauer, *Playing by the Rules: A Philosophical Examination of Rule-Based Decision-Making in Law and in Life* (Oxford: Clarendon Press, 1991); Cass R. Sunstein and Edna Ullman-Margalit, "Second-Order Decisions," *Ethics* 110 (1999): 5; Kenneth J. Vandevelde, *Thinking Like a Lawyer: An Introduction to Legal Reasoning* (Boulder, CO: Westview Press, 1996).

11. Though she earned her law degree from Columbia, Ruth Bader Ginsburg began her education in law at Harvard.

12. See, for example, Jonathan Todres, "A Healthier Legal Profession Starts with Law Schools," *Bloomberg Law,* March 15, 2022, https://news.bloomberglaw.com/ us-law-week/a-healthier-legal-profession-starts-with-law-schools ("Law school is where the next generation of lawyers is first taught the expectations and culture of the legal profession").

13. See, for example, Michael Zilis, "The Political Consequences of Supreme Court Consensus: Media Coverage, Public Opinion, and Unanimity as a Public-Facing Strategy," *Washington University Journal of Law and Policy* 54 (2017): 229 ("The Roberts Court has an affinity for consensus. In recent years, many, including Chief Justice Roberts himself, have remarked on the Court's desire to reach unanimous decisions"). See also Adam Liptak, "Justices Are Long on Words, Short on Guidance," *New York Times*, November 17, 2010, A1 ("Chief Justice Roberts . . . early on expressed his preference for unanimous opinions even as he seemed to recognize a potential cost in providing guidance to the lower courts").

14. See Adam Liptak and Alicia Palipiano, "Tracking the Major Supreme Court Decisions This Term," *New York Times*, July 1, 2021, https://www.nytimes.com/ interactive/2021/06/01/us/major-supreme-court-cases-2021.html.

"5-to-4" has become symbolic and representative of division, not just on the Supreme Court of the United States, but also in America. On the Court, the percentage of 5–4 rulings has generally trended upward. In the 2014, 2015 and 2016 terms, the percentage of 5–4 rulings was 26, 25, and 29, respectively. In 2017, 2018, and 2019, the percentages were 74, 40, and 71, respectively.

15. See Maureen Dowd, "Too Much Church in the State," *New York Times,* May 15, 2022, SR11 (writing of the ideological approach by the Court's majority, "There are prior world views at work in this upheaval").

16. See Schauer, "Is There a Psychology of Judging?" Prof. Schauer is among those who refers to "second-order reasoning"—the ability required of judges to see beyond present circumstances and to develop solutions that can be properly applied to future situations as well as those in the present.

So even if humans are temperamentally, physiologically, or genetically averse to second-order reasoning, there is little reason to believe that this aversion is so hardwired as to be incapable of change. Perhaps one form of education, including one form of moral education, is aimed, at least in part, at fostering various forms of second-order reasoning. Ibid.

17. Sonia Sotomayor, *My Beloved World* (New York: Vintage Books, 2014), 11 (describing the "fragile world of my childhood" as "a state of constant tension punctuated by explosive discord, all of it caused by my father's alcoholism and my mother's response to it, whether family fight or emotional flight").

18. See, for example, Shamus Khan, "Kavanaugh Is Lying. His Upbringing Explains Why," *Washington Post*, September 28, 2018, https://www.washingtonpost .com/outlook/kavanaugh-is-lying-his-upbringing-explains-why/2018/09/27 /2b596314-c270-11e8-b338-a3289f6cb742_story.html (describing Justice Kavanaugh's upbringing and suggesting that it created a sense of privilege). See also Jackie Calmes, *Dissent: The Radicalization of the Republican Party and Its Capture of the Court* (New York: Twelve, 2021), 7–19 (describing Kavanaugh's early years).

19. See "Justice Agreement—All Cases," ScotusBlog, https://www.scotusblog.com /wp-content/uploads/2019/07/StatPack_OT18-7_5_19_23-26.pdf.

20. See "Statistics," ScotusBlog, July 2, 2021, https://www.scotusblog.com/ statistics/ (showing that for the October 2020 Term, Justice Kavanaugh agreed with the Court's majority in 97 percent of cases, Justice Sotomayor 69 percent—the widest disparity between any two justices).

21. See "Justice Agreement—Highs and Lows," ScotusBlog, https://www .scotusblog.com/wp-content/uploads/2019/07/StatPack_OT18-7_5_19_23-26.pdf (Alito-Sotomayor and Alito-Kagan agree in 5 percent of all 5–4 rulings).

22. *Jones v. Mississippi*, 141 S. Ct. 1307 (2021).

23. Colin Kalmbacher, "Sotomayor Pens 'Brutal' Dissent by Repeatedly Citing Kavanaugh Back at Himself as Conservative Majority 'Guts' Precedent in Juvenile Punishment Case," *Law and Crime*, April 22, 2021, https://lawandcrime.com/ supreme-court/sotomayor-pens-brutal-dissent-by-repeatedly-citing-kavanaugh-back -at-himself-as-conservative-majority-guts-precedent-in-juvenile-punishment-case/.

24. Marcia Coyle, "Sotomayor Clashes with Kavanaugh, as Justices Feud about Following Precedent," Law.com, April 22, 2021, https://www.law.com/ nationallawjournal/2021/04/22/sotomayor-clashes-with-kavanaugh-as-justices-feud -about-following-precedent/?slreturn=20220014132202.

25. *Jones v. Mississippi*, 141 S. Ct. 1307, 1337 (2021) (Sotomayor, J. dissenting).

26. See Mark Joseph Stern, "Sotomayor Calls Out Kavanaugh For Breaking His Promise to Death Row Inmates," *Slate*, May 24, 2021, https://slate.com/news-and-politics/2021/05/sotomayor-kavanaugh-supreme-court-death-penalty.html.

27. Robert Barnes, Carol D. Leonnig, and Ann E. Marimow, "How the Future of Roe Is Testing Roberts on the Supreme Court," *Washington Post*, May 7, 2022, https://www.washingtonpost.com/politics/2022/05/07/supreme-court-abortion-roe-roberts-alito/ ("Roberts has sometimes sided with the liberals in some . . . disputes, particularly when he thought the authority or reputation of the court was at stake").

28. Tom Nichols, *The Death of Expertise: The Campaign Against Established Knowledge and Why It Matters* (New York: Oxford University Press, 2017), 47.

29. See, for example, "Cherry Picking: When People Ignore Evidence that They Dislike," *Effectiviology*, accessed June 25, 2022, https://effectiviology.com/cherry-picking ("Cherry picking is a logical fallacy that occurs when someone focuses only on evidence that supports their stance, while ignoring evidence that contradicts it").

30. See "Public's Views of Supreme Court Turned More Negative Before News of Breyer's Retirement," Pew Research Center, February 2, 2022, https://www.pewresearch.org/politics/2022/02/02/publics-views-of-supreme-court-turned-more-negative-before-news-of-breyers-retirement (showing that 16 percent surveyed believe Justices do an excellent or good job in keeping their views out of their decisions).

31. Adam Liptak, "A Supreme Court Term Marked by a Conservative Majority in Flux," *New York Times*, September 30, 2021, https://www.nytimes.com/2021/07/02/us/supreme-court-conservative-voting-rights.amp.html.

32. Devins and Baum, "Split Definitive: How Party Polarization Turned the Supreme Court into a Partisan Court."

33. See, for example, Todd C. Peppers, *Courtiers of the Marble Palace: The Rise and Influence of the Supreme Court Law Clerk* (Stanford, CA: Stanford University Press, 2006), 170 (describing Justice Fortas writing a draft opinion, throwing it on his law clerk's desk. "'Decorate it,' he ordered. The 'decorations' consisted of legal cases that would justify a decision Fortas had already reached").

34. See, for example, David Luban, "What's Pragmatic About Legal Pragmatism?" *Cardozo Law Review* 18 (September 1996): 43. See also Ronald Dworkin, *Justice in Robes* (Cambridge: Harvard University Press, 2006), 21–24, 36–48.

35. Hector H. Cárdenas Jr., "United States v. Alvarez-Machain: Result Oriented Jurisprudence." *Houston Journal of International Law* 16 (Fall 1993): 124. Cárdenas's analysis pertains to treaties. Liberty was taken here to substitute "text" for "treaty."

36. Louis Fischer, "When Courts Play School Board: Judicial Activism in Education," *Education Law Reporter* 51, no. 3 (April 1989): 697. See also Jeff Shesol, "The Willful Naïveté of Stephen Breyer," *New York Times*, January 27, 2022, https://www.nytimes.com/2022/01/27/opinion/breyer-supreme-court.html (writing that some justices engage in "outcome-driven judicial activism . . . [that] works its way backward, by twists and turns and pirouettes, from precooked conclusions").

37. See, for example, Linda Greenhouse, "This Is What Judicial Activism Looks Like on the Supreme Court," *New York Times*, April 8, 2021, https://nytimes.com /2021/04/08/opinion/Supreme-Court-religion-activism.amp.html (suggesting that legislating from the bench is an example of improper activism). But see Rebecca L. Brown, "Activism Is Not a Four-Letter Word," *University of Colorado Law Review* 73 (Fall 2002): 1273 (writing that judicial activism is arguably "a way for a Court to live up to its obligation to serve as citadel of the public justice"). See also Keenan D. Kmiec, "The Origin and Current Meanings of 'Judicial Activism,'" *California law Review* 92 (October 2004): 1442 ("one can scarcely make an observation about judicial activism today without appending definitions, provisos, and qualifications").

38. See Jim Hornfischer, "The Conscience of a Constitutionalist: A Recipe for Living?" "Review of *Living the Bill of Rights: How to Be an Authentic American*, by Nat Hentoff," *Texas Journal on Civil Liberties and Civil Rights* 5 (Summer/Fall 2000): 218 (writing that to originalists, "the idea of a '*living Constitution*' is a front for reckless judicial activism") (emphasis in original). But see Erwin Chemerinsky, *The Conservative Assault on the Constitution* (New York: Simon & Schuster, 2010), 32 (writing that on the Supreme Court, "conservative justices are very willing to be activist in striking down laws and overturning precedents").

39. See, for example, Philippa Strum, *Brandeis: Beyond Progressivism* (Lawrence, KS: University of Kansas Press, 1993), 89 (discussing Justice Louis Brandeis's belief in judicial restraint).

40. See, for example, Adam Cohen, *Supreme Inequality: The Supreme Court's Fifty-Year Battle for a More Unjust America* (New York, Penguin Press, 2020), xxix. See also Stefanie A. Lindquist, Joseph L. Smith, and Frank B. Cross, "The Rehnquist Court in Empirical and Statistical Retrospective: The Rhetoric of Restraint and the Ideology of Activism," *Constitutional Commentary* 24 (Spring 2007): 103:

> Criticism of judicial activism has become commonplace in political debate. In recent years it has been political conservatives who have most often sounded the alarm that unelected, activist judges are intruding on the prerogatives of the elected branches. This criticism traces to the Warren Court era, when conservatives called for "judicial restraint" or "strict constructionism" in place of liberal judicial activism, contending that "when liberal Courts overturn democratically enacted laws in favor of liberal, activist constitutionalism, they destroy citizens' rights to democratic participation and self-government" (footnote omitted).

41. See Nina Totenberg, "Supreme Court Justices Aren't 'Scorpions,' But Not Happy Campers Either," *NPR*, January 18, 2022, https://www.npr.org/2022/01/18 /1073428376/supreme-court-justices-arent-scorpions-but-not-happy-campers-either (noting that some constitutional scholars "see the kind of conservative judicial activism that is unfolding as posing a danger to the court itself not too far down the road").

42. See, for example, Rebecca E. Zietlow, "The Judicial Restraint of the Warren Court (and Why it Matters)," *Ohio State Law Journal* 69 (2008): 271 ("Many of the Court's critics argued that the [Warren] Court had exceeded its proper role within the system of separation of powers"). See also Jeffrey Rosen, "Court Approval," *New Republic*, July 23, 2007, 9, 12 ("For more than 50 years, conservatives have

insisted that judges should defer to legislatures and let citizens resolve their disputes politically. But, at the very moment they consolidated their majority, they have abandoned this principle and embraced the activism they once deplored"); Jeffrey Toobin, "Activism v. Restraint," *New Yorker*, May 24, 2010, 19 ("Chief Justice John G. Roberts, Jr., and his conservative fellow-Justices, like their ideological kinsmen in the nineteen-thirties, are engaging in what's known as judicial activism").

43. Jeffrey F. Addicott, "Reshaping American Jurisprudence in the Trump Era: The Rise of 'Originalist' Judges," *California Western Law Review* 55 (Spring 2019): 346.

44. Ibid., 346. But see *Bostock v. Clayton County*, 140 S. Ct. 1731 (2020) (ruling an employer who fires an individual merely for being gay or transgender violates Title VII. Justice Neil Gorsuch wrote the Court's opinion relying on his textualist originalism in reading Title VII. Those who joined him included nonoriginalists Justices Ginsburg, Breyer, Sotomayor, and Kagan).

45. See Lino A. Graglia, "Some Comments on Posner," review of *The Federal Judiciary: Strengths and Weaknesses* by Richard Posner, *Texas Review of Law and Politics* 25 (Fall 2020): 152 (calling originalists and proponents of a living Constitution opposites). But see Jack M. Balkin, *Living Originalism* (Cambridge: Harvard University Press, 2011); Jack M. Balkin, "Jack Balkin's Constitutional Text and Principle: Nine Perspectives on Living Originalism." *University of Illinois Law Review* (2012): 815–16 (writing that his book, *Living Originalism*, "argues that the best versions of originalism and living constitutionalism, correctly understood, are compatible rather than opposed"); Cary Franklin, "Living Textualism," 2020 *Supreme Court Review* (2020): 119.

46. See Marc J. Hetherington and Jonathan Weiler, *Prius or Pickup? How the Answers to Four Simple Questions Explain America's Great Divide* (Boston: Houghton Mifflin Harcourt, 2018), 34 (explaining that public feelings about Constitutional interpretation contain this expected fixed-fluid split).

47. Keith E. Whittington, "The New Originalism," *Georgetown Journal of Law and Public Policy* 2 (Summer 2004): 599. See also Ozan O. Varol, "The Origins and Limits of Originalism: A Comparative Study," *Vanderbilt Journal of Transnational Law* 44 (November 2011): 1248 ("In simple terms, originalism is a method for interpreting a constitutional provision by seeking to uncover its meaning at the time of its adoption"). Prof. Varol continued:

> At its inception, originalism focused on original intention. Prominent from the 1960s to the mid-1980s, intentionalism sought to interpret the Constitution by determining the subjective intentions and expectations of its drafters. Intentionalism focuses on what the framers "intended—or expected or hoped—would be the consequence" of the language they used in a specific constitutional provision. Intentionalism . . . was one of the interpretive presuppositions of the Constitution; the framers expected that their intent would govern how their posterity interpreted the Constitution. Ibid. at 1248–49 (footnote omitted).

48. Robert Post and Reva Siegel, "The Rehnquist Court and Beyond: Revolution, Counter-Revolution, or Mere Chastening of Constitutional Aspirations? Originalism as a Political Practice: 'The Right's Living Constitution.'" *Fordham Law Review* 75 (November 2006): 547. See also Adrain Vermeule, "Beyond Originalism," *Atlantic*,

March 31, 2020, https://www.theatlantic.com/ideas/archive/2020/03/common-good
-constitutionalism/609037/ ("originalism has prevailed, mainly because it has met
the political and rhetorical needs of legal conservatives struggling against an overwhelmingly left-liberal legal culture"); Kim Isaac Eisler, *A Justice for All: William
J. Brennan Jr., and the Decisions that Transformed America* (New York: Simon and
Schuster, 1993), 179 (quoting Justice Brennan: "It was in the years from 1962 to 1969
that the face of the law changed"). The Court acquired a liberal majority in 1962.
Chief Justice Warren retired in 1969.

49. 47 U.S. 483 (1954) (establishing that under the Fourteenth Amendment, racial
segregation in public schools is unconstitutional).

50. See, for example, Calvin TerBeek, "'Clocks Must Always Be Turned Back':
Brown v. Board of Education and the Racial Origins of Constitutional Originalism,"
American Political Science Review 115, no. 3 (2021). See also Jack M. Balkin,
"Constitutional Interpretation and Change in the United States: The Official and the
Unofficial," *Jus Politicum*, accessed July 15, 2022, http://juspoliticum.com/article/
Constitutional-Interpretation-and-Change-in-the-United-States-The-Official-and-the
-Unofficial-1088.html (explaining the Court's nonoriginalist constitutional approach
in *Brown v. Board of Education*):

> The doctrine of Brown developed in the course of trying to make sense of and apply the
> Fourteenth Amendment to a particular problem—and a very difficult problem, too, in
> the context of American politics. It was not the generally accepted original construction
> of the Fourteenth Amendment . . . Brown reversed older constructions of the Fourteenth
> Amendment, and, in the process, it became a symbol of American equality and civil rights.
> The example of Brown, by the way, demonstrates a very important feature of American
> constitutional interpretation. It is that the original meaning of a constitutional text is not
> the same as the original expected application of the text (emphases in original).

51. Post and Siegel, "The Rehnquist Court and Beyond," 558. See also Vermeule,
Beyond Originalism ("In recent years, allegiance to the constitutional theory known
as originalism has become all but mandatory for American legal conservatives").

52. Logan E. Sawyer III, "Principle and Politics in the New History of Originalism," *American Journal of Legal History* 57, no. 2 (2017): 205. See also Mark Graber,
"Clarence Thomas and the Perils of Amateur History," in *Rehnquist Justice: Understanding the Court Dynamic*, ed. Earl M. Maltz (Lawrence, KS: University of Kansas
Press, 2003), 70 (writing of Justice Thomas, "his originalism in major cases generally
buttresses conservative policy preferences").

53. TerBeek, "'Clocks Must Always Be Turned Back,'" 821 ("The Republican
Party has adopted constitutional 'originalism' as its touchstone"). See also Erwin
Chemerinsky, *Worse Than Nothing: The Dangerous Fallacy of Originalism* (New
Haven: Yale University Press, 2022), 6 (writing that Reagan administration Attorney
General Edwin Meese especially championed originalism).

54. TerBeek, "'Clocks Must Always Be Turned Back,'" 822 ("[Originalism], too,
serves as the de facto official theory of the Federalist Society, conservative academ-
ics, and the elite conservative bar").

55. Sawyer, "Principle and Politics in the New History of Originalism," 199.

56. See generally Stephen M. Teles, *The Rise of the Conservative Legal Movement: The Battle for Control of the Law* (Princeton, NJ: Princeton University Press, 2010). To be fair, progressive activism arguably has had similar goals—that is, changing the law and nation. Advocates, however, note that progressive living constitutionalism expands rights and liberties whereas conservative originalism tends to limit them.

57. See, for example, James Madison, "The Federalist No. 37," in *The Federalist Papers* ed. Clinton Rossiter (New York: Penguin Books, 1961), 229 ("All new laws, though penned with the greatest technical skill, and passed on the fullest and most mature deliberation, are considered as more or less obscure and equivocal, until their meaning be liquidated and ascertained by a series of particular discussions and adjudications"); Alexander Hamilton, "The Federalist No. 78," in *The Federalist Papers* ed. Clinton Rossiter (New York: Penguin Books, 1961), 440 (defending judicial authority to interpret the constitution); Ronald Dworkin, *Taking Rights Seriously* (Cambridge: Harvard University Press, 1977) (contending that the framers intended future interpreters to develop their own "conceptions" of certain provisions of the Constitution within the framework of the adopters' general "concept" of the same provision); Lawrence Lessig, "Fidelity in Translation," *Texas Law Review* 71 (May 1993): 1225 (expressing skepticism about how the original regulatory balance struck by the Framers can be applied faithfully without actually considering how that balance has changed over time); Thomas O. Sargentich, "Is the Supreme Court Undoing the New Deal: The Impact of the Rehnquist Court's New Federalism: The Rehnquist Court and State Sovereignty: Limitations of the New Federalism," *Widener Law Journal* 12 (2003): 506–7 (2003) ("an original intent argument can be turned against itself by contending that the founders did not intend the Constitution to be interpreted in terms of their own limited frames of reference, which is why the Constitution employs such spare language and open-ended phrases").

58. See, for example, Peter Brandon Bayer, "Deontological Originalism: Moral Truth, Liberty, and Constitutional 'Due Process': Part I—Originalism and Deontology," 43 *Thurgood Marshall Law Review* (Fall 2019): 98.

59. Jesse Wegman, "The Supreme Court Is Out of Step with Most Americans," *New York Times*, May 3, 2022, https://www-nytimes-com.ezproxy1.lib.asu.edu/2022 /05/03/opinion/supreme-court-roe-wade.html:

> *Roe v. Wade* is one of those interpretations, an effort to bring Americans' expanding concept of rights and freedoms into line with the Constitution's broadly worded guarantees, to connect the past with the present and the future. It is not perfect—no Supreme Court ruling is—but it was an essential step on the path to achieving full equality for more than half of the nation's population.

60. Bayer, "Deontological Originalism: Moral Truth, Liberty, and Constitutional 'Due Process': Part I—Originalism and Deontology," 98. See also Jeffrey M. Shaman, "The End of Originalism," *San Diego Law Review* 47, no. 1 (2010): 83.

61. Erwin Chemerinsky, *The Conservative Assault on the Constitution*, 32. See also Adam Serwer, "The Constitution Is Whatever the Right Wing Says It Is," *Atlantic*, June 25, 2022, https://www.theatlantic.com/ideas/archive/2022/06/roe-overturned -supreme-court-samuel-alito-opinion/661386/:

Conservatives have long attacked the left for supporting a "living constitutionalism," which they say renders the law arbitrary and meaningless. But the current majority's approach is itself a kind of undead constitutionalism—one in which the dictates of the Constitution retrospectively shift with whatever Fox News happens to be furious about. Legal outcomes preferred by today's American right conveniently turn out to be what the Founding Fathers wanted all along (emphasis in original).

62. Chemerinsky, *Worse Than Nothing*, 8 ("[O]riginalism should be resoundingly rejected as a way of interpreting the Constitution . . . [It] is an emperor with no clothes"). Ibid.

63. See, for example, Thomas B. Colby and Peter J. Smith, "Living Originalism," *Duke Law Journal* 59 (November 2009): 244–45 (arguing that originalists' work consists of a "smorgasbord of distinct constitutional theories" that are "rapidly evolving").

64. Mitchell N. Berman, "Originalism Is Bunk," *New York University Law Review* 84 (April 2009): 6 ("the arguments for hard originalism are based on faulty logic or erroneous premises and that even the best case for soft originalism is extremely implausible").

65. See, for example, Whittington, "The New Originalism," 599 (suggesting the emergence of a "new originalism").

66. See "12 Questions That Would Actually Tell Us Something About Ketanji Brown Jackson," *Politico*, March 22, 2022, https://www.politico.com/news/magazine/2022/03/22/senate-confirmation-questions-ketanji-brown-jackson-00018982 (quoting law professor Peggy Cooper Davis: "Those who interpret the Constitution through the lens of the original founders must reconcile their interpretations with the compromises that enabled the continuation of human slavery").

67. Amy Coney Barrett, "Originalism and Stare Decisis," *Notre Dame Law Review* 92 (May 2017): 1921. See also Kate Shaw and John Bash, "We Clerked for Justices Scalia and Stevens. America Is Getting Heller Wrong," *New York Times*, May 31, 2022, https://www.nytimes.com/2022/05/31/opinion/supreme-court-heller-guns.html (writing that Scalia was "the foremost proponent of originalism").

68. Barrett, "Originalism and Stare Decisis." See also "Amy Coney Barrett Senate Confirmation Hearing Day 2 Transcript," October 13, 2020, https://www.rev.com/blog/transcripts/amy-coney-barrett-senate-confirmation-hearing-day-2-transcript ("Justice Scalia was obviously a mentor, and . . . his philosophy is mine too. He was a very eloquent defender of originalism . . . [T]he judge approaches the text as it was written with the meaning it had at the time and doesn't infuse our own meaning into it").

69. Antonin Scalia, "Originalism: The Lesser Evil," *University of Cincinnati Law Review* 57 (1989): 849–65. See also Jamal Greene, "Selling Originalism," *Georgetown Law Journal* 97 (March 2009): 664 ("The central conceit behind originalism as a mode of judicial constitutional interpretation is that it is more consistent with constitutional democracy than are its competitors").

70. Scalia, "Lesser Evil," 863. See also *Bd. of Cty. Comm'rs v. Umbehr*, 518 U.S. 668, 688–89, 711 (Scalia, J., dissenting):

What secret knowledge, one must wonder, is breathed into lawyers when they become Justices of this Court, that enables them to discern that a practice which the text of the Constitution does not clearly proscribe, and which our people have regarded as constitutional for 200 years, is in fact unconstitutional? . . . The Court must be living in another world. Day by day, case by case, it is busy designing a Constitution for a country I do not recognize.

71. But see Christian Farias, "Post-*Roe*, the Supreme Court Is on a Collision Course with Democracy," *Vanity Fair*, August 25, 2022, https://www.vanityfair.com /news/2022/08/post-roe-scotus-is-on-a-collision-course-with-democracy ("In practice, [originalists have] become Republican orthodoxy, embraced by party officials, scholars, and activists to wield power").

72. See Ian Millhiser, "The Nihilism of Neil Gorsuch," *Vox*, October 2, 2021, https://www.vox.com/22431044/neil-gorsuch-nihilism-supreme-court-voting-rights -lgbt-housing-obamacare-constitution#content. See also Ian Millhiser, "Originalism, Amy Coney Barrett's Approach to the Constitution, Explained," *Vox* October 12, 2020, https://www.vox.com/21497317/originalism-amy-coney-barrett-constitution -supreme-court ("As it turns out, originalism potentially gives judges—or, at least, Supreme Court justices—tremendous discretion to decide whether to upend foundational legal principles that few Americans would care to see unsettled").

73. See Jennifer McCoy and Benjamin Press, "What Happens When Democracies Become Perniciously Polarized," Carnegie Endowment for International Peace, January 22, 2022, https://carnegieendowment.org/2022/01/18/what-happens-when -democracies-become-perniciously-polarized ("Binary choice is deeply embedded in the U.S. electoral system, creating a rigid two-party system that facilitates binary divisions of society"). See also Jonathan Chait, "Why Liberals Like Compromise and Conservatives Hate It," *New Republic*, March 2, 2011, https://newrepublic .com/article/84630/why-liberals-compromise-and-conservatives-hate-it ("conservatives tend to err toward the black-and-white worldview, and liberals toward the shades-of-gray worldview").

74. Kaiya M.A. Arroyo, "Originalism and Constitutional Construction: A Shelby County Case Study," 18 *University of Pennsylvania Journal of Constitutional Law Online* (April 2016): 26.

75. Jamal Greene, "Let's Talk About How Truly Bizarre Our Supreme Court Is," interview by Ezra Klein, "The Ezra Klein Show," *New York Times* podcast, February 4, 2022, audio 58:30, https://www.nytimes.com/2022/02/04/opinion/ezra-klein -podcast-jamal-greene.amp.html.

76. See, for example, Mary Ziegler, "Grassroots Originalism: Judicial Activism Arguments, the Abortion Debate, and the Politics of Judicial Philosophy," *University of Louisville Law Review* 51 (2013): 201 (noting that "political leaders, judges, and lawyers have cultivated popular support for originalism").

77. See, for example, Ibid., 201 (writing that political leaders "made apparent that originalism would often produce outcomes that social conservatives found satisfactory").

78. Ian Millhiser, "Chief Justice Roberts's Lifelong Crusade Against Voting Rights, Explained," *Vox*, September 18, 2020, https://www.vox.com/21211880/supreme -court-chief-justice-john-roberts-voting-rights-act-election-2020.

79. 410 U.S. 113 (1973). See also Ziegler, "Grassroots Originalism," 201 (writing of the central role of originalism in the debate around *Roe v. Wade*).

80. See Eisler, *A Justice for All*, 178 (quoting Justice William Brennan: "With five votes around here you can do anything").

81. See, for example, *Dobbs v. Jackson Women's Health Organization*, 142 S. Ct. 2228, 2262 (2022) ("[O]ur Constitution is notoriously hard to amend"). See also Bruce Ackerman, "2006 Oliver Wendell Holmes Lecture: The Living Constitution," *Harvard Law Review* 120 (May 2007) ("America's political identity is at war with the system of constitutional revision left by the Framers").

82. See, for example, J. Harvie Wilkinson III, "Of Guns, Abortions, and the Unraveling Rule of Law," *Virginia Law Review* 95 (April 2009). See also David A. Kaplan, *The Most Dangerous Branch: Inside the Supreme Court in the Age of Trump* (New York: Broadway Books, 2018), xiii ("More than congress, sometimes more than the president, it is the Court that holds sway").

83. See Linda Greenhouse, "Stephen Breyer Was the Right Justice for the Wrong Age," *New York Times*, January 26, 2022, https://www.nytimes.com/2022/01/26/ opinion/breyer-supreme-court-retirement.html (referring to the era as "heroic" when the Court pushed "post-World War II America into recognizing the equality of the races and the rights of criminal suspects").

84. See Geoffrey R. Stone and David A. Strauss, *Democracy and Equality: The Enduring Constitutional Vision of the Warren Court* (New York: Oxford University Press, 2020), 2 ("[T]he Constitution, as we know it today, is very much the work of the Warren Court . . . [Yet] conservative critics attack it—now as they did then—as 'lawless'").

85. Shesol, "The Willful Naïveté of Stephen Breyer." See also Barry Friedman, *The Will of the People: How Public Opinion Has Influenced the Supreme Court and Shaped the Meaning of the Constitution* (New York: Farrar, Straus and Giroux, 2009), 280–83 (suggesting that the originalist perspective of "strict constructionism" entered the political arena during the Nixon administration).

86. Mark Joseph Stern, "Republicans Don't Need to Win Elections. They Already Won the Supreme Court," *Slate*, January 24, 2022, https://slate.com/news-and -politics/2022/01/supreme-court-affirmative-action-republican-policy.amp.

87. Ziegler, "Grassroots Originalism," 202.

88. See Adrian Vermeule, "Supreme Court Justices Have Forgotten What the Law Is For," *New York Times*, February 3, 2022, https://www.nytimes.com/2022/02/03 /opinion/us-supreme-court-nomonation.html (writing that originalism "pretends to separate law from justice, [and] rests on an invented tradition that has projected itself back into the past").

89. Post and Siegel, "The Rehnquist Court and Beyond," 549. "As a political practice, in short, originalism aspires to 'return to Constitutional authenticity' only insofar as it perceives authenticity to make sense in the present. Originalism uses political

and litigation strategies to infuse the law of the Constitution with contemporary political meanings that originalists find compelling." Ibid., 560 (footnotes omitted).

90. See Robert H. Bork, "Neutral Principles and Some First Amendment Problems," *Indiana Law Journal* 47 (Fall 1971): 8 ("Where constitutional materials do not clearly specify the value to be preferred, there is no principled way to prefer any claimed human value to any other"). See also Lawrence B. Solum, "Original Ideas on Originalism: District of Columbia v. Heller and Originalism," *Northwestern University Law Review* 103 (Spring 2009): 927 (describing Bork's article as one "that is sometimes considered the opening move in the development of contemporary originalist theory").

91. Post and Siegel, "The Rehnquist Court and Beyond," 569. See also Ibid., 561 (characterizing modern originalism as an effort "to alter the Constitution so as to infuse it with conservative political principles").

92. Reva B. Siegel, "Constitutional Culture, Social Movement Conflict and Constitutional Change: The Case of the de facto ERA; 2005–2006 Brennan Center Symposium Lecture," *California Law Review* 94 (October 2006): 1347. See also Sawyer (tellingly dividing originalism into "principled" and "political" categories).

93. Post and Siegel, "The Rehnquist Court and Beyond," 554. "Conservative groups that have mobilized in the name of originalism are not inspired by professional historical research. These groups are instead stirred by those dimensions of the past that can sustain a present political perspective that is persuasive and attractive." Ibid., 559.

94. Post and Siegel, "The Rehnquist Court and Beyond," 569. See also Greenhouse, *Justice on the Brink*, 125 (referring to a "conservative legal ecosystem" formed by the blending of originalism and politics).

95. See Maeva Marcus, "Is the Supreme Court a Political Institution?" *George Washington Law Review* 72 (December 2003): 95 ("Is the Supreme Court a 'political' institution? Of course—in every sense of the word. And it was meant to be").

96. Sawyer, "Principle and Politics in the New History of Originalism," 200.

97. See, for example, David B. Anders, "Justices Harlan and Black Revisited: The Emerging Dispute Between Justice O'Connor and Justice Scalia Over Enumerated Fundamental Rights," *Fordham Law Review* 61 (March 1993): 924 (writing of originalist icon Antonin Scalia, "he reverses precedent to reach his originalist goal of limiting rights").

98. TerBeek, "'Clocks Must Always Be Turned Back,'" 821 (writing that conservatives viewed *Brown v. Board of Education* "as an affront to their developing ideology . . . The intellectual core of the resistance was a turn to constitutional history that first privileged revivified antebellum constitutional theories . . . The development of constitutional originalism was part and parcel of the parties' secular realignment on race as Southern conservatives joined coalitional forces with movement conservatives across the nation") (citations omitted).

99. See, for example, *Brown v. Board of Education*, 47 U.S. 483 (1954) (establishing that racial segregation in public schools is unconstitutional); *Gideon v. Wainwright*, 372 U.S. 335 (1963) (ruling that the Sixth Amendment requires states to provide attorneys to criminal defendant who cannot afford one); *New York Times*

v. Sullivan, 376 U.S. 254 (1964) (establishing a standard making it more difficult for public official plaintiffs to win libel cases, noting that debate on public issues should be "uninhibited, robust and wide-open"); *Griswold v. Connecticut*, 381 U.S. 479 (1965) (ruling that the U.S. Constitution protects the liberty of married couples to buy and use contraceptives without government restriction); *Miranda v. Arizona*, 384 U.S. 436 (1966) (ruling that the Fifth Amendment forbids prosecutors from using statements made as part of police interrogations unless they can show that the person was informed of the right to consult with an attorney before and during questioning); *Loving v. Virginia*, 388 U.S. 1 (1967) (ruling that laws banning interracial marriage violate the Equal Protection and Due Process Clauses of the Constitution); *Tinker v. Des Moines Independent School District*, 393 U.S. 503 (1969) (applying the First Amendment to public school students, that they do not "shed their constitutional rights to freedom of speech or expression at the schoolhouse gate"); *Brandenburg v. Ohio*, 395 U.S. 444 (1969) (ruling that the government cannot punish inflammatory speech unless that speech is "directed to inciting or producing imminent lawless action and is likely to incite or produce such action").

100. See TerBeek, "'Clocks Must Always Be Turned Back,'" 822 (quoting the influential conservative journalist James Kilpatrick responding to Warren: "[in] constitutional cases clocks must always be turned back").

101. David A. Kaplan, *The Most Dangerous Branch: Inside the Supreme Court in the Age of Trump* (New York: Broadway Books, 2018), 14 ("Conservatives, usually committed to preserving that fossilized status quo, conveniently gravitate toward originalism"). See also Erwin Chemerinsky, *The Case Against the Supreme Court* (New York: Penguin Books, 2015), 21–53 (writing in chapter 1, "Protecting Minorities," that the modern Supreme Court's guardianship of minority rights has been lacking).

102. See Chemerinsky, *Worse Than Nothing*, 7 (writing that for most constitutional provisions, there is no "original meaning" to be discovered, but instead "a range of possibilities").

In many areas where an original meaning can be discovered, it would lead to abhorrent results. Partly for this reason, originalist justices frequently abandon the theory when it does not yield the outcomes they want. All of this matters enormously because originalism is a dangerous approach to constitutional law that would jeopardize many basic rights and advances in equality. Ibid.

103. Greene, "Let's Talk About How Truly Bizarre Our Supreme Court Is," audio 59:56.

104. See Jim Hornfischer, "The Conscience of a Constitutionalist: A Recipe for Living?" review of *Living the Bill of Rights: How to Be an Authentic American,* by Nat Hentoff, *Texas Journal on Civil Liberties and Civil Rights* 5 (Summer/Fall 2000): 218 (writing that living constitutionalists believe the Constitution "does not possess *fixed* meaning") (emphasis added).

105. See David A. Strauss, "The Living Constitution," University of Chicago School of Law, September 27, 2010, https://www.law.uchicago.edu/news/living -constitution ("A living Constitution is one that evolves, changes over time, and adapts to new circumstances, without being formally amended"). See also Charlie

Savage, "Abortion Ruling Poses New Questions About How Far Supreme Court Will Go," *New York Times*, June 24, 2022, https://www.nytimes.com/2022/06/25/us /supreme-court-abortion-contraception-same-sex-marriage.html ("Liberals and Democrats tend to argue that the framers defined rights in general terms to permit future evolution in their scope and meaning by applying them in new ways in response to new societal understandings and conditions").

106. See, for example, Calvin TerBeek, "The Search for an Anchor: Living Constitutionalism from the Progressives to Trump," *Law and Social Inquiry* 46 (August 2021): 861 (crediting Princeton's Edward Corwin with developing the notion in 1924 that the Constitution is necessarily "a living statute, to be interpreted in the light of living conditions").

107. Mark W. Hendrickson, "The U.S. Constitution: Living, Breathing Document or Dead Letter?" *Center For Vision and Values*, May 28, 2009, http://www .visionandvalues.org/2009/05/the-us-constitution-living-breathing-document-or-dead -letter/.

108. Oliver Wendell Holmes, *The Common Law* (Boston: Little Brown, 1881), 1.

109. See, for example, Craig Anthony Arnold, "The Reconstitution of Property: Property as a Web of Interests," *Harvard Environmental Law Review* 26 (2002): 295, n.73.

110. See, for example, Marc O. DeGirolami and Kevin C. Walsh, "Judge Posner, Judge Wilkinson, and Judicial Critique of Constitutional Theory," *Notre Dame Law Review* 90 (December 2014): 646 (grouping pragmatism and living constitutionalism); Stephen M. Feldman, "Free Speech Jurisprudence and Its Interactions with Social Justice: Free Speech Formalism and Social Injustice," *William and Mary Journal of Race, Gender and Social Justice* 26 (Fall 2019): 53 ("In current constitutional jurisprudence, many scholars endorse interpretive pluralism, eclecticism, or pragmatism, or in other words, living constitutionalism").

111. But see J. Harvie Wilkinson III, "Subjective Art; Objective Law," *Notre Dame Law Review* 85 (June 2010): 1664 ("Judges feel a strong and understandable temptation, evinced in evocations of judicial empathy, evolving social norms, and living constitutionalism, to do justice as they feel it should be done rather than adhering to the strictures of text and structure").

112. See, for example, Lackland H. Bloom, Jr., "The Legacy of Griswold," *Ohio Northern University Law Review* 16, no. 3 (1989): 513 (describing the right to privacy as defined in *Griswold v. Connecticut* as stemming from First, Third, Fourth, Fifth, Ninth and Fourteenth Amendments).

113. See Samuel Warren and Louis Brandeis, "The Right to Privacy," *Harvard Law Review* 4, no. 5 (December 1890): 193–220 (expressing dissatisfaction with abusive press tactics, expanded gossip columns, and the "yellow journalism" of the late 1800s, and advocating for the right to be let alone).

114. Ackerman, "2006 Oliver Wendell Holmes Lecture: The Living Constitution," 1756.

115. U.S. Const., art. III, § 1: ("The judicial power of the United States, shall be vested in one Supreme Court . . . ").

116. 5 U.S. (1 Cranch) 137 (1803).

117. Transcript of Oral Argument, 22:8–14, *Dobbs v. Jackson Women's Health Organization*, 142 S. Ct. 2228 (2022) (emphasis added).

118. See Graglia, "Some Comments on Posner," 153 (explaining the premise of living constitutionalism: "[T]he meaning of the Constitution's provisions may and does change over time, which is to say that judges, and ultimately the Justices of the Supreme Court, are authorized to change them").

119. U.S. Const., Amend. XXVII ("No law, varying the compensation for the services of the Senators and Representatives, shall take effect, until an election of Representatives shall have intervened").

120. Strauss, "The Living Constitution."

121. See, for example, "Constitutional Amendment Process," National Archives, Office of the Federal Register, https://www.archives.gov/federal-register/constitution ("The Constitution provides that an amendment may be proposed either by the Congress with a two-thirds majority vote in both the House of Representatives and the Senate or by a constitutional convention called for by two-thirds of the State legislatures").

122. See, for example, David M. Rabban, *Free Speech in Its Forgotten Years* (Cambridge: Cambridge University Press, 1997), 175:

> A general hostility to free expression permeated the judicial system . . . The overwhelming weight of judicial opinion in all jurisdictions before World War I offered little recognition and even less protection of free speech interests . . . A general hostility to the value of free expression permeated the judicial system . . . Judges often emphasized the sanctity of free speech in the very process of reaching adverse decisions in concrete cases.

See also *Patterson v. Colorado*, 205 U.S. 454, 462 (1907) ("[T]he main purpose of [the First Amendment's speech protection] provisions is 'to prevent all such *previous restraints* upon publications as had been practiced by other governments'") (emphasis in original) (internal citations omitted).

123. *Masses Publishing Co. v. Patten*, 244 F. 535 (S.D.N.Y 1917) (ruling that government refusal to allow the circulation of an antiwar journal violated the First Amendment).

124. *Abrams v. United States*, 250 U.S. 616, 624 (1919) (Holmes, J., dissenting) (best known for Holmes's dissent, disagreeing with a 7–2 majority that upheld a conviction for distributing antiwar leaflets).

125. *Whitney v. California*, 274 U.S. 357, 372 (1927) (Brandeis, J., concurring) (upholding a conviction for threatening speech, but best known for Brandeis's seminal opinion that defended political speech by explaining its value in a democratic society).

126. See, for example, Joseph Russomanno, "Cause and Effect: The Free Speech Transformation as Scientific Revolution," *Communication Law and Policy* 20 (Summer 2015) (analyzing the parallel paths of (1) how advances in social science contributed to understanding how speech affects people, and (2) how the legal and cultural views toward speech freedom developed). See also Jack M. Balkin, "The Roots of the Living Constitution," *Boston University Law Review* 92 (July 2012): 1141 (stating that these dissents of Holmes and Brandeis did not contain new ideas, but instead

concepts that "had been around in American political culture for a long time" but that "were not well developed in federal judicial doctrines").

127. See, for example, Margaret Bendroth, "Christian Fundamentalism in America," *Oxford Research Encyclopedias*, February 27, 2017, https://oxfordre.com/religion/view/10.1093/acrefore/9780199340378.001.0001/acrefore-9780199340378-e-419.

128. Roger Wolsey, "Progressive Christianity Isn't Progressive Politics," Huffington Post, February 10, 2012, https://www.huffpost.com/entry/progressive-christianity-isnt-progressive-politics_b_1897381 ("Progressive Christianity is a post-liberal movement that seeks to reform the faith via the insights of post-modernism and a reclaiming of the truth beyond the verifiable historicity and factuality of the passages in the Bible by affirming the truths within the stories that may not have actually happened").

129. John Cornyn, "Jackson Confirmation Hearing, Day 1," CSPAN, March 21, 2022, https://www.c-span.org/video/?518341-1/jackson-confirmation-hearing-day-1 (audio 58:34).

130. Thom Tillis, "Tillis Delivers Opening Remarks in SCOTUS Confirmation Hearings," March 21, 2022, https://www.tillis.senate.gov/2022/3/tillis-delivers-opening-remarks-in-scotus-confirmation-hearings.

131. Chuck Grassley, "Grassley Opening Statement," Senate Judiciary Committee, March 21, 2022, https://www.judiciary.senate.gov/scotus_grassley-opening-statement.

132. Marsha Blackburn, "Blackburn Raises Concerns Over Judge Ketanji Brown Jackson's Judicial Record," March 21, 2022, https://www.blackburn.senate.gov/2022/3/blackburn-raises-concerns-over-judge-ketanji-brown-jackson-s-judicial-record.

133. Jon Ossoff, "Sen. Ossoff's Opening Statement in Supreme Court Nomination Hearing," March 21, 2022, https://www.ossoff.senate.gov/press-releases/watch-sen-ossoffs-opening-statement-in-supreme-court-nomination-hearing/.

134. See Charles M. Blow, "The Supreme Court as an Instrument of Oppression," *New York Times*, May 8, 2022, https://www.nytimes.com/2022/05/08/opinion/supreme-court-oppression.html (referring to American freedoms and rights, "the originalists know that they can turn that clock back"). See also Linda Greenhouse, "The Supreme Court, Weaponized," *New York Times*, December 16, 2021, https://www.nytimes.com/2021/12/16/opinion/supreme-court-trump.html (writing the Court's "path of destruction of settled precedent and long-established norms is breathtaking").

135. It is acknowledged that the fixed-originalist approach expands Second Amendment rights, but it does so arguably by denying another constitutional right—life and liberty, guaranteed by the Fourteenth Amendment.

PART 2

A Weaponized Court

Chapter 3

Voting Rights

Among his many noteworthy viewpoints, Justice Antonin Scalia believed that while the U.S. Constitution is the core of the American judicial process, it is not suited to resolving moral dilemmas. "Moral issues are intractable," he wrote. "The vast majority of political issues, though often polemicized in moral terms, ultimately boil down to questions of prudence or utility, to disagreement about the most effective means to more or less agreed-upon moral ends."[1] As the Justice knew, however, moral issues embedded in case law arrive at the Supreme Court now and then. When they did so during his tenure, he was not reluctant dive in, armed with originalism.

In dealing with moral/legal issues, however, an originalist fixed worldview is troublesome given its demand to disregard contemporary perspectives. It is a problem, according to Columbia law professor Jamal Greene, when "the Court pretends that what it's doing when it makes these moral decisions is making them on the basis of what James Madison thinks, as opposed to making them on the basis of the actual benefits and burdens associated with government action."[2]

It is especially these kinds of cases in which the worldview perspective of the Court's supermajority is exposed. That fixed worldview was front and center in the tumultuous summer of 2022.[3] By way of introduction to phenomena embodied by a series of 6–3 rulings across several crucial issues, *West Virginia v. EPA*[4] was the culmination. It was the final muscle flex of the term by the Court's conservative supermajority, demonstrating its willingness—even eagerness—to read texts narrowly, then to decide the law by locking it in the past. As Rodney A. Smolla points out in this book's foreword, in this case the majority justified its narrow interpretation by announcing a new rule. Though a bold step, it should not be perceived as any sort of progressivism given that its purpose was the polar opposite—to prevent a broad reading of the Environmental Protection Agency's mandate. Instead, the majority predictably utilized an originalist reading that adhered strictly to the text.[5] The dissent was not only highly critical of this approach, it sought a more fluid, expansive reading that, in this instance, would allow the EPA to address a "pressing environmental challenge."[6] Justice Elena Kagan's blistering dissent concluded by criticizing the Court's majority for appointing itself as the decision maker on environmental policy rather than relying on Congress or the EPA. Targeting the majority view in this ruling, but perhaps also expressing concern for the future, she wrote, "I cannot think of many things more frightening."[7]

As with the rulings analyzed below, *West Virginia v. EPA* exhibited classic tension not merely between conservative and progressive, but also a clash of worldviews and constitutional approaches—of fixed-originalists and fluid-living constitutionalists. The cases examined in the following pages represent a selected sample that highlights the Court's worldview divide. As these rulings are considered, it is important to remember that cases do not arrive at the Supreme Court by happenstance. No case appears on the Court's docket without the vote of at least four justices. That is, no cases, including those embedded with moral issues, are being forced on the Court. When a case is heard, that means that at least 44 percent of the Court *wants* to hear it, with the opportunity to rule on the issue(s) at hand. It is noteworthy, for example, that within months of Justice Amy Coney Barrett's confirmation, the Court chose to hear cases in which moral issues were central—cases dealing with gun rights, abortion, and religion.[8] The significance resides less in the cases individually, and more in viewing them collectively—an illustration of the Court's ability to consciously shift the direction of the law and the nation, and to issue its own imprimatur of morality.[9] That begins with its case selection process.

Because of the vital role that elections play in a functioning democracy,[10] the first topic addressed here in some depth is voting rights. As important as voting is, however, it is not always protected to the extent many believe necessary.[11] The right to vote is thus an area of law that is particularly worthy of attention, in part to due to the contemporary attempts to restrict those rights.[12] The 2021 Presidential Commission on the Supreme Court, for example, concluded that "the Court has whittled away the Voting Rights Act (VRA) and other cornerstones of democracy."[13] According to Ryan Rebe, election law cases at the Supreme Court have "raised serious questions about the justices' independence and dedication to neutral decision-making." Rebe also alleges "a pattern of bias" and "partisan loyalty" on the Court leading to suspicion that "the justices were reshaping America's electoral institutions to further a partisan agenda," and doing so through an allegiance to originalism and textualism that he characterizes as disingenuous.[14]

In *The Partisan Court*, Rebe concludes that the twenty-first century has been "one of the most politically contentious eras in Supreme Court history" in election law cases. It was a period, he claims, when serious questions were raised about "the justices' independence and dedication to neutral decision-making" and when the Court "failed to rise above the increased partisanship of the time."[15]

With the foregoing as backdrop, it is difficult to be surprised by Justice Kagan's view that there has been a "deep fault" within American democracy—"the historical and continuing attempt to withhold from a race of citizens their fair share of influence on the political process" by limiting their ability to vote in elections.[16] To combat this fault, Congress passed the VRA in 1965 and renewed its provisions periodically. At nearly every turn, there was significant conservative opposition. Disapproval was present not only within Congress—though never enough to thwart reauthorization—but also from outside. Among those leading the opposition beginning in the early 1980s was John Roberts, then working in the Reagan administration's Justice Department. Later as Chief Justice of the United States, Roberts's efforts to limit voting rights did not wane, with one analyst characterizing his approach as a "lifelong crusade."[17]

Rationales for consistent conservative opposition to the VRA and its renewals typically have been masked by constitutionally based claims. For example, in *Shelby County v. Holder*,[18] an Alabama county challenged the constitutionality of Section 4 and Section 5 of the VRA. Some states and counties, due to their histories of discrimination, were required by the VRA to obtain "preclearance"—that is, approval—from the Justice Department before local jurisdictions could change their voting procedures. While acknowledging that the intent of these VRA sections was to address the history of discriminatory voting practices, Shelby County argued that its Tenth Amendment right that grants states the power to regulate elections was being violated.[19]

During oral arguments in 2013, Justice Scalia referred to "a phenomenon that is called the perpetuation of racial entitlement."[20] In doing so, he tipped his conservative-fixed worldview hand, making clear both his opposition to Section 5 and his view that a judicial solution to return the nation to a prior era was necessary. Unhappy that most legislators felt obligated to maintain voting protections, Scalia recognized the political reality of the VRA: "I am fairly confident it will be reenacted in perpetuity unless—unless a court can say it does not comport with the Constitution."[21] The *Shelby County* Court was just the one to establish a judicial "solution" to the conservatives' legislative problem.

In ruling for Shelby County, the Court's five-member majority determined that Section 4 was no longer necessary because the discrimination it sought to prevent had been significantly reduced. The majority seemed to miss not only the fact that discrimination was declining *because* of Section 4, but also that eliminating the law would very likely result in an increase in discriminatory practices. The faulty reasoning prompted a now-famous response from Justice Ruth Bader Ginsburg in her dissenting opinion: "Throwing out preclearance when it has worked and is continuing to work to stop discriminatory *changes* is like throwing away your umbrella in a rainstorm because you are not getting wet."[22] The dissenters in this case—Ginsburg's opinion was joined by Justices Breyer, Sotomayor, and Kagan—demonstrated a fluid worldview by recognizing a changing environment and the need for evolving, updated law to keep pace with it.

The majority's conclusion was reached in the face of Congress' determination that "without the continuation of the Voting Rights Act of 1965 protections, racial and language minority citizens will be deprived of the opportunity to exercise their right to vote, or will have their votes diluted, undermining the significant gains made by minorities in the last 40 years."[23] Congress had not only passed the VRA in 1965, but as part of its periodic reauthorization process, studied whether conditions warranted its approval. The Court's rationale resulted in its self-empowerment—that is, removing Congress' authority (as granted by the 15th Amendment[24]) and substituting its own to reject the VRA's Section 4 as being unnecessary.

The dissenting opinion is mentioned 16 times in the Court's *Shelby County* opinion—not surprisingly delivered by Chief Justice Roberts given his history of opposition to voting rights. The majority's members embraced a fixed worldview from the start, expressing a desire to return to a pre-VRA era. Section 4's approval requirement, and that it applied only to some states, was criticized as a "dramatic departure" from basic principles of federalism and equal sovereignty.[25] The law was destined to prevail for several more years but, in the majority's view, unnecessarily. Admitting that discrimination still occurred, the Court nevertheless opined that the "extraordinary measures" being enforced were overly burdensome. "[T]he conditions that originally justified these measures no longer characterize voting in the covered jurisdictions."[26]

"[H]istory did not end in 1965," wrote Chief Justice Roberts, suggesting that the fight waged against discrimination since the passage of the VRA was successful. The approach represents what Guy-Uriel Charles and Luis Fuentes-Rohwer call "the majority's attempt to free the present from the past . . . History is not relevant to the present."[27] By focusing merely on the trajectory of historical developments, the majority ignored the present—one in which discrimination not only persists, but also where it is being expanded. "For the majority, and thus for the Court, in order to free the states and the present, they must be liberated from the past."[28] In this instance, the majority's desired past predates the VRA. *Shelby County* is a nod to the era of state sovereignty when the notion of adherence to the federal regulation of "state business" was only a bad dream.[29]

Shelby County v. Holder was prelude to *Brnovich v. Democratic National Committee*.[30] The two rulings are equal parts attempts to dismantle the VRA, one piece at a time. In the *Brnovich* "sequel," the VRA's Section 2 was targeted.[31] As explained by Justice Kagan, Section 2 "guarantees that members of every racial group will have equal voting opportunities. Citizens of every race will have the same shot to participate in the political process and to elect representatives of their choice. They will all own our democracy together—no one more and no one less than any other."[32] Fortified by the door of opportunity opened by the *Shelby County* ruling, Arizona had passed two new election-procedure measures.[33] Ostensibly designed to prevent voter fraud, it was alleged they resulted in reduced voting opportunities, particularly for minorities. A federal appeals court agreed that Arizona had violated the VRA's Section 2.[34] "For over a century," that court wrote, "Arizona has repeatedly targeted its American Indian, Hispanic, and African American citizens, limiting or eliminating their ability to vote and to participate in the political process."[35] The new laws, that court determined, brought that history into the present.

On appeal to the Supreme Court, and as in *Shelby County*, oral arguments in *Brnovich* were especially telling, revealing a core reason for the desire by some to revert to a pre-VRA time. In response to a question from Justice Barrett about the interest of the Arizona Republican Committee in the new laws, the attorney supporting the new Arizona laws, Michael Carmin, said that without them, "it puts us at a competitive disadvantage relative to Democrats. Politics is a zero-sum game, and every extra vote they get through unlawful interpretations of Section 2 hurts us."[36] The intent was clear: because every vote "they" get hurts "us," suppressing their votes is a path to success. The us-versus-them dynamics of tribalism were apparent.

Justice Kagan explained the double-edged nature of the VRA. On the one hand, she wrote, it represents the best of America, marrying two great ideals: democracy and racial equality.[37] On the other hand, it reminds us of the worst of America, because it was—and remains—so necessary.[38] The Court's majority—this time 6–3 given Justice Ginsburg being succeeded by Amy Coney Barrett—disagreed, finding that the Arizona laws did not violate Section 2.

Justice Kagan's dissenting opinion is instructive, in part because it highlights the fixed-fluid worldview divide. The majority, she wrote, sought to undermine Section 2 and the right it provides because it "*fears* that the statute Congress wrote is too 'radical'—that it will invalidate too many state voting laws."[39] Several states, emboldened by *Shelby County*,[40] had passed new laws that restricted voting,[41] most with discriminatory overtones.[42] "Wherever it can," Kagan wrote, "the [Court's] majority gives a *cramped reading* to broad language. And then it uses that reading to uphold two election laws from Arizona that discriminate against minority voters."[43]

Noting again the vital role of the Voting Right Act in upholding a pillar of the nation, Kagan wrote, "Democratic ideals in America got off to a glorious start; democratic practice not so much."[44] Repeating an approach it used in *Shelby County*, the Court's majority sought to return to the days of "ideal," not practice. This is a page from the fixed worldview playbook—reverting to the comfort and safety of what was while avoiding the new and nuanced of the present. The VRA, after all, represents unwanted change and creates conditions in opposition to the safety, security, and predictability especially prized by fixed-originalists.

Kagan's dissenting opinion, joined by Justices Breyer and Sotomayer, was clearly a response to Justice Samuel Alito's opinion for the Court—a passionate reply. How the two squared off dramatically in *Brnovich* highlights the fixed-fluid divide. It was captured by Linda Greenhouse:

> This decision offered two mutually exclusive visions of what the right to vote means today . . . The competing visions . . . reflected profoundly different understandings of what law needs to do to keep the basic mechanics of democracy functioning. In that, it offered an almost perfect mirror of the partisan divide over the seemingly simple concept of the right to vote . . . Justice Alito called Justice Kagan's interpretation of [Section 2's] language "radical"; Justice Kagan called his "tragic." What could lead the two wings of the court to diverge so completely in interpreting that language?[45]

The answer: worldview.

Perhaps the best of the *Brnovich* examples lies in Justice Kagan's description of not only the VRA's purpose, but also when she placed her finger on why Justice Alito and the Court's majority so fervently opposed Section 2: "[The law] was meant to *disrupt the status quo*, not to preserve it—to eradicate then-current discriminatory practices, not to set them in amber."[46] The last thing those with fixed worldviews want is to disrupt the status quo; instead, preserving or returning to it is a foundational value. Thus, *Brnovich* became another opportunity to restore the past, to turn back the clock to a time prior to the VRA. Dismantling the law, even piece by piece, moves the nation toward a state that approximates a pre-VRA reality.

Congressional redistricting is another tool that can be used as a weapon in skewing voting rights and election outcomes. As populations shift, redistricting is necessary. Done fairly, each district becomes a representative of the whole. However, gerrymandering—that is, manipulating district boundaries, typically in a way to favor a political party—is a practice that, according to the Brennan Center for Justice, "has been a thorn in the side of democracy for centuries."[47] It is a "thumb on the scale . . . empower[ing] politicians to choose their voters" rather than vice versa.[48] In short, the practice is antidemocratic.[49]

Though executed at the state level—often by legislatures controlled by one party—redistricting cases have come before the Supreme Court. In 2019's *Rucho v. Common Cause*,[50] for example, Chief Justice Roberts wrote for a 5–4 majority that sidestepped gerrymandering claims in North Carolina, ruling that this was not an issue for federal courts because the Framers, aware of the practice, chose to empower state legislatures to handle such matters. Justice Kagan filed a dissent highly critical of the majority for refusing to "remedy a constitutional violation because it thinks the task beyond judicial capabilities."[51] But this was not just any constitutional violation, she continued. This one "deprived citizens of the most fundamental of their constitutional rights."[52] Kagan argued that by choosing not to intervene in the political gerrymandering, the Court effectively "encourage[s] a politics of polarization and dysfunction" that "may irreparably damage our system of government."[53] In addition to being another example of Roberts's opposition to voting rights,[54] this ideological confrontation classically pitted the fixed-originalist approach of relying exclusively on the past to maintain a status quo against a progressive-living constitutionalist method advocating for the Court to adapt to evolving circumstances.

In early 2022, the Court remained steadfast on this trajectory when it reinstated an Alabama congressional map that a lower court had said diluted the power of Black voters.[55] Another shadow docket decision, the 5–4 provisional order prevented the execution of an Alabama court decision. While suggesting that the case would ultimately move forward to a full hearing, that would not happen until the Court's next term. As a result, the Fall 2022 elections were conducted according to a plan deemed inadequate by Alabama's legislature, governor, and a unanimous three-judge federal court panel. The Supreme Court's decision, reported the *New York Times'* Adam Liptak, once again "indicated that the court is open to weakening the role race may play in drawing voting districts for federal elections, setting up a major new test of the VRA in a court that has gradually limited the reach of the law in other contexts."[56] Linda Greenhouse was more direct, describing the decision as "a raw power play by a runaway majority that seems to recognize no stopping point."[57] Particularly within the context of *Shelby County* and *Brnovich*, she added, "It's impossible not to conclude that what we see at work is not some neutral principle guiding the Supreme Court's intervention but simply whether a majority likes or doesn't like what a lower court has done."[58] Returning the Court—and the nation—to pre-VRA law, and doing so in ways "at odds with settled precedent and without any sense of the moment"[59] reveals those with a fixed worldview pushing back against living constitutionalism.

Even when the contemporary Court's rulings in this area seem to serve pro-democracy values, it comes with a caveat. In March 2022, for example, in two shadow docket hearings, the Court opted to leave in place congressional maps drawn by the Pennsylvania and North Carolina Supreme Courts, respectively. Both maps were thought to be favorable to progressive interests.[60] Each order, however, was likely temporary, deferring to a predicted "grand showdown"[61] over whether state lawmakers should be the last word in redistricting. To answer this question affirmatively would be to accept the "independent state legislature doctrine" which proponents say stems from the U.S. Constitution's original meaning.[62] The doctrine is rooted in the fixed-originalist mindset and would, according to one commentator, "turn the clock back on our constitutional order, with states acting more like the quasi-independent entities they were before the Civil War and less like the subordinate units of a national polity."[63]

This doctrine appears to have support on the current Court. While Justice Kavanaugh wrote the Court's order in the North Carolina case, Justices Alito, Thomas, and Gorsuch dissented. This suggests an ominous future if and when the larger issue of completely empowering state legislatures on redistricting emerges from the shroud of the Court's emergency shadow docket and is subjected to a complete hearing.[64] Liptak, for example, reported there are indications that at least four justices would rule that courts must defer entirely to state legislatures when it comes to redistricting. He added, "Such a ruling would fundamentally alter how congressional elections are conducted and amplify partisan gerrymandering, allowing the party that controls the legislature to draw voting districts favoring its candidates."[65] On the last day of June 2022, the Court announced it would provide a full hearing of the North Carolina case.[66] The "thumb on the scale" and the burden on democracy inherent in partisan redistricting grew heavier.

That thumb had been on the scale again in March 2022, and again was done within a shadow docket action. This one reversed a Wisconsin Supreme Court ruling that had selected a redistricting map drawn by that state's governor.[67] In a move rich with irony, the majority said the state court had not considered carefully enough whether the same VRA the Court had gutted required the addition of a district in which Black voters made up a majority. The Court's unsigned order, permitted by shadow docket procedures, was opposed by Justice Sotomayor's dissent contending that the Court's action was unprecedented.

Three months later a 6–3 Court granted a stay to a judgment by a lower court federal judge.[68] The judge had ruled that a Republican-drawn map for Louisiana diluted the power of Black voters. The Court's decision reinstated the map, ensuring that congressional elections that Fall would proceed according to the map's boundaries. The Court's decision to hear the case concerned some because of its "potential to fundamentally rework the relationship between state legislatures and state courts in protecting voting rights in federal elections."[69] Observers noted this as further indication of the Court's disregard for the role that race should play in drawing a state's voting districts for elections to federal office.[70]

In sum, voting rights are under assault, and the Supreme Court is a significant part of the political offensive. Collectively, the rulings examined here support the notion of a Court-backed conservative strategy to empower states, granting them a level of autonomy that shields them from federal enforcement of laws and standards that comport with the U.S. Constitution. Particularly regarding the VRA, the approach has been to eviscerate its provisions, then to utilize the newly created formulations to empower states to exercise power and deny equality. These rulings occurred within a period in which there was "an impulse in American society and politics today to unmoor the present from the country's history of racial discrimination,"[71] as explained by Charles and Fuentes-Rohwer. They describe hostility toward a "voting rights project"—a long-term effort to protect the opportunity for everyone to cast a ballot. As a representation of this effort, the *Brnovich* ruling, they write, " . . . is so troubling and potentially destructive because it is not operating within the confines of the VRA project. The decision is a repudiation of the core aims of that project . . . [T]he opinion is best understood as setting up a series of legal obstacles designed to protect the supposedly vulnerable states."[72]

In short, repudiating the VRA project and creating obstacles are done with the intent of conforming to the fixed worldview mantra of reinstating the status quo of a previous era, exercising wariness of "the other," increasing predictability by eliminating the unknown and relieving the fear and discomfort that accompany a "new" world of equal, widespread justice and opportunity.

NOTES

1. Antonin Scalia, "Morality, Pragmatism and the Legal Order," *Harvard Journal of Law and Public Policy* 9, no. 1 (1986): 123–24. See also Nichole Dunsmore, "Justice Antonin Scalia Says Constitution Not Meant to Answer Moral Questions," *GW Hatchet*, September 6, 2013, https://www.gwhatchet.com/2013/09/16/justice-antonin-scalia-says-he-is-not-philosopher-king-cant-answer-moral-questions/

2. Jamal Greene, "Let's Talk About How Truly Bizarre Our Supreme Court Is," interview by Ezra Klein, "The Ezra Klein Show," *New York Times* podcast, February 4, 2022, audio 59:42, https://www.nytimes.com/2022/02/04/opinion/ezra-klein-podcast-jamal-greene.amp.html.

3. See Adam Liptak, "Gridlock in Congress Has Amplified the Power of the Supreme Court," *New York Times*, July 2, 2022, https://www.nytimes.com/2022/07/02/us/supreme-court-congress.html (describing the Court's 2021–2022 term as "turbulent").

4. 142 S. Ct. 2587 (2022).

5. Ibid., 2609 (expressing reluctance to read into "ambiguous statutory text" EPA authority not explicitly stated).

6. Ibid., 2626 (Kagan, J., dissenting). See also Ibid., 2627 (citing Section 111 of the Clean Air Act which directs the EPA "to regulate stationary sources of any substance that 'causes, or contributes significantly to, air pollution' and that 'may reasonably be anticipated to endanger public health or welfare'")(42 U.S.C. §7411(b)(1)(A)).

7. Ibid., 2644 (Kagan, J., dissenting). See also Christian Farias, "Post-*Roe*, the Supreme Court is On a Collision Course with Democracy," *Vanity Fair*, August 25, 2022, https://www.vanityfair.com/news/2022/08/post-roe-scotus-is-on-a-collision-course-with-democracy ("the conservative justices are already smelling blood . . . The Supreme Court is on a collision course with democracy itself").

8. Linda Greenhouse, "The Supreme Court, Weaponized," *New York Times*, December 16, 2021, https://www.nytimes.com/2021/12/16/opinion/supreme-court-trump.html (noting the significance of the Court accepting this group of cases—"handpicked by the justices . . . from among the thousands of cases the court receives each term—5,227 in the last term to be precise").

9. Ibid. (noting that the group of appeals granted hearings "involves a touchstone issue for conservatives: easing restrictions on firearms, overturning Roe v. Wade and elevating the place of religion in a secular society").

10. See, for example, David J. Zeitlin, "Revisiting *Richardson v. Ramirez*: The Constitutional Bounds of Ex-Felon Disenfranchisement," *Alabama Law Review* 70, no. 1 (2018): 287 ("The nation's progress toward empowering citizens to hold all of their political representatives accountable underscores the importance of citizens' ability to vote within a democracy"), 259–92.

11. See, for example, Joshua A. Douglas, "Is the Right to Vote Really Fundamental?" *Cornell Journal of Law & Public Policy* 18, no. 1 (Fall 2008): 145 ("The problem, however, is that our legal system has not always given an individual's right to vote the same venerated status as it has given many other important rights").

12. See, for example, "Voting Laws Roundup: February 2022," Brennan Center for Justice, February 9, 2022, https://www.brennancenter.org/issues/ensure-every-american-can-vote/voting-reform/state-voting-laws: "The efforts to restrict voting have continued into [2022]. As of January 14, legislators in at least 27 states have introduced, pre-filed, or carried over 250 bills with restrictive provisions, compared to 75 such bills in 24 states on January 14, 2021."

13. Presidential Commission on the Supreme Court of the United States, December 7, 2021, 77, https://www.whitehouse.gov/wp-content/uploads/2021/12/SCOTUS-Report-Final-12.8.21-1.pdf.

14. Ryan J. Rebe, *The Partisan Court: The Era of Political Partisanship on the U.S. Supreme Court* (Lanham, MD: Lexington Books, 2021), 1–2:

While the justices extolled the virtues of originalism and textualism, the reality was quite different. A close examination of their opinions revealed a politically divided court that regularly brushed aside decades-long precedent and statutes. The result was inconsistency and unpredictability in election law decisions. Most striking was the court's unwillingness to stand up to partisan efforts to manipulate the electoral system at the expense of average voters. The justices presided over unlimited corporate campaign spending, partisan gerrymandering, purged registration rolls, unwarranted voting restrictions, and the deterioration of America's faith in its electoral system. The justices allowed themselves to become pawns in the nation's political battles, instead of stalwart defenders of the Constitution.

15. Ibid., 1.

16. *Brnovich v. Democratic Nat'l Committee*, 141 S. Ct. 2321, 2372 (2021) (Kagan, J., dissenting).

17. Ian Millhiser, "Chief Justice Roberts's Lifelong Crusade Against Voting Rights, Explained," *Vox*, September 18, 2020, https://www.vox.com/21211880/supreme -court-chief-justice-john-roberts-voting-rights-act-election-2020.

18. 570 U.S. 529 (2013).

19. U.S. Const., Amend. X. "The powers not delegated to the United States by the Constitution, nor prohibited by it to the States, are reserved to the States respectively, or to the people."

20. Transcript of Oral Argument, 47:7–8, *Shelby County v. Holder*, 570 U.S. 529 (2013) (No. 12–96), February 27, 2013.

21. Transcript of Oral Argument, 47:14–16, *Shelby County v. Holder*, 570 U.S. 529 (2013) (No. 12–96), February 27, 2013.

22. *Shelby County, v. Holder*, 570 U.S. 529, 590 (Ginsburg, J., dissenting) (emphasis added).

23. Ibid., 566 (internal citation omitted).

24. U.S. Const., Amend. XV. "Section 1: The right of citizens of the United States to vote shall not be denied or abridged by the United States or by any State on account of race, color, or previous condition of servitude. Section 2: The Congress shall have the power to enforce this article by appropriate legislation."

25. *Shelby County*, 535 (Roberts, C.J.).

26. Ibid.

27. Guy-Uriel Charles and Luis Fuentes-Rohwer, "The Court's Voting-Rights Decision Was Worse Than People Think," *Atlantic*, July 8, 2021, https://www .theatlantic.com/ideas/archive/2021/07/brnovich-vra-scotus-decision-arizona-voting -right/619330/.

28. Ibid.

29. See Vann R. Newkirk II, "How Shelby County v. Holder Broke America," *Atlantic*, July 10, 2018, https://www.theatlantic.com/politics/archive/2018/07/ how-shelby-county-broke-america/564707/:

The results have been predictable. Voter-identification laws, which experts suggest will make voting harder especially for poor people, people of color, and elderly people, have advanced in several states, and some voting laws that make it easier to register and cast ballots have been destroyed. For many of the jurisdictions formerly under preclearance, voting became rapidly more difficult after the *Shelby County* decision, particularly for poor and elderly black people and Latinos.

30. *Brnovich v. Democratic Nat'l Committee*, 141 S. Ct. 2321 (2021). Mark Brnovich was Arizona's attorney general and an authorized representative of the state.

31. Section 2 was enacted to forbid, in all 50 States, any standard, practice, or procedure imposed or applied to deny or abridge the right of any citizen of the United States to vote on account of race or color (42 USCS § 1973 (a)). With updates, the current version forbids any standard, practice, or procedure *that results in* a denial or abridgment of the right of any citizen of the United States to vote on account of race or color (42 USCS § 1973j(d)) (emphasis added).

32. *Brnovich*, 2350 (Kagan, J., dissenting).

33. Ariz. Rev. Stat. Ann. § 16–584 (Cum. Supp. 2020) (enforcing the requirement that voters who chose to vote in person on election day had to do so in their assigned precincts; votes cast in an unassigned precinct do not count); Ariz. Rev. Stat. Ann. § 16–542(D) (limiting those authorized to collect and submit completed ballots).

34. *Democratic Nat'l Comm. v. Hobbs*, 948 F.3d 989 (2021) (9th Cir.).

35. Ibid., 998.

36. Transcript of Oral Argument, 37:25–38:1–4, *Brnovich v. Democratic Nat'l Committee*, 141 S. Ct. 2321 (2021) (No. 19–1257), March 2, 2021.

37. See Charles Blow, "Seven Steps to Destroy a Democracy," *New York Times*, March 13, 2022, https://www.nytimes.com/2022/03/13/opinion/republicans-democracy.html:

Chipping away at voter protections has become a theme of the court. Ever since its 2013 decision gutting a key part of the Voting Rights Act, which forced states with a history of racial discrimination to seek federal approval before changing their voting laws, the court has made it increasingly difficult for liberals to prove that state officials are violating the law.

38. *Brnovich*, 2350 (Kagan, J., dissenting).

39. Ibid. (emphasis added).

40. See Ibid., 2354 ("Indeed, the problem of voting discrimination has become worse since that time—in part because of what this Court did in *Shelby County*").

41. See, for example, "Voting Laws Roundup: December 2021," Brennan Center for Justice, December 21, 2021, https://www.brennancenter.org/our-work/research-reports/voting-laws-roundup-december-2021 ("Between January 1 and December 7 [2021], at least 19 states passed 34 laws restricting access to voting. More than 440 bills with provisions that restrict voting access have been introduced in 49 states in the 2021 legislative sessions"). See also Ed Pilkington, "Report Shows the Extent of Republican Efforts to Sabotage Democracy," *Guardian*, December 24, 2021, https://www.theguardian.com/us-news/2021/dec/23/voter-suppression-election-interference-republicans:

A year that began with the violent insurrection at the US Capitol is ending with an unprecedented push to politicize, criminalize or in other ways subvert the nonpartisan administration of elections . . . [N]o fewer than 262 bills introduced in 41 states that hijack the election process. Of those, 32 bills have become law in 17 states. Ibid.

42. See, for example, LaShawn Warren, "Voting Discrimination is Getting Worse, Not Better," ScotusBlog, February 18, 2021, https://www.scotusblog.com/2021/02/voting-discrimination-is-getting-worse-not-better/.
43. *Brnovich*, 2352 (Kagan, J., dissenting) (emphasis added).
44. Ibid.
45. Linda Greenhouse, "On Voting Rights, Justice Alito Is Stuck in the 1980s," *New York Times*, July 15, 2021, https://www.nytimes.com/2021/07/15/opinion/Voting-rights-supreme-court.html.
46. *Brnovich,* 2363–64 (2021) (Kagan, J., dissenting) (emphasis added).
47. Julia Kirschenbaum and Michael Li, "Gerrymandering Explained," Brennan Center for Justice, August 12, 2021, https://www.brennancenter.org/our-work/research-reports/gerrymandering-explained.
48. Ibid.
49. See Jesse Wegman, "Gerrymander, U.S.A.," *New York Times*, July 12, 2022, https://www.nytimes.com/2022/07/12/opinion/texas-redistricting-maps-gerrymandering.html ("Partisan politicians draw lines in order to distribute their voters more efficiently, ensuring they can win the most seats with the fewest votes. They shore up their strongholds and help eliminate any meaningful electoral competition. It's the opposite of how representative democracy is supposed to work").
50. 139 S. Ct. 2484 (2019).
51. Ibid., 2509 (Kagan, J., dissenting).
52. Ibid.
53. Ibid.
54. See, for example, *Arizona State Legislature v. Arizona Independent Redistricting Commission*, 576 U.S. 787 (2015) (ruling a bipartisan commission appointed to handle redistricting was constitutional). Roberts dissented: "The Court's position has no basis in the text, structure, or history of the Constitution." Ibid., 825 (Roberts, C.J., dissenting).
55. *Merrill v. Milligan*, 142 S. Ct. 1358 (2022).
56. Adam Liptak, "Supreme Court Restores Alabama Voting Map That a Court Said Hurt Black Voters," *New York Times*, February 7, 2022, https://www.nytimes.com/2022/02/07/us/politics/supreme-court-alabama-redistricting-congressional-map.html.
57. Linda Greenhouse, "The Supreme Court Has Crossed the Rubicon," *New York Times*, February 9, 2022, https://www.nytimes.com/2022/02/09/opinion/supreme-court-voting-rights.html.
58. Ibid.
59. Ibid.
60. See, for example, Adam Liptak, "Supreme Court Allows Court-Imposed Voting Maps in North Carolina and Pennsylvania," *New York Times*, March 7, 2022, https://www.nytimes.com/2022/03/07/us/supreme-court-voting-maps.html (describing the maps as "giving Democrats an advantage in this year's election in two key states").

61. Ian Millhiser, "A Grand Supreme Court Showdown Over Gerrymandering Ends in a Whimper," *Vox*, March 7, 2022, https://www.vox.com/platform/amp/22966311/supreme-court-gerrymandering-toth-moore-harper-chapman-north-carolina-pennsylvania-redistricting.

62. U.S. Const., art. I, § 4: "[T]he Times, Places and Manner of holding Elections for Senators and Representatives shall be prescribed in each State by the Legislature thereof; but the Congress may at any time by Law make or alter such Regulations, except as to the Places of choosing Senators."

63. Jamelle Bouie, "The Supreme Court Did the Right Thing. Still, I'm Worried," *New York Times*, March 11, 2022, https://www.nytimes.com/2022/03/11/opinion/north-carolina-pennsylvania-gerrymandering.html.

64. See Mark Sherman and Gary D. Robertson, "Justices Seem Poised to Hear Election Cases Pressed by GOP," Associated Press, June, 19, 2022, https://apnews.com/article/2022-midterm-elections-us-supreme-court-pennsylvania-constitutions-north-carolina-b1aaaf54cda0deada714a4eb57643d94 ("The Supreme Court seems poised to take on a new elections case being pressed by Republicans that could increase the power of state lawmakers over races for Congress and the presidency, as well as redistricting, and cut state courts out of the equation").

65. Liptak, "Supreme Court Allows Court-Imposed Voting Maps in North Carolina and Pennsylvania." See also Jessica Levinson, "Conservative Supreme Court's Gerrymandering Flip-Flops Spell Trouble," MSNBC, March 10, 2022, https://www.msnbc.com/opinion/msnbc-opinion/supreme-court-election-hypocrisy-north-carolina-alabama-n1291360:

> State lawmakers may soon have virtually unfettered power to draw congressional district lines. If this happens, it could undermine the democratic process and upend a century's worth of case law. And it will only happen with the deeply hypocritical blessing of the Supreme Court's conservative wing.

66. *Moore v. Harper*, 142 S. Ct. 1089 (2022) (*cert. granted* June 30, 2022).

67. *Wisconsin Legislature v. Wisconsin Elections Commission*, 142 S. Ct. 1245 (2022).

68. *Ardoin v. Robinson*, 37 F.4th 208 (5th Cir. 2022).

69. Richard L. Hasen, "It's Hard to Overstate the Danger of the Voting Case the Supreme Court Just Agreed to Hear," *Slate,* June 30, 2022, https://slate.com/news-and-politics/2022/06/supreme-court-dangerous-independent-state-legislature-theory.html ("It also could provide the path for election subversion in congressional and presidential elections").

70. See, for example, Adam Liptak, "Supreme Court Revives Republican-Drawn Voting Map in Louisiana," *New York Times*, June 30, 2022, https://www.nytimes.com/2022/06/28/us/supreme-court-louisiana-voting-map.html.

71. Charles and Fuentes-Rohwer, "The Court's Voting-Rights Decision Was Worse Than People Think."

72. Ibid.

Chapter 4

Gun Rights

Compared to other nations, gun ownership in the United States is ubiquitous. It is the world's only nation with more guns than people—120 guns for every 100 Americans.[1] A 2020 Gallup survey reported that 44 percent of American households have at least one firearm, and 32 percent of American adults say they own a gun.[2] In January 2021, Americans purchased more than two million firearms, an 80 percent increase from the same month the year before, and the third-highest one-month total on record at that time.[3] There are more deaths per capita from gun violence in the United States than in any other developed nation,[4] with gun-related deaths reaching the highest level ever recorded in 2020.[5] In short, when it comes to guns, the United States and its gun culture are global outliers.[6]

The history surrounding the right to firearms possession in the United States is long, complex, and contentious. Guns are embedded in the stories of the nation's settlement, its founding, and its history thereafter. With the ratification of the Bill of Rights, and specifically the Second Amendment,[7] the right to bear arms was established in the new nation's Constitution. Its precise meaning, then and now, has been the subject of debate, one in which originalism and living constitutionalism play prominent roles.[8] This issue, in fact, may best exemplify the ideological clash between the two camps, with living constitutionalists especially passionate in their view that contemporary circumstances demand a Second Amendment interpretation different and more nuanced than anything the Founders may have intended. It is also a debate that is replete with political overtones. In general, conservatives defend the right to possess firearms, sometimes in an absolute fashion, with progressives/liberals typically being those who support measures to limit possession.[9] It bears repeating here that those who advocate for, and support, gun rights are more likely to have a fixed worldview—an orientation that prioritizes safety and eliminating danger, real or perceived.[10] Guns, they believe, enhance safety. Similarly, a jurist with a fixed worldview often sees Constitutional law through a lens in which the weak need to be protected, with the state's proper role being the enhancement of safety by augmenting the right to have the tools necessary to ward off danger.[11]

Particularly as shootings occurred and increased across the country—some of them resulting in mass casualties and some with children as victims[12]— the debates extended into the propriety and constitutionality of gun control. Some laws to limit possession were passed, including one by the District of Columbia in 2001.[13] That measure prohibited the possession of unregistered firearms, and limited the opportunity to register handguns. Thus, the possession of handguns was illegal, in effect, unless special permission was granted.

A District of Columbia special police officer, Dick Heller, challenged this law. Given his job, Heller was authorized to carry a handgun while on duty. He also wanted to keep one at home. When his application to do so was denied, he filed a lawsuit challenging the D.C. regulations on Second Amendment grounds. The case was ultimately heard by the Supreme Court, one that was "long awaited by many, long feared by others."[14] In addition, the case produced "the most thoroughgoing originalist opinion in the Court's history,"[15] in large part due to its author being Justice Antonin Scalia, the iconic champion and standard bearer of originalism.[16]

While *Heller* is regarded as a quintessential example of the application of originalism—and it is[17]—its plot line contains some twists. First, within his opinion, Justice Scalia engaged in a deep textual dissection of the Second Amendment, phrase by phrase, clause by clause, one that would make any etymologist, linguist, or lexicologist proud. Lawrence Solum asserts that this represents the most important feature of *Heller*—methodology:

> The Court examined each of the operative words and phrases in the Second Amendment, examining the semantic content of "the people," "keep," "bear," and "arms." The Court concluded its examination as follows: "Putting all of these textual elements together, we find that they guarantee the individual right to possess and carry weapons in case of confrontation."[18]

This approach, of course, is directly from the originalist manual. It also represents what many find unacceptable about an approach that relies on, and microanalyzes, text. Reflecting how any reader of Scalia's *Heller* opinion might react, David Sosa writes that "textualism risks devolving into absurdity."[19] The primary problem, he suggests, stems from the focus on form, writing "the rule of law is emphatically not about form. It is 'about' meaning."[20]

Second, Justice Stevens's lead dissenting opinion in *Heller* seems to be just as concerned with the Second Amendment's text and original intent as was his adversary's opinion. It is an approach that attracted critics, from Justice Scalia[21] himself to scholars such as Jamal Greene and Rory Little who, respectively, described Stevens's opinion as an effort to engage Scalia rather than challenge him,[22] and a "fruitless tilting at the Champion of Originalism."[23]

The roots of a fixed-originalist approach—in part a response to rulings of the Warren Court, as previously examined in this volume—surface on the fringes of *Heller*. Specifically, for some, *Brown v. Board of Education*,[24] the ruling that race-based segregation in public schools violates the Constitution, engendered fear of increased crime. In response, a social movement to expand law-and-order and self-defense opportunities took root, in part seeking the expansion of Second Amendment rights.[25] Reva Siegel writes that this movement illustrates how battles "over the Constitution's meaning can endow courts with authority to change the way they interpret its provisions."[26] Ultimately, these new interpretations are recognized as the (new) Constitution. This "Second Amendment movement" was not unlike others in which participants patiently play a long game, waiting for the "right" case opportunity to submit to the Supreme Court. This reinforces the notion that any shift in the law and interpretation of the Constitution precipitated by an agenda-driven Supreme Court begins not so much with its rulings, but with the decisions about which cases to hear.

Though worthy of being placed on a pedestal in the school of originalism, Scalia's *Heller* opinion arguably veers off those rails to some degree. Jack Balkin, for example, makes the almost counterintuitive assertion that the *Heller* ruling shows that "living constitutionalism is alive and well."[27] His reasoning is straightforward:

> [T]he Supreme Court revise[d] existing law to match changes in public opinion . . . In *Heller*, the Court changed existing law dramatically to adopt a new interpretation of the Second Amendment that is actually fairly close to the center of public opinion. It struck down one of the most restrictive gun control laws in the country and it recognized Americans' right to use handguns to defend their home.[28]

To be sure, the *Heller* majority changed the law by expanding Second Amendment rights, but it did so consistent with the tenets of a fixed worldview. In this case, that meant returning to the state of gun control law that existed prior to the 2001 District of Columbia regulations that triggered *Heller*. A status quo regime of minimal regulation of firearms was restored.

There is irony in the Court's *Heller* opinion. Offered as "an exemplar of originalist reasoning,"[29] its author was an advocate of that approach because it constrained judges, forced them to view the Constitution as law, not politics, and to eschew any inclination to consider "current societal values."[30] Yet, in applying fixed-originalist textualism, Justice Scalia and the majority worked at the edges of these principles, injecting the very politics into the opinion that originalism claims to avoid, and did so precisely by taking "current social values" into account. Rather than utilizing fixed meaning, Siegel notes, "*Heller*'s originalism enforces understandings of the Second Amendment that were forged in the late twentieth century through popular constitutionalism."[31] Thus, two flaws in the originalist approach are exposed: First, as noted previously, there is a lack of precision in determining not only the exact meaning of the Constitution's text at the time of its authorship, but also what it means now.[32] Even reasonable people can disagree about the meaning. Second, even when this problem clearly surfaces, a fixed worldview fails to allow the necessary flexibility. At its core, originalism remains rigid. This, in turn, reveals the presence of result orientation (i.e., confirmation bias) on the Court. Winning is the goal.[33] And vice versa. That is not merely politics, but politics at its worst.

In his *Heller* dissent, Justice Stevens noted that not only did the majority contradict the Court's own precedent[34]—a harbinger of what would surface emphatically in subsequent terms—but also that "hundreds of judges have relied on the view of the [Second] Amendment we endorsed" previously.[35] Stevens added, "No new evidence has surfaced since," nor did the *Heller* majority "identify any new evidence supporting the view that the Amendment was intended to limit the power of Congress to regulate civilian uses of weapons."[36] For nearly a half-century, lower courts had been virtually unanimous in rejecting the view that the Second Amendment creates an individual right to use guns for nonmilitary purposes. This then begs the question: What changed? The answer is political circumstances,[37] starting with the politics of the nation—including the "Second Amendment movement" noted above.

That change in the political environment affected the Court itself. All members of the *Heller* majority were Reagan/Bush nominees.[38] Like the Trump nominees who later followed them, all possessed fixed worldviews. Supported and encouraged by like-minded citizens and politicians—and armed with an approach that included selectively choosing social developments to support their goal—they succeeded in returning to a time of a Second Amendment largely unfettered by regulatory limitations.

As a landmark precedent, and with the subsequent growth of a fixed-originalist majority on the Court, *Heller* served as a springboard for rulings that take a broad view of the Second Amendment. Though Justice Scalia's death in 2016 was a significant loss in originalist leadership on the Court, his seat was ultimately filled by Neil Gorsuch, a successor in whom originalists took comfort.[39]

For several years, however, the Court sidestepped major Second Amendment cases,[40] frustrating Justices Thomas and Alito who believed the Second Amendment was being turned into a second class right.[41] The inability to acquire four votes in favor of hearing a case that could significantly expand Second Amendment rights post-*Heller* may have been based in pragmatism— part of an effort to "turn down the heat on perceptions that the Supreme Court is merely another political body."[42] Cooling those perceptions, however, was challenging given other factors such as the matter of timing and the presence of reliable votes on the Court. That is, with Amy Coney Barrett's replacement of Ruth Bader Ginsburg in October 2020, a conservative supermajority was created. Not only were there now at least four votes in place to favor hearing a gun rights case, there was confidence in its outcome.[43]

That case arrived officially in April 2021 when the Court agreed to hear *New York State Rifle & Pistol Association, Inc. v. Bruen.*[44] At issue was a New York state law that limited a person's ability to obtain a license to carry a gun outside of the home. The law required license seekers to show "proper cause exists" to carry the gun outside the home.[45]

This was the second time in less than two years that Second Amendment challenges led by the New York State Rifle & Pistol Association (NYSRPA) were argued at the Court. It was the product of efforts to "convince the jus- tices that the Second Amendment is being treated as a second-class right in need of their support,"[46] a phrase characterized as a "dog whistle that signi- fied sympathy for the gun rights cause."[47] In both cases, turnover on the Court played key roles. It was "a widely held theory" that the Court had not ruled on a Second Amendment case for many years "because Justice Anthony Kennedy was reluctant to vote in favor of granting certiorari to such cases."[48] Kennedy's retirement and replacement by Brett Kavanaugh in 2018 tilted the Court in a pro–Second Amendment direction.[49] Just a few months after Kavanaugh took his seat, the Court agreed to hear *New York State Rifle & Pistol Association, Inc. v. City of New York.*[50]

In what was ultimately a double-barreled effort by an affiliate of the conservatively aligned National Rifle Association, efforts to expand *Heller* unfolded. The first round is noteworthy not so much for any new law or policy stemming from the decision, but instead for how it revealed that three members of the Court's conservative pro-gun bloc accepted the torch passed by Justice Scalia and sought to advance the *Heller* doctrine. Illustrating again how political agendas on the Court are first revealed by which cases are heard,[51] the Kavanaugh-for-Kennedy exchange was crucial.

In an unsigned two-page opinion, the Court deemed the case moot because New York had amended the challenged laws. Justice Alito, joined by Justices Thomas and Gorsuch, filed a strong dissent. "This case is not moot," Alito wrote in a 17-page opinion. "The city violated petitioners' Second Amendment right, and we should so hold."[52]

Apparently as dissatisfied as Alito, and believing that Second Amendment issues remained, a new but similar challenge to the now-revised New York law was filed by the NYSRPA, this time supporting two individual plaintiffs who had been denied gun licenses. The case was dismissed by a federal district court, and that decision was affirmed by a federal appeals court. The Supreme Court, however, accepted the case, this time after a personnel change arguably more significant than the Kavanaugh-for-Kennedy exchange. The Court agreed to hear *New York State Rifle & Pistol Association, Inc. v. Bruen* almost six months to the day after the Barrett-for-Ginsburg exchange, a seismic ideological shift on the Court.

The petitioners had asked the Supreme Court to review their case, specifically on the question "whether the Second Amendment allows the government to prohibit ordinary law-abiding citizens from carrying handguns outside the home for self-defense." The NYSRPA wanted the rights that apply to home possession expanded to outside the home—that is, to apply *Heller* outside the home. This was clear in oral arguments where, for example, in response to a question from Justice Gorsuch, NYSRPA attorney Paul Clement played to his audience of originalists in the majority by suggesting that "text, history, and tradition"[53] should be the standards in evaluating the meaning of Second Amendment rights—as the Court had done in *Heller*—and applying that equally to settings inside and outside the home.[54]

Predictably—and not unlike some of his colleagues who asked leading questions so that the answers would place their preconceived notions on the record—Justice Alito asked about the "original understanding" of what the Second Amendment protects. The response included the benefits of looking at tradition to understand the meaning of constitutional rights.[55] Alito later doubled down, suggesting that "traditions" such as late-nineteenth century and early-twentieth century rulings should not be substituted for evidence of the Constitution's original meaning.[56]

Lastly in terms of the oral arguments in *New York State Rifle & Pistol Association, Inc. v. Bruen*, it is important to cite a specific statement given the degree to which viewpoint-friendly justices provided license to a stunningly insensitive closing rebuttal by the Rifle and Pistol association's attorney: "In a country with the Second Amendment as a fundamental right, simply having more firearms cannot be a problem and can't be a government interest just to put a cap on the number of firearms."[57] While those words may have appealed to a majority of his nine audience members, others found it antithetical to common sense and fuel to the fire of a nation already with more guns than people,[58] and where more people per capita die from gun violence than in any other developed nation.[59]

The Court's predictable[60] 6–3 ruling was written by the leader of the Second Amendment-as-second-class-right tribe, Clarence Thomas.[61] By expanding possession opportunities, he addressed what he had viewed as a problem. For the first time, the Court defined the "keep and bear arms" clause and did so by making it easier to carry a weapon outside the home.

Falling into the fixed/originalist framework, Justice Thomas wrote that with any weapons regulation, the state must demonstrate that its law "is consistent with the Nation's historical tradition of firearms regulation. Only if a firearm regulation is consistent with this Nation's historical tradition may a court conclude that the individual's conduct falls outside the Second Amendment's 'unqualified command.'"[62] That last phrase is especially stunning, apparently declaring the Second Amendment to be the only constitutional provision without boundaries. The declaration is rooted in originalist textualism, lacking sound interpretation and reasoning. The *Heller* ruling—one issued twelve years prior to *NYSRPA*—Thomas wrote, "demands a [licensing] test rooted in the Second Amendment's text, as informed by history."[63] A state must demonstrate that any attempt to restrict possession "is consistent with the Nation's historical tradition of firearms regulation."[64]

The reliance on *Heller* is also notable given its author—the original originalist, Justice Scalia, who was joined by Chief Justice Roberts and Justices Kennedy, Alito, and Thomas himself. The overlap in this ruling was notable, with Justices Gorsuch, Kavanaugh, and Barrett as newer members of the tribe who replaced the departed Scalia and Kennedy.

Further relying on *Heller*, Thomas described the approach used by the majority there. It "canvassed the historical record," finding support in the fact that state constitutions adopted arms-bearing rights immediately before and after the ratification of the Second Amendment.[65] As Thomas wrote, "*Heller*'s methodology centered on constitutional text and history."[66] And nothing else. This clearly ignores anything resembling contemporary circumstances, notably the proliferation of firearms and the deaths at their hands. In his concurring opinion, Justice Alito specifically questioned the relevance of "mass shootings that have occurred in recent years"[67] mentioned by Justice Breyer in dissent.

Though relying on *Heller*, this ruling went further, scaling down the limitations articulated in that 2008 ruling that allowed for firearms regulation in some circumstances.[68] Those limitations were a stipulation by Justice Kennedy, his price for joining the majority.[69] A dozen years later, Kennedy was retired, replaced by Kavanaugh, a jurist with a history of strong Second Amendment support.[70]

Thomas doubled down on his originalist approach, writing that "the Second Amendment's historically *fixed meaning* applies to new circumstances: Its reference to 'arms' does not apply only [to] those arms in existence in the 18th century."[71] Moreover, the Court's opinion seems to specifically reject any notion of considering the evolution of both firearms and society since

1791, expressing distrust of present-day judges to properly evaluate regulations consistent with the nation's history.

Breyer's dissent—joined by Justices Sotomayor and Kagan—was rooted in contemporary circumstances, clearly suggesting the need for a fluid worldview reading of the Second Amendment. He added that the majority "wrongly limits its analysis to focus nearly exclusively on history."[72] Even then, Breyer contends, that misguided focus included only parts of history, "ignoring an abundance of historical evidence supporting" the kind of regulation at issue here.[73] He exhaustively examined periods of history that support evolving (i.e., fluid) standards for firearms regulation. Breyer continued, "The question before us concerns the extent to which the Second Amendment prevents democratically elected officials from enacting laws to address the serious problem of gun violence. And yet the Court today purports to answer that question without discussing the nature or severity of that problem."[74]

Breyer suggests that unlike what the majority did in *NYSRPA*, courts have an obligation to consider current conditions—the situations that lead states to consider regulating firearms in the first place. The many statistically supported assertions that he made included citing that along with the world's highest per capita gun possession rate, the trajectory of gun violence in America was rising.[75] This highlights the stark contrast in how the Constitution—including the Second Amendment here—and other texts are read. Breyer's dissenting opinion is replete with fluid-living constitutionalism; the majority's opinion is steeped in fixed-originalism.

It is common in the aftermath of mass shootings—and those in 2022 were no exception—that the issue of gun control laws vs. Second Amendment rights acutely surfaces within the national conversation. Some contend that placing the issue within the context of politics is misplaced.[76] It is suggested here that by ruling as it did in *NYSRPA*—only weeks after mass shootings in Buffalo, New York, and Uvalde, Texas, by gunmen armed with what were called "weapons of war"[77]—a fixed-originalist Court majority that ignored evolving social realities not only made it clear that the issue is, in fact, a political one, it placed itself squarely within that realm.

As they often are, the words from a Supreme Court ruling from another era seem appropriate to recall. Though the case was much different than those examined herein, the principle invoked is highly relevant. Justice Robert Jackson admonished his colleagues and the institution itself in 1949 for how the Constitution was sometimes viewed: "There is danger that, if the Court does not temper its doctrinaire logic with a little practical wisdom, it will convert the constitutional Bill of Rights into a suicide pact."[78]

NOTES

1. Kara Fox, Krystina Shveda, Natalie Croker, and Marco Chacon, "How US Gun Culture Stacks Up with the World," CNN, November 26, 2021, https://amp.cnn.com/cnn/2021/11/26/world/us-gun-culture-world-comparison-intl-cmd/index.html.

2. Lydia Saad, "What Percentage of Americans Own Guns?" Gallup, November 13, 2020, https://news.gallup.com/poll/264932/percentage-americans-own-guns.aspx.

3. Hannah Denham and Andrew Ba Tran, "Fearing Violence and Political Uncertainty, Americans Are Buying Millions More Firearms," February 3, 2021, *Washington Post*, https://www.washingtonpost.com/business/2021/02/03/gun-sales-january-background-checks (attributing the increase, in part, to the January 6, 2021, attack on the U.S. Capitol).

4. Fox, Shveda, Croker and Chacon, "How US Gun Culture Stacks Up with the World" ("The [death] rate in the US is eight times greater than in Canada, which has the seventh highest rate of gun ownership in the world; 22 times higher than in the European Union and 23 times greater than in Australia, according to Institute for Health Metrics and Evaluation (IHME) data from 2019").

5. Roni Caryn Rabin, "Gun Deaths Surged During the Pandemic's First Year, the C.D.C. Reports," *New York Times*, May 10, 2022, https://www.nytimes.com/2022/05/10/health/cdc-gun-violence-pandemic.html.

6. Fox, Shveda, Croker, and Chacon, "How US Gun Culture Stacks Up with the World." See also David Frum, "America's Gun Plague," *Atlantic*, May 14, 2022, https://www.theatlantic.com/ideas/archive/2022/05/buffalo-shooting-great-replacement-ideology/629870/ ("Almost every country on Earth has citizens filled with vitriol, but no comparably advanced country has a gun-violence epidemic quite like America's").

7. U.S. Const., Amend. II ("A well regulated Militia, being necessary to the security of a free State, the right of the people to keep and bear Arms, shall not be infringed").

8. When it comes to interpretation, it is worth noting that onetime Chief Justice Warren Burger, a Nixon nominee and generally acknowledged to be a conservative, referred to the Second Amendment as "the subject of one of the greatest pieces of fraud—I repeat the word fraud—on the American public by special interest groups that I have ever seen in my lifetime." See Warren Burger, "PBS News Hour," interview by Charlene Hunter-Gault, PBS, December 16, 1991, https://www.youtube.com/watch?v=Eya_k4P-iEo. Elsewhere Burger wrote that the Second Amendment does not provide unfettered gun rights for individuals. See Michael Waldman, "How the NRA Rewrote the Second Amendment," *Politico*, May 19, 2014, https://www.politico.com/magazine/story/2014/05/nra-guns-second-amendment-106856/.

9. See Saad, "What Percentage of Americans Own Guns?" (reporting that 50 percent of Republican adults own a gun compared to 18 percent of Democrats).

10. Marc J. Hetherington and Jonathan Weiler, *Prius or Pickup? How the Answers to Four Simple Questions Explain America's Great Divide* (Boston: Houghton Mifflin Harcourt, 2018), 4 ("conservatives erect more barriers—more defense mechanisms—between themselves and their environment").

11. See, for example, Michelle Goldberg, "America May be Broken Beyond Repair," *New York Times*, May 27, 2022, https://www.nytimes.com/2022/05/27/opinion/uvalde-shooting.html (writing of the belief citizens need guns as a defense against government, "Guns, in this worldview, are a guarantor against government overreach. And government overreach includes attempts to regulate guns").

12. See, for example, Aaron Smith, "Eight Years After Sandy Hook, Mass Shootings Are Up, But Federal Gun Control Remains the Same," *Forbes*, December 11, 2020, https://www.forbes.com/sites/aaronsmith/2020/12/11/eight-years-after-sandy-hook-mass-shootings-are-up-but-federal-gun-control-remains-the-same. See also Christine Hauser, "A Partial List of Mass Shootings in the United States in 2022," *New York Times*, May 23, 2022, https://www.nytimes.com/article/mass-shootings-2022.html.

13. D. C. Code §§ 7-2501.01(12), 7-2502.01(a), 7-2502.02(a)(4) (2001).

14. Reva B. Siegel, "Dead or Alive: Originalism as Popular Constitutionalism in Heller," *Harvard Law Review* 122 (November 2008): 191.

15. Jamal Greene, "Selling Originalism," *Georgetown Law Journal* 97 (March 2009): 659.

16. See Antonin Scalia and Bryan A. Garner, *Reading the Law: The Interpretation of Legal Texts* (Eagan, MN: Thomson/West, 2012), 402 ("Originalism is not perfect. But it is more certain than any other criterion. And this is not even a close question").

17. *District of Columbia v. Heller*, 554 U.S. 570, 576 (2008) ("In interpreting this text, we are guided by the principle that 'the Constitution was written to be understood by the voters; its words and phrases were used in their normal and ordinary as distinguished from technical meaning'") (internal citations omitted). See also Rory Little, "Heller and Constitutional Interpretation: Originalism's Last Gasp," *Hastings Law Journal* 60 (June 2009): 1418 (describing the application of originalism in *Heller* as "laborious historical detail [that] is unprecedented for a constitutional Supreme Court decision").

18. Lawrence B. Solum, "Original Ideas on Originalism: District of Columbia v. Heller and Originalism," *Northwestern University Law Review* 103 (Spring 2009): 939 (quoting *Heller*, 592).

19. David Sosa, "'The Unintentional Fallacy,' review of *A Matter of Interpretation*, by Antonin Scalia," *California Law Review* 86 (July 1998): 927.

20. Ibid., 927.

21. *Heller*, 590 (Scalia, J.) ("It is always perilous to derive the meaning of an adopted provision from another provision deleted in the drafting process").

22. Greene, "Selling Originalism," 659.

23. Little, "Heller and Constitutional Interpretation," 1421.

24. 347 U.S. 483 (1954) (ruling that race-based segregation in public schools violates the Constitution).

25. See Linda Greenhouse, *Justice on the Brink: The Death of Ruth Bader Ginsburg, the Rise of Amy Coney Barrett, and Twelve Months That Transformed the Supreme Court* (New York: Random House, 2021), 171 ("A mobilized social movement had succeeded in propelling *Heller* to the Supreme Court"). See also Jack Balkin, "Balkinization," June 27, 2008, http://balkin.blogspot.com/2008/06/this-decision-will-cost

-american-lives.html ("The result in *Heller* would have been impossible without . . . social movement actors who, over a period of about 35 years, succeeded in changing Americans' minds about the meaning of the Second Amendment").

26. Siegel, "Dead or Alive," 194 ("[B]y the 1990s, proponents of this law-and-order Second Amendment came to differentiate their claims from those of the modern militia movement, emphasizing that the Second Amendment entitled the citizen to arms needed to defend his family against crime, not against the government").

27. Balkin, "Balkinization."

28. Ibid.

29. Reva B. Siegel, "Symposium: The Second Amendment and the Right to Bear Arms After D.C. v. Heller: Heller & Originalism's Dead Hand—In Theory and Practice," *UCLA Law Review* 56 (June 2009): 1412.

30. Antonin Scalia, "Originalism: The Lesser Evil," *University of Cincinnati Law Review* 57 (1989): 854.

31. Siegel, "Dead or Alive," 192. See also J. Harvie Wilkinson III, "Of Guns, Abortions, and the Unraveling Rule of Law," *Virginia Law Review* 95 (April 2009): 254 ("*Heller* encourages Americans to do what conservative jurists warned for years they should not do: bypass the ballot and seek to press their political agenda in the courts").

32. Compare, for example, *Heller*, 592 (Scalia, J.) ("The very text of the Second Amendment implicitly recognizes the pre-existence of the right and declares only that it 'shall not be infringed'") with *Heller*, 646 (Stevens, J., dissenting) ("The 'right to keep and bear Arms' protects only a right to possess and use firearms in connection with service in a state-organized militia").

33. See Ezra Klein, *Why We're Polarized* (New York: Avid Reader Press, 2020), 74 (writing that as the stakes rise in a polarized society, so does "our willingness to do anything to make sure our side wins"). See also Charles M. Blow, "The Supreme Court as an Instrument of Oppression," *New York Times*, May 8, 2022, https://www.nytimes.com/2022/05/08/opinion/supreme-court-oppression.html ("There are no inviolable rules for those bent on oppression. There is only winning, at all costs, no matter the casualties. Conservatives would abide a boor like Donald Trump because he could give them the judges they wanted").

34. *United States v. Miller*, 307 U.S. 174 (1939) (protecting the right to keep and bear arms for certain military purposes but affirming the legislature's power to regulate the nonmilitary use and ownership of weapons). See also Greenhouse, *Justice on the Brink*, 170 ("*Heller* was a stunning constitutional departure").

35. *Heller*, 638 (Stevens, J., dissenting). See also *United States v. Miller*, 307 U.S. 174 (1939); *Lewis v. United States*, 445 U.S. 55 (1980); *McDonald v. City of Chicago*, 561 U.S. 742 (2010) (the right of an individual to "keep and bear arms," as protected under the Second Amendment, is incorporated by the Due Process Clause of the Fourteenth Amendment and is thereby enforceable against the states).

36. *Heller*, 638–39 (Stevens, J., dissenting).

37. See Cass R. Sunstein, "Second Amendment Minimalism: Heller as Griswold." *Harvard Law Review* 122 (November 2008): 252 (2008) (writing that *Heller*'s originalism "has everything to do with the particular context in which the *Heller* Court

wrote—the context that led the Court to be composed as it was and to have the inclinations that it did").

38. *District of Columbia v. Heller*: "Judges: Scalia, J., delivered the opinion of the
Court, in which Roberts, C. J., and Kennedy, Thomas, and Alito, JJ., joined."

39. See Neil Gorsuch, *A Republic, If You Can Keep It* (New York: Crown Forum,
2020), 131 (extolling the virtues of textualism: "When interpreting statutes, it tasks
judges with discerning (only) what an ordinary English speaker familiar with the
law's usages would have understood the statutory text to mean at the time of its
enactment").

40. But see *McDonald v. City of Chicago*, 561, U.S. 742 (2010) (largely affirming
Heller and citing the 14th Amendment as supporting the right to bear arms).

41. See, for example, Silvester v. Becerra, 138 S. Ct. 945, 945 (2018) (Thomas,
J., dissenting from denial of certiorari) (bemoaning "lower courts' general failure
to afford the Second Amendment the respect due an enumerated constitutional
right"); Peruta v. California, 137 S. Ct. 1995, 1999 (2017) (Thomas, J., joined by
Gorsuch, J., dissenting from denial of certiorari) (lamenting the "distressing trend"
of "the treatment of the Second Amendment as a disfavored right"); Friedman v.
City of Highland Park, 577 U.S. 1039, 1039 (2015) (Thomas, J., joined by Scalia,
J., dissenting from denial of certiorari) (criticizing "noncompliance with our Second
Amendment precedents" by "several Courts of Appeals"); Jackson v. City & Cty. of
San Francisco, 576 U.S. 1013, 1014 (2015) (Thomas, J., joined by Scalia, J., dissent-
ing from denial of certiorari) ("lower courts, including the ones here, have failed to
protect [the Second Amendment right]").

42. Jessica Levinson, "Trump's Supreme Court Is About to Reshape Gun Control,"
MSNBC, April 27, 2021, https://www.msnbc.com/opinion/trump-s-supreme-court
-about-reshape-gun-control-n1265424.

43. Ibid.:

> Advocates of more gun control measures have reasonably worried for years about the next
> time the court takes up a big Second Amendment question. But now, with the addition of
> three conservative justices appointed by former President Donald Trump—Justices Neil
> Gorsuch, Brett Kavanaugh and Amy Coney Barrett—that worry has turned to outright
> terror.

44. *New York State Rifle & Pistol Assn. v. Bruen*, 142 S. Ct. 2111 (2022).

45. Ibid., 2122–23.

46. Richard Wolf, "Supreme Court Sidesteps Major Second Amendment Case,
a Setback for NRA," *USA Today*, April 27, 2020, https://www.usatoday.com/story
/news/politics/2020/04/27/guns-supreme-court-setback-national-rifle-association
/2634492001/.

47. Greenhouse, *Justice on the Brink*, 175.

48. Garrett Cleveland, "Shooting America Straight: Why the Time Is Now for
the Supreme Court to Fortify Gun Rights in America Post-Heller," *Texas A&M Law
Review Arguendo* 7 (February 2020): 16.

49. Ibid., 16 ("In his time on the bench for the U.S. Court of Appeals for the District
of Columbia, Justice Kavanaugh has displayed some pro-gun rights-ideals").

50. 140 S. Ct. 1525 (2020).

51. See David A. Kaplan, *The Most Dangerous Branch: Inside the Supreme Court in the Age of Trump* (New York: Broadway Books, 2018), 260 (writing of Court politics within the context of *Heller* and "Getting the right appeal before the Court" and at the right time).

52. 140 S. Ct. 1525, 1544 (2020) (Alito, J., dissenting). Kavanaugh concurred with the Court's opinion, but actually seemed most in step with Alito's dissent, including an admonition of the Court to address the enforcement of the Second Amendment in a pending case. Ibid., 1527.

53. Transcript of Oral Argument, 46: 21–23, *New York State Rifle & Pistol Assn. v. Bruen*, 142 S. Ct. 2111 (2022).

54. See Greenhouse, "The Supreme Court, Weaponized" (writing that oral arguments "strongly suggested that the court will expand the boundaries of the Second Amendment well beyond" *Heller*).

55. Transcript of Oral Argument, 105: 1–23, *New York State Rifle & Pistol Assn. v. Bruen*, 142 S. Ct. 2111 (2022).

56. Ibid., 107: 2–8.

57. Ibid., 118: 10–14. See also Petition for Writ of Certiorari, *New York State Rifle & Pistol Association v. Cortlett,* Dec. 15, 2020, 15 (Clement: "Regimes like New York's 'proper cause' criteria ration constitutional rights instead of protecting them. Government may not reserve to a select few what the Constitution guarantees to all").

58. Fox, Shveda, Croker, and Chacon, "How US Gun Culture Stacks Up with the World" (reporting that there are 120 guns for every 100 people in the U.S.).

59. Ibid.

60. See Ruth Marcus, "The Supreme Court Hangs a Gun on the Wall," *Washington Post,* April 27, 2021, https://www.washingtonpost.com/opinions/the-supreme-court-hangs-a-gun-on-the-wall/2021/04/27/352af482-a780-11eb-8c1a-56f0cb4ff3b5_story.html ("This court didn't take up this case without a plan to pull the trigger. It's a safe bet that it is not hearing a Second Amendment dispute for the purpose of limiting gun rights").

61. Ibid. ("The conservative justices have been itching to clarify the scope of the constitutional protection the court first established 13 years ago—and to make clear that the Second Amendment is not being treated, as some justices have complained, as a second-class right"). See also Adam Liptak, "Clarence Thomas Is the Court's Most Committed Advocate for Gun Rights," in "Live Updates: Supreme Court and Senate Take Rare, Divergent Steps on Gun Safety," *New York Times*, June 23, 2022, https://www.nytimes.com/live/2022/06/23/us/gun-control-senate-supreme-court#clarence-thomas-gun-rights-supreme-court.

62. *New York State Rifle & Pistol Assn. v. Bruen*, 142 S. Ct. 2111 (2022). But see Saul Cornell, "The Supreme Court's Latest Gun Case Made a Mockery of Originalism," *Slate*, November 10, 2021, https://slate.com/news-and-politics/2021/11/bruen-supreme-court-guns-mockery-originalism.html (noting after oral arguments that the Court ignored a record of firearms regulation in densely populated areas: "The court appears to be perfectly happy to trot out originalist rhetoric when it serves its

interests and abandon it entirely when the historical record does not support its political goals").

63. *New York State Rifle & Pistol Assn.*, 2126.

64. Ibid., 2130.

65. Ibid., 2126.

66. Ibid., 2128–29.

67. Ibid., 2157 (Alito, J., concurring).

68. *Heller*, 627.

69. See Ruth Marcus, "How Low Will the Supreme Court Go on Guns?" *Washington Post,* June 10, 2022, https://www.washingtonpost.com/opinions/2022/06/10/supreme-court-second-amendment-brett-kavanaugh.

70. See, for example, *Heller v. District of Columbia*, 670 F.3d 1244, 1269 (2011 D.C. Cir.) (Kavanaugh, J., dissenting).

71. *New York State Rifle & Pistol Assn.*, 2118 (internal citation omitted) (emphasis added).

72. Ibid., 2164 (Breyer, J., dissenting).

73. Ibid., 2181:

> Laws addressing repeating crossbows, launcegays, dirks, daggers, skeines, stilladers, and other ancient weapons will be of little help to courts confronting modern problems. And as technological progress pushes our society ever further beyond the bounds of the Framers' imaginations, attempts at "analogical reasoning" will become increasingly tortured. In short, a standard that relies solely on history is unjustifiable and unworkable. Ibid.

74. Ibid., 2164.

75. Ibid., 2165–66.

76. See, for example, Acacia Coronado and Sara Burnett, "Beto O'Rourke Interrupts Briefing, Echoing US Debate on Guns," Associated Press, May 26, 2022, https://apnews.com/article/beto-orourke-texas-shooting-press-conference-7dfd6a0b44b9d0f739e4fd6b02ac3cf9 (quoting Texas Lt. Gov. Dan Patrick after the Uvalde mass shooting: "This is not a partisan issue. This is not a political issue"). See also Ronald Brownstein, "The Real Reason America Doesn't Have Gun Control," *Atlantic*, May 25, 2022, https://www.theatlantic.com/politics/archive/2022/05/senate-state-bias-filibuster-blocking-gun-control-legislation/638425/ (writing that the stalemate over gun control legislation rests on "the growing crisis of majority rule in American politics").

77. See, for example, Reese Oxner, "Uvalde Gunman Legally Bought AR Rifles Days Before Shooting, Law Enforcement Says," *Texas Tribune*, May 25, 2022, https://www.texastribune.org/2022/05/25/uvalde-shooter-bought-gun-legally/ (quoting President Joe Biden: "The idea that an 18-year-old could walk into a store and buy weapons of war designed and marketed to kill is, I think, just wrong. It just violates common sense").

78. *Terminiello v. City of Chicago*, 337 U.S. 1, 107 (1949) (Jackson, J. dissenting).

Chapter 5

Religious Liberty

Religious freedom is constitutionally protected in the United States. The "central value and animating purpose"[1] of the First Amendment's opening clauses prevent the passage of any "law respecting an establishment of religion, or prohibiting the free exercise thereof."[2] These words have become a quintessential representation of a constitutional passage open to—and even one that engenders—conflicting interpretations. This especially applies to whether the words require a separation between church and state. To be certain, there are views that are both supportive of,[3] and in opposition to,[4] that notion—a debate that often embodies the tenets of fluid-living constitutionalism vs. fixed-originalism.[5]

Pushback against separation is genuine. Pew Research reported in 2021, for example, that a segment of "Americans clearly long for a more avowedly religious and explicitly Christian country."[6] By mid-2022, NPR reported on "an influential minority of Americans who envision the United States as a Christian nation."[7] That sentiment, according to some analysts, extends to a majority of the Supreme Court's members. Lee Epstein and Eric Posner maintain that the right to religious liberty has not merely influenced what happens on the Court, but it has "transformed" it.[8] More to the point, they write that the majority of the Roberts Court has advanced conservative Christian values with its rulings. The numbers make the point clear: From 1953 to 2005—the Warren, Burger, and Rehnquist Court eras—the Supreme Court ruled in favor of religious parties in roughly 50 percent of those cases. Under Chief Justice Roberts, that figure rose to almost 90 percent.[9]

This phenomenon is especially recent: Of all the justices since 1953, those who voted most often for the religious side of a case belong to the Court's current conservative bloc—Brett Kavanaugh (100 percent), Neil Gorsuch (100 percent), Clarence Thomas (94 percent), John Roberts (93 percent), and Samuel Alito (93 percent).[10] The addition of Justice Barrett will likely continue this trend: "The newest Supreme Court Justice [as of mid-2022] isn't just another conservative—she's the product of a Christian legal movement that is intent on remaking America."[11] Referring to the Court more broadly, another commentator wrote in early 2021, "[T]he new supermajority conservative Court is already changing the law on religious liberty."[12]

Epstein and Posner attribute this shift to politics—justices being appointed by Republican presidents, with nominees adhering to the party line in ways that did not occur previously.[13] "Renegotiating the boundary between church and state was part of the unstated charge to the most recent nominees," writes Greenhouse.[14] Worldview is also integral—the fixed approach that finds safety and comfort by returning to the standards of the past—has surfaced and revealed itself in an unprecedented manner. Like the possession of firearms, for some religiosity, particularly extended into the public sphere, is an emotional security blanket. For them, guns and God are reassuring. A faithfulness to party and an ideology that results in pro-Christian rulings is an outgrowth of partisan polarization on religious issues on the Roberts Court that is "unmistakable," according to Epstein and Posner.[15] They continue:

> The conservative bloc on the Supreme Court sees the promotion of religious rights as a legitimate way to push back on the socially liberal rulings of the court [from the Warren era]. For over 50 years, conservatives have railed against rulings that have established constitutional protection for contraception, pornography, nontraditional family arrangements, abortion and the rights of sexual minorities, including the right to same-sex marriage.[16]

Same-sex marriage is, indeed, a good example. The argument that such a right could be found within the Constitution was historically opposed largely on moral and religious grounds[17]—a movement that was fortified by a strong desire to avoid change and preserve the status quo. When the Court found the right to same-sex marriage in the Constitution, it did so by utilizing a fluid-living constitutionalism perspective. In writing for a 5–4 majority, Justice Anthony Kennedy wrote that "rights come not from ancient sources alone,"[18] but also develop "from a better-informed understanding of how constitutional imperatives define a liberty that remains urgent *in our own times*."[19] In *Obergefell v. Hodges*, Kennedy based his view on a contemporary approach to, and application of, both the Due Process and Equal Protection clauses of the Fourteenth Amendment.[20]

In his opinion, Kennedy referred multiple times to "new insights" about marriage that were revealed through both the study of the issue and analysis of the Equal Protection Clause. For example, he wrote, "in interpreting the Equal Protection Clause, the Court has recognized that new insights and societal understandings can reveal unjustified inequality within our most fundamental institutions that once passed unnoticed and unchallenged."[21]

In contrast, the dissenting opinion of Chief Justice Roberts rejected new insights and enhanced perspectives of constitutional analysis, as well as Kennedy's approach:

> Over and over, the majority exalts the role of the judiciary in delivering social change. In the majority's telling, it is the courts, not the people, who are responsible for making "new dimensions of freedom . . . apparent to new generations," for providing "formal discourse" on social issues, and for ensuring "neutral discussions, without scornful or disparaging commentary."[22]

In short, similar to the Alito-Kagan clash of worldviews in *Brnovich* described in chapter 3, Kennedy and Roberts demonstrated prototypical fluid-fixed friction.

Religion can permeate a variety of case circumstances, sometimes indirectly. A 2020–2021 pandemic-era case is revealing within the worldview context. The Court determined whether COVID-related restrictions that had been mandated in California were discriminatory.[23] The restrictions included temporary limitations on church attendance as stipulated in an executive order by Governor Gavin Newsom. One church, the South Bay United Pentecostal Church, challenged the order, requesting emergency relief. That triggered its placement on the Court's expedited docket, its "shadow docket"—as noted previously, cases and applications decided without full briefing and argument. "[W]e cannot afford to let tyranny against religion rise in the guise of well-meaning police power of the State,"[24] South Bay's attorneys told the Court, clearly framing the case to appeal to the fixed worldview conservative bloc.

On initial consideration, the Court upheld the restrictions by a 5–4 margin, denying a request for injunctive relief. The dissent was led by Justice Kavanaugh who rallied on behalf of Christians' growing expectation of support from the Court. He expressed his belief that churchgoers were being subjected to discrimination by the state restrictions. Attending church, he wrote, should be viewed no differently than secular activities.[25] He saw little or no difference between the transient experience of visiting a retail establishment, for example—untouched by the California order—and the sedentary occurrence of sitting for an hour within close proximity of others in an enclosed space. Kavanaugh's approach, Linda Greenhouse wrote, "gave us more proof that the polarization roiling the country has the Supreme Court in its grip."[26]

The Kavanaugh dissent foreshadowed what would follow in *South Bay*. On reconsideration, justified in part by the Ginsburg-to-Barrett succession, the Court changed course, with a majority opting to enjoin the California restrictions. The Court's statements—again, not "opinions" because this was not a "full" hearing that included oral arguments—reveal a Court at war with itself, with religion clashing with science at the core of this disagreement. Mirroring the division between holders of fixed and fluid worldviews, the Court's rift included whether to accept science-based evidence in favor of any desire to find a result sympathetic to religious interests (see "Science and the Pursuit of Truth" in chapter 1).

"Justices of this Court are not scientists," began Justice Kagan's dissent. "Nor do we know much about public health policy. Yet today the Court displaces the judgments of experts about how to respond to a raging pandemic."[27] While Chief Justice Roberts acknowledged that "the Constitution principally entrusts the safety and the health of the people to the politically accountable officials of the States,"[28] he concurred with the Court's decision to move away from reliance on the relevant science. "[T]he Constitution also entrusts the protection of the people's rights to the Judiciary." Deference to the state—and apparently to science—Roberts wrote, "has its limits."[29]

Kagan decried what she called the Court's error, complete with a not-so-subtly-articulated skepticism about her colleagues' grasp of the science:

> In forcing California to ignore its experts' scientific findings, the Court impairs the State's effort to address a public health emergency. . . . To state the obvious, judges do not know what scientists and public health experts do. I am sure that, in deciding this case, every Justice carefully examined the briefs and read the decisions below. But I cannot imagine that any of us delved into the scientific research on how COVID spreads or studied the strategies for containing it. So it is alarming that the Court second-guesses the judgments of expert officials, and displaces their conclusions with its own.[30]

The conclusion of Justice Gorsuch served as a reminder that religion and the Court's protection of it was at the heart of the *South Bay* decision: "Since the arrival of COVID–19, California has openly imposed more stringent regulations on religious institutions than on many businesses . . . When a State so obviously targets religion for differential treatment, our job becomes that much clearer."[31]

To further understand how this ruling symbolizes the fixed-fluid divide, it is useful to return to the role of religion within the context of worldview. First, there is a significant split in beliefs about the role and importance of religion in the lives of the fixed and fluid. Religion is important or very important in the lives of 77 percent of those with a fixed worldview. For fluid people, 49 percent said religion is not important at all to them.[32] Second, reactions to the word "faith" is "an especially telling symptom of the worldview divide."[33] In a study asking people to rate the word "faith" 0-to-100, with 100 the most favorable, fixed people averaged 81, fluid 44. Next, those with a fixed worldview prefer that texts are read, understood, and interpreted literally.

This pertains to both religious texts and the U.S. Constitution.[34] Deferring to the text is paramount for both followers and (judicial) leaders. In turn, and as explored previously in chapter 1, skepticism of science is an especially common trait to card-carrying members of the fixed worldview. This phenomenon only increased during the COVID era.

Textualism is an important measure. A study asked whether judges should consider the original intent of the authors of the Constitution, or instead consider changing times when applying principles of the Constitution.[35] Seventy-four percent of holders of the fixed worldview chose originalism/textualism. Fewer than 20 percent of the fluid favored a literal interpretation of the Constitution.[36] This is relevant here because biblical literalism follows a similar path.[37] As Marc Hetherington and Jonathan Weiler write, those with a fixed worldview favor "the straightforward, unnuanced approach."[38] Again, not surprising—simple and safe, little or no interpretation required.

In early 2022, two cases that the Supreme Court agreed to hear served as a reminder that the execution of a judicial agenda begins with the decision whether to place cases on its docket. First, the Court agreed to hear the appeal of a high school football assistant coach whose year-by-year contract was not renewed after he refused to stop praying on the field immediately after games.[39] Officials in the Bremerton, Washington, public school district repeatedly reminded the coach, Joseph Kennedy, of a policy that prohibited school staff members from indirectly encouraging or discouraging students to engage in religious activity because it could be perceived as endorsing religious activity.

Kennedy had prayed with some students at the center of the field at the conclusion of games in which he coached. Given their policy, school officials were less concerned with Kennedy praying than with whether students felt compelled or pressured—even indirectly—to join him. It was there that the district's First Amendment-based concern about Establishment Clause violations resided—freedom *from* religion, separating "church" from a state-operated school. Though several alternatives to his public display were offered by the district, Kennedy believed his freedom *of* religion was at stake.

The district insisted that he stop mixing faith with football in public. Kennedy responded by advocating for his rights in local news outlets and continued his 50-yard line praying. The publicity transformed it into a media event. He was placed on administrative leave and at the recommendation of his supervisor, his contract was not renewed. Kennedy followed with his legal claim that his First Amendment rights were violated.

Lower courts denied his claim, but the Supreme Court eventually decided to hear his appeal—*eventually* because three years prior, the Court had denied Kennedy's appeal.[40] What changed over that period? Not the facts of the case, but instead the Court's ideological balance. During his 2016 presidential campaign, Donald Trump described the coach's treatment as "very, very sad and outrageous."[41] The Supreme Court that accepted Kennedy's appeal in 2022 contained three Trump nominees and had the momentum of a 6–3 supermajority in place. "The court's new conservative majority has been protective of individual religious rights," wrote Robert Barnes at the time, "and it was not a surprise it took the case."[42]

Not unexpectedly given the Court's recent penchant for navigating the tension in the First Amendment's two religion clauses by favoring "freedom of" over "freedom from," a 6–3 Court sided with Kennedy.[43] The ruling was consistent with the Roberts Court's (world)view. "Bolstering religious rights, and notably those of Christians," wrote Adam Liptak in reporting on this ruling, "has been a signature project of the court led by Chief Justice John G. Roberts Jr."[44] The ruling was called the worst of the Court's 2021–2022 term—there was stiff competition—by columnist Pamela Paul: "[T]he one that best captures the majority's brazen efforts to inflict its political and religious agenda on the rest of the country."[45]

Both the Opinion of the Court and Justice Sotomayor's dissent—joined by Justices Breyer and Kagan—are detailed in justifying their views. Consistent with other case analyses herein, attention will be confined to those elements that highlight this volume's premise of worldview-driven decisions. As would be expected, the majority's over-simplified analysis is one steeped in fixed-originalism, relying on "history and tradition."

The case and its analysis were complicated by the fact that three First Amendment clauses—Establishment, Free Exercise, and Speech—and the interplay between them were at issue. Navigating that landscape is rarely straightforward. Justice Gorsuch's Opinion for the Court, for example, admonished both those who lack a "proper understanding" of the Establishment Clause and those who would conclude that the coach's prayers potentially violated it.[46] On the other hand, Justice Sotomayor's dissenting opinion recognized that the Free Exercise and Establishment Clauses "often exert conflicting pressures."[47] The majority, she wrote, gave "almost exclusive attention to the Free Exercise Clause's protection for individual religious exercise while giving short shrift to the Establishment Clause's prohibition on state establishment of religion."[48] She added that the Court's decision rested "on an erroneous understanding of the Religion Clauses."[49]

Sotomayor also criticized the majority for inaccurately implying that lower courts in *Kennedy* relied on a rule that the Establishment Clause must always prevail over the Free Exercise Clause.[50] "In focusing almost exclusively on Kennedy's free exercise claim . . . and declining to recognize the conflicting rights at issue, the Court substitutes one supposed blanket rule for another."[51] Sotomayor added that rather than identifying the tension between the clauses and balancing the interests, the majority simply ignored the conflict.[52]

Relying heavily on the Establishment Clause, Gorsuch wrote that it does not require the government to single out private religious speech for special disfavor. "The Constitution and the best of our traditions counsel mutual respect and tolerance, not censorship and suppression, for religious and nonreligious views alike."[53] To single out "private religious speech," he wrote, conveys an improper understanding of the Constitution.[54] Yes, Justice Sotomayor replied, respect and tolerance stem from the Constitution, but to achieve them, some singling out of religious speech by the government is necessary. To do so, she wrote, is consistent with "the lesson of history that was and is the inspiration for the Establishment Clause, the lesson that in the hands of government what might begin as a tolerant expression of religious views may end in a policy to indoctrinate and coerce."[55] This not only turned the majority's reliance on history on its ear, it also addressed the Bremerton concern that by praying in the presence of students, Kennedy, whether or not intentionally, coerced some to participate. To allow that to continue, the school district believed, would betray its obligation to the Establishment Clause.

Gorsuch regularly invoked tradition throughout his opinion, not only as it applied to interpretations of the Constitution,[56] but also regarding Bremerton's traditions of prayer.[57] Sotomayor found it unacceptable that the Court relied on tradition and history at the exclusion of its own tradition by overruling a long-relied on precedent.[58] The majority, she wrote, called into question "decades of subsequent precedents that it deems 'offshoot[s]' of that decision."[59] One of those precedents was the Court's 2000 ruling in which the issue was student-led prayers before high school football games that were broadcast through a stadium's public address system. "The delivery of a pregame prayer has the improper effect of coercing those present to participate in an act of religious worship," Justice John Paul Stevens wrote for the majority in that case.[60] This also highlights that given the role of the Establishment Clause in public school settings, coercion—real or perceived, intended or inadvertent—is a significant concern. When a prayer is not only not private, but so public that it becomes a media event—in this case, thanks largely to publicity solicited by Coach Kennedy[61]—then the potential for the materialization of coercion increases.

Emphasizing the critical nature of the Court rewriting history, Justice Sotomayor continued: "The Court relies on an assortment of pluralities, concurrences, and dissents by Members of the current majority to effect fundamental changes in this Court's Religion Clauses jurisprudence, all the while proclaiming that nothing has changed at all."[62] This addresses a recent and disturbing development in how some members of the Court attempt to rationalize their rulings: "We say it is so, so it is."

Rather than relying on precedent, and while displaying his originalist colors, Gorsuch wrote, "the Establishment Clause must be interpreted by 'reference to historical practices and understandings,'"[63] adding that distinguishing the permissible from the impermissible must "faithfully reflect the understandings of the Founding Fathers."[64] In a word, the conservative *Kennedy* majority was exercising precisely what it so often claims to abhor, activism. It assumed that role not merely by rejecting "longstanding concerns surrounding government endorsement of religion," but also with its creation of a new standard, a "history and tradition test,"[65] to legitimize its ruling. Further weakening it position, according to Sotomayor, the majority failed to provide support for its new test: "The Court reserves any meaningful explanation of its history-and-tradition test for another day, content for now to disguise it as established law and move on."[66]

Further cementing the foundation of his (world)view, Gorsuch wrote that the Court has stressed that "analysis focused on original meaning and history . . . has long represented the rule rather than some 'exception' within the 'Court's Establishment Clause jurisprudence.'"[67] While the majority leaned on tradition and history, it seemed to ignore history when it suited its objectives. This included the history of the case, misrepresenting facts related to Kennedy's role,[68] wrote Sotomayor, including that he "consistently invited others to join his prayers and for years led student athletes in prayer at the same time and location."[69]

The dissent, already critical for the majority's opinion for misrepresenting the facts of the case,[70] wrote the "decision goes beyond merely misreading the record."[71] Gorsuch and Sotomayor presented conflicting narratives of the events surrounding the case—"starkly" different, according to one observer.[72] Another described the Court's characterization of Kennedy's praying to be private as "preposterous."[73] "This particular court of 'originalists,'" wrote the *Seattle Times*' Danny Westneat, "is increasingly looking to historical tradition, back to the days of the Founding Fathers when the Constitution was written, to determine modern-day rights . . . If they're going to parse 250-year-old histories, it's worrisome how much trouble they had getting a seven-year-old story straight."[74]

Sotomayor concluded her dissent by expressing concern about the Roberts Court's trajectory on issues of religion: "[T]he court sets us further down a perilous path in forcing states to entangle themselves with religion, with all of our rights hanging in the balance."[75] This was echoed by Rachel Laser, the president of Americans United for Separation of Church and State, which represented the Bremerton school board: "[T]he court continued its assault on church-state separation, by falsely describing coercive prayer as 'personal' and stopping public schools from protecting their students' religious freedom . . . This decision represents the greatest loss of religious freedom in our country in generations."[76]

In addition to the *Kennedy* case, in February 2022 the Court announced it would hear another appeal that, according to Adam Liptak, would be "returning the justices to a battleground in the culture wars pitting claims of religious freedom against laws prohibiting discrimination on the basis of sexual orientation."[77] The owner of a website design company challenged Colorado's law forbidding discrimination because it conflicted with her preference to withhold service to those seeking her work for same-sex weddings. Owner Lorie Smith was represented by the conservative Alliance Defending Freedom, whose website described the Colorado law as one that "censors and coerces the speech of creative professionals whose religious beliefs do not conform to state orthodoxy."[78] In their submission to the Court, Smith's lawyers wrote, "She cannot create websites that promote messages contrary to her faith, such as messages that condone violence or promote sexual immorality, abortion or same-sex marriage."[79]

The decision to hear this case seemed to tee up an opportunity for the Court's conservatives to clarify their position. In a 2021 ruling, *Fulton v. City of Philadelphia*,[80] Justice Alito, joined by Justices Thomas and Gorsuch, concurred with a unanimous opinion, but also wrote of a missed opportunity that failed to correct what Alito called the Court's error in a 1990 decision.[81] There, the Court held that general laws that do not single out religion cannot be challenged on the grounds that they violate the First Amendment's protection of the free exercise of religion.[82] The Colorado website case afforded the chance to address the missed opportunity. As for *Fulton*, the *New York Times'* Liptak wrote, "The unanimous ruling was further evidence that claims of religious liberty almost always prevail in the current court."[83] Again, the decision to hear this case was another example of the Court's inclination to continue its integration of church and state.

Another 2022 case seemed to remove any remaining doubt where the Court's supermajority stands on separation of church and state. A tuition assistance program in Maine had required recipients of aid to choose from secular schools only. The rationale rested on the belief that funding tuition with taxpayer money at religious schools violated the First Amendment's restriction on the state establishing or respecting religion. The program's constitutionality was challenged, with the First Circuit Court of Appeals upholding the program.[84] When the Supreme Court agreed to hear the appeal,[85] it was clear it was not doing so to affirm.

Indeed, in a 6–3 ruling precisely along ideological lines, the Court declared the Maine program unconstitutional.[86] It discriminated against religion, Chief Justice Roberts wrote in his opinion of the Court: "[W]e have repeatedly held that a State violates the Free Exercise Clause when it excludes religious observers from otherwise available public benefits."[87]

Two dissenting opinions by Justices Breyer and Sotomayor revealed very different interpretations of the First Amendment. Exuding fluid worldview living constitutionalism, Justice Breyer cited a previously established concept,[88] the "play in the joints" between the First Amendment's two religion clauses that provides states some legislative leeway. He added that the Court's majority failed to account for the flexibility (i.e., fluidity) permitted by the concept and instead was rigid (i.e., fixed) in its reading of the First Amendment: "To interpret the two Clauses as if they were joined at the hip will work against their basic purpose: to allow for an American society with practitioners of over 100 different religions, and those who do not practice religion at all, to live together without serious risk of religion-based social divisions."[89] Justice Sotomayor dissented more vigorously, including observations about where the Court has been and where it is going: "This Court continues to dismantle the wall of separation between church and state that the Framers fought to build."[90]

As this chapter has demonstrated, the "promotion of religious rights" that Epstein and Posner claim the Supreme Court's conservatives have advanced since the 1970s casts a wide net. Moreover, it is a net whose threads are particularly tied to the political right.[91]

NOTES

1. Michael W. McConnell, "Accommodation of Religion," *Supreme Court Review* (1985): 1.

2. U.S. Const., Amend. I.

3. See, for example, *Everson v. Bd. of Education*, 330 U.S. 1, 18 (1947) ("The First Amendment has erected a wall between church and state. That wall must be kept high and impregnable. We could not approve the slightest breach"). See also Howard Gillman and Erwin Chemerinsky, *The Religion Clauses: The Case for Separating Church and State* (New York: Oxford University Press, 2020), xi ("The Establishment Clause should be interpreted, to the greatest extent practical, to require separation of church and state"); Chelsea Brown, "Not Your Mother's Remedy: A Civil Action Response to the Westboro Baptist Church's Military Funeral Demonstrations," *West Virginia Law Review* 112 (Fall 2009): 236 ("The Founding Fathers considered the separation of church and state to be so vital that they established this separation in the First Amendment to the Constitution").

4. See, for example, Patrick M. Garry, "The Myth of Separation: America's Historical Experience with Church and States," *Hofstra Law Review* 33 (Winter 2004): 476 ("Not only does the 'wall of separation' metaphor have almost no historical basis, but it is actually contradicted by the relationship between religion and government in eighteenth century America"); Arlin M. Adams and Charles J. Emmerich, "A Heritage of Religious Liberty," *University of Pennsylvania Law Review* 137 (May 1989): 1598

("the Founders intended the establishment and free exercise clauses to be complementary co-guarantors of a single end").

5. See, for example, Laurie Messerly, "Reviving Religious Liberty in America," *Nexus: A Journal of Opinion* 8 (2003): 156 (describing how views on religious freedom and separation of church and state are driven by a literal reading of the First Amendment—nowhere is "separation" specifically stated—vs. a reading that is interpretive in ascertaining meaning).

6. "In U.S., Far More Support Than Oppose Separation of Church and State," Pew Research Center, October 28, 2021, https://www.pewresearch.org/religion/2021/10/28/in-u-s-far-more-support-than-oppose-separation-of-church-and-state.

7. Ashley Lopez, "The Christian Right Is Winning Cultural Battles While Public Opinion Disagrees," NPR, July 1, 2022, https://www.npr.org/2022/07/01/1109141110/the-christian-right-is-winning-cultural-battles-while-public-opinion-disagrees.

8. Lee Epstein and Eric Posner, "How the Religious Right Has Transformed the Supreme Court," *New York Times*, September 22, 2020, https://www.nytimes.com/2020/09/22/opinion/supreme-court-religion.amp.html.

9. Ibid. See also Linda Greenhouse, Justice on the Brink: *The Death of Ruth Bader Ginsburg, the Rise of Amy Coney Barrett, and Twelve Months That Transformed the Supreme Court* (New York: Random House, 2021), 19 ("[S]ince the advent of the Roberts court, religious claims have prevailed nearly 90 percent of the time and the voting patterns of the court's Republican- and Democratic-appointed justices have diverged sharply").

10. Epstein and Posner, "How the Religious Right Has Transformed the Supreme Court." (These statistics were compiled prior to Justice Barrett's confirmation.)

11. Margaret Talbot, "Amy Coney Barrett's Long Game," *New Yorker*, February 7, 2022, https://www.newyorker.com/magazine/2022/02/14/amy-coney-barretts-long-game/amp. See also Epstein and Posner, "How the Religious Right Transformed the Supreme Court" (writing immediately after Ruth Bader Ginsburg's death, "If Justice Ginsburg, who had the most secular voting record of any justice since 1953, is replaced with a religious conservative like Justices Kavanaugh, Gorsuch or Thomas, the court's jurisprudence will veer even farther from the values she brought to the law").

12. Leah Litman, "COVID at the Court: South Bay United Pentecostal," *Take Care*, February 6, 2021, https://takecareblog.com/blog/covid-at-the-court-south-bay-united-pentecostal. See also Greenhouse, *Justice on the Brink*, 233 ("[W]hen Amy Coney Barrett's Thanksgiving eve vote, only weeks after her confirmation, abruptly shifted the balance the court had previously struck between religion and public health in the context of the COVID pandemic, the country saw what it meant to have the court 'differently composed than it was'").

13. See Laurence Baum and Neal Devins, "Federalist Court: How the Federalist Society Became the De Facto Selector of Republican Supreme Court Justices," *Slate*, January 31, 2017, https://slate.com/news-and-politics/2017/01/how-the-federalist-society-became-the-de-facto-selector-of-republican-supreme-court-justices.html.

14. Greenhouse, *Justice on the Brink*, 238–39. See also Epstein and Posner, "How the Religious Right Has Transformed the Supreme Court" (writing that the Roberts

Court is converting the First Amendment's religion clauses from protections for religious dissenters to means for advancing conservative Christian values).

15. When a Justice strays from party "loyalty," critics are plentiful. See, for example, David A. Kaplan, *The Most Dangerous Branch: Inside the Supreme Court in the Age of Trump* (New York: Broadway Books, 2018), 55 (writing how conservatives saw George H.W. Bush nominee David Souter as a "turncoat" and "the process that produced his selection as a catastrophe"). See also Joan Biskupic, "John Roberts' Argument for Saving Obamacare Helping Power Legal Challenge," CNN, July 10, 2019, https://www.cnn.com/2019/07/10/politics/john-roberts-affordable-care-act-5th -circuit/index.html (reporting that conservatives viewed Chief Justice Roberts with skepticism after he sided with the Court's progressives in a 2012 challenge to the Affordable Care Act even though his record "remains solidly on the right").

16. Epstein and Posner, "How the Religious Right Has Transformed the Supreme Court." See also Greenhouse, *Justice on the Brink*, 179 ("With Amy Coney Barrett on the Court, the conservatives now had the votes to shape the law of religion to their liking").

17. See Frank Newport, "Religion Big Factor for Americans Against Same-Sex Marriage," Gallup Research, December 5, 2012, https://news.gallup.com/poll/159089 /religion-major-factor-americans-opposed-sex-marriage.aspx (Americans who oppose the legalization of same-sex marriage "are most likely to explain their position on the basis of religious beliefs and/or interpretation of biblical passages dealing with same-sex relations").

18. *Obergefell v. Hodges*, 576 U.S. 644, 671 (2015) (Kennedy, J.).

19. Ibid., 706 (emphasis added).

20. U.S. Const., Amend. XIV,§ 1:

All persons born or naturalized in the United States, and subject to the jurisdiction thereof, are citizens of the United States and of the state wherein they reside. No state shall make or enforce any law which shall abridge the privileges or immunities of citizens of the United States; nor shall any state deprive any person of life, liberty, or property, without due process of law; nor deny to any person within its jurisdiction the equal protection of the laws.

21. *Obergefell*, 673.

22. Ibid., 708 (Roberts, C.J, dissenting) (quoting Kennedy's Opinion for the Court). See also *Dobbs v. Jackson Women's Health Organization*, 142 S. Ct. 2228, 2301 (2022) (suggesting, especially given Kennedy's retirement, that the Court's majority may target the rights inherent in *Obergefell* and other precedents: "[I]n future cases, we should reconsider all of this Court's substantive due process precedents, including Griswold, Lawrence, and Obergefell") (Thomas, J., concurring).

23. *S. Bay United Pentecostal Church v. Newsom*, 140 S. Ct. 1613 (2020).

24. Petition of Writ of Cert., 5, S. Bay United Pentecostal Church, 140 S. Ct. 1613 (2020).

25. 140 S. Ct. 1613, 1614 (Kavanaugh, J., dissenting).

26. Linda Greenhouse, "The Supreme Court, Too, Is on the Brink," *New York Times*, June 4, 2020, https://www.nytimes.com/2020/06/04/opinion/sunday/supreme -court-religion-coronavirus.html.

27. *S. Bay United Pentecostal Church v. Newsom*, 141 S. Ct. 716, 720 (Kagan. J., dissenting).

28. Ibid., 716 (Roberts, C.J., concurring) (internal quotation omitted).

29. Ibid., 717.

30. Ibid., 722–23 (Kagan, J., dissenting).

31. Ibid., 717 (Roberts, C.J. concurring).

32. Marc J. Hetherington and Jonathan Weiler, *Prius or Pickup? How the Answers to Four Simple Questions Explain America's Great Divide* (Boston: Houghton Mifflin Harcourt, 2018), 81.

33. Ibid., 83.

34. Ibid., 34 (citing a study that asked whether judges should consider the original intent of the authors of the Constitution or consider changing times and apply principles of the Constitution, with 74 percent of the fixed choosing the first option and fewer than 20 of the fluid favoring that literal interpretation of the Constitution).

35. See Kaplan, *The Most Dangerous Branch*, 15 (stating that living constitutionalism reflects on changing times—"a country of 325 million rather than 4 million people, with a global rather than a rural economy, dominated by technologies and industries unknown in the 18th century").

36. Hetherington and Weiler, *Prius or Pickup?* 34.

37. See, for example, Ibid., 80 (writing that evangelicals are more likely to possess fixed worldviews and that they are among the most likely to endorse a literal interpretation of the Bible—consistent with people with a fixed worldview).

38. Ibid., 80. See also Ibid., 41 (writing that suspicion of people who belong to different groups is consistent with a fixed worldview).

39. *Kennedy v. Bremerton School District*, 142 S. Ct. 2407 (2022).

40. *Kennedy v. Bremerton School District*, 139 S. Ct. 634 (2019).

41. Michael Gryboski, "Trump Meets Coach Kennedy: Suspension for Praying After Games 'Outrageous,' 'Very Sad,'" *Christian Post*, October 4, 2016, https://www.christianpost.com/news/donald-trump-meets-coach-kennedy-suspension -praying-football-games-outrageous-very-sad.html.

42. Robert Barnes, "Supreme Court to Hear Case of High School Football Coach Who Lost Job After Praying with Players," *Washington Post*, January 14, 2022, https://www.washingtonpost.com/politics/courts_law/supreme-court-football-coach -joseph-kennedy/2022/01/14/d9a98630-7585-11ec-8b0a-bcfab800c430_story.html

43. *Kennedy v. Bremerton School District*, 142 S. Ct. 2407 (2022).

44. Adam Liptak, "Supreme Court Sides with Coach Over Prayers at the 50-Yard Line," *New York Times,* June 27, 2022, https://www.nytimes.com/2022/06/27/us/ politics/supreme-court-coach-prayers.html.

45. Pamela Paul, "In the Face of Fact, the Supreme Court Chose Faith," *New York Times*, July 17, 2022, https://www.nytimes.com/2022/07/17/opinion/kennedy -bremerton-supreme-court.html.

46. *Kennedy*, 2416.

47. Ibid., 2447 (Sotomayor, J., dissenting).

48. Ibid., 2434.

49. Ibid., 2446.

50. Ibid., 2447.

51. Ibid.

52. Ibid.

53. Ibid., 2416.

54. Ibid.

55. Ibid., 2447.

56. Ibid., 2431 (referring to the Court's "traditional understanding" of the Free Exercise Clause). See also Ibid., 2433 (Thomas, J., concurring) (invoking the "history" and "tradition" of the Free Exercise Clause).

57. Ibid., 2416 (noting that pregame and postgame prayers were a "school tradition" at Bremerton).

58. *Lemon v. Kurtzman*, 403 U.S. 602 (1971) (establishing standards for determining whether a law is constitutional considering the Establishment Clause).

59. *Kennedy*, 2434.

60. *Santa Fe Independent School District v. Doe*, 530 U.S. 290, 312 (2000).

61. See *Kennedy v. Bremerton School District*, 4 F. 4th 910, 926 (4th Cir. 2021) (ruling that Kennedy staged public praying in an "everybody watch me pray" event). See also Brief for Bremerton Community Members as Amici Curiae Supporting Respondents, *Kennedy v. Bremerton School District*, 142 S. Ct. 2407 (2022) (including student testimony that described Kennedy's final prayer as expected, with 500 people storming the field, including media).

62. *Kennedy*, 2446.

63. Ibid., 2450 (internal citation omitted).

64. Ibid., 2428 (internal citations omitted).

65. Ibid., 2450 (Sotomayor, J., dissenting).

66. Ibid.

67. Ibid., 2428.

68. See Paul, "In the Face of Fact, the Supreme Court Chose Faith":

[T]his court's right-wing majority is following the dictum of our Trumpian age: Objective truth doesn't matter. Subjective belief—specifically the beliefs of the court's religious-right majority—does. The Kennedy decision wasn't based on the facts but on belief in the face of facts. Moreover, those six justices are determined to foist their beliefs on the rest of the country.

69. *Kennedy*, 2434.

70. Ibid. ("The majority misconstrues the facts").

71. Ibid.

72. Liptak, "Supreme Court Sides with Coach Over Prayers at the 50-Yard Line." See also Danny Westneat, "The Myth at the Heart of the Praying Bremerton Coach Case," *Seattle Times*, June 29, 2022, https://www.seattletimes.com/seattle-news/politics/the-myth-at-the-heart-of-the-praying-bremerton-coach-case/ ("[T]o get around this problem, Kennedy, his lawyers and, ultimately, six U.S. Supreme Court

justices made up an alternate storyline. In this new telling, students were nowhere around and had nothing to do with Kennedy's praying").

73. Westneat, "The Myth at the Heart of the Praying Bremerton Coach Case."

74. Ibid. ("The dishonesty at the heart of this case though suggests the movement that brought it—and the justices that bought it—are hardly going to be content to stop at that").

75. *Kennedy*, 2453.

76. Rachel Laser, "Supreme Court Ruling Is Greatest Loss of Religious Freedom in Decades," Americans United, June 27, 2022, https://www.au.org/the-latest/press/supreme-court-kennedy-bremerton-decision/.

77. Adam Liptak, "Supreme Court to Hear Case of Web Designer Who Objects to Same-Sex Marriage," *New York Times*, February 22, 2022, https://www.nytimes.com/2022/02/22/us/colorado-supreme-court-same-sex-marriage.html.

78. "US Supreme Court to Hear Case of Artist Threatened Under 'Orwellian' Colorado Law," Alliance Defending Freedom, February 22, 2022, https://adflegal.org/press-release/us-supreme-court-hear-case-artist-threatened-under-orwellian-colorado-law?sourcecode=10020697_r200.

79. Petition for a Writ of Certiorari, *303 Creative LLC v. Elenis*, No. 21–476.

80. *Fulton v. City of Philadelphia*, 141 S. Ct. 1868, 1924 (2021) (Alito, J., concurring) ("Smith was wrongly decided. As long as it remains on the books, it threatens a fundamental freedom. And while precedent should not lightly be cast aside, the Court's error in Smith should now be corrected").

81. *Employment Division v. Smith*, 494 U.S. 872 (1990).

82. See Mark Joseph Stern, "The Supreme Court Broke Its Own Rules to Radically Redefine Religious Liberty," *Slate*, April 12, 2021, https://slate.com/news-and-politics/2021/04/supreme-court-religious-liberty-covid-california.html (writing of the Court overturning the *Smith* precedent).

83. Adam Liptak, "Supreme Court Backs Catholic Agency in Case on Gay Rights and Foster Care," *New York Times*, June 17, 2021, https://www.nytimes.com/2021/06/17/us/supreme-court-gay-rights-foster-care.html.

84. *Carson v. Makin*, 979 F. 3d (2020 1st Cir.).

85. *Carson v. Makin*, 141 S. Ct. 2883 (2021).

86. *Carson v. Makin*, 142 S. Ct. 1987 (2022).

87. Ibid., 1996.

88. *Locke v. Davey*, 540 U.S. 712, 728 (2004) (" . . . a refusal to apply any principle when faced with competing constitutional directives . . . If the Religion Clauses demand neutrality, we must enforce them, in hard cases as well as easy ones") (emphasis in original).

89. *Carson*, 2005 (Breyer, J., dissenting).

90. Ibid., 2012 (Sotomayor, J., dissenting). See also Adam Liptak, "Supreme Court Rejects Maine's Ban on Aid to Religious Schools," *New York Times*, June 22, 2022, https://www.nytimes.com/2022/06/21/us/politics/supreme-court-maine-religious-schools.html (calling *Carson* "the latest decision by a conservative majority that has increasingly favored the role of religion in public life").

91. See, for example, Elizabeth Dias and Ruth Graham, "The Growing Religious Fervor in the American Right: 'This Is a Jesus Movement,'" *New York Times*, April 6, 2022, https://www.nytimes.com/2022/04/06/us/christian-right-wing-politics.html (writing of "a right-wing political movement powered by divine purpose, whose adherents find spiritual sustenance in political action").

Chapter 6

Abortion Rights

In 1927, the Supreme Court ruled 8–1 that a state law sanctioning the sterilization of certain American women was legal.[1] Justice Oliver Wendell Holmes wrote the Court's opinion, claiming it was "better for the world"[2] to uphold the law than to allow "feeble-minded"[3] people to reproduce. Among many others, constitutional law expert Erwin Chemerinsky has derided the decision, calling it inhumane and an injustice.[4] "The Court sided with the government," he wrote, "and failed to protect an individual from a horrific abuse of power."[5]

Almost a century later, the Court ruled to remove constitutional protection for women to decide the fate of their pregnancies.[6] It is not difficult to extrapolate that the Court was just as inhumane in 2022 as it was in 1927, abusing its power in both cases. Margaret Atwood, author of the dystopian novel, *The Handmaid's Tale*, suggests that both rulings are bookends of the same narrative—"a 'deeply rooted' tradition . . . that women's reproductive organs do not belong to the women who possess them. They belong only to the state."[7]

"It was always about abortion,"[8] wrote Linda Greenhouse. Indeed. In this instance, "it" includes the battle for control of the Supreme Court. But "it" can also be construed as the originalist movement, at least post-*Roe*. "It" drove not only judicial nominations, but also presidential election votes cast to ensure that specific kinds of nominees ascended to the Court.[9] And with its 2022 ruling on this issue, "it" propelled the Court into what may be the ultimate exemplar of its worldview divides.

Though many issues have transformed the Supreme Court into a political institution over the last half-century, abortion tops the list.[10] This manifested itself and culminated in 2022's decision in *Dobbs v. Jackson Women's Health Organization*[11] that overturned the precedent established by *Roe v. Wade*,[12] a ruling largely upheld by *Planned Parenthood v. Casey*.[13] Like the death of a long-ill family member, the *Dobbs* ruling was expected yet stunning.

"This didn't happen by accident," wrote Jesse Wegman. "Republicans have spent the past several years twisting the court into an aggressive right-wing supermajority for precisely this purpose."[14]

Little else, if anything, has done more to polarize and politicize America than abortion.[15] This especially includes the role of the Supreme Court. According to Mary Ziegler, "the growing divide in the abortion debate reflects the polarization of both American party politics and media."[16] Because politics has significantly infiltrated the Supreme Court, it also reflects the polarization of that institution. The divides in the Court especially surfaced in *Dobbs*, revealed in splits both according to ideology as well as within the fixed-originalist majority. These are described below.

Like much of history, this story is not about a single event—though one stands out, the *Roe* decision.[17] Instead, a confluence of events and various responses to each shaped this issue. They include the rulings of, and the reactions to, the Warren Court; the rise of the religious right and its embrace by political conservatives in government, especially including the White House;[18] and, as described by Ziegler, "a dialogue between social-movement members, elite and grassroots actors" that forged justifications for originalism.[19] "This suggests that ordinary citizens are not simply consumers, students, or members of an audience," she continues. "At least in the abortion context, they are also contributors and creators."[20]

Though having a shorter history than that of firearms, the issue of abortion is at least as complex and contentious, with the debate consistently "ugly."[21] The areas of disagreement continually multiply.[22] In her introduction to *Abortion Wars*, historian Rickie Sollinger notes that whereas in the mid-twentieth century when the issue was not spoken about in public, by the beginning of the next century the subject occupied space within public discourse that expressed fear, outrage and hatred, with clashes over ideology and justice.[23] It was generally unimagined in the 1950s that abortion practitioners would one day wear bullet-proof vests or that the practice would be coupled with civil rights for women.

Just before the dawn of the twentieth century's last quarter, abortion's social, political, and legal landscape shifted. In 1973, the Supreme Court issued its ruling in *Roe v. Wade*. Nothing has been the same since. The movement opposing *Roe* gained traction in large part because of the alliance between conservatives and the religious right.[24] Together, they exerted leverage on the political process, including the judiciary. Jamal Greene points out the importance of events coinciding with the *Roe* ruling—when "politics [was] beginning to polarize around it"[25]—and occurring during "a period of the rise of a post-Goldwater conservative movement, the rise of Ronald Reagan" and an American right pushing back against what it perceived as government activism.[26]

The cultural transformation was relatively gradual. Twenty years after *Roe*, for example, during her Supreme Court confirmation hearing in the U.S. Senate, Ruth Bader Ginsburg expressed unequivocal support for abortion rights—"a reminder, perhaps," writes Greenhouse, "that the country and the court were not always engulfed by the polarizing politics of abortion."[27] Ginsburg's nomination was approved 96–3, hardly imaginable today of a nominee who clearly expressed support for the Court's decisions in *Roe* and the subsequent, mostly affirming *Planned Parenthood v. Casey*.[28] In the latter, Justice Scalia suggested that, in the abortion context, the public has expected and even demanded that the Court adhere to originalism.[29] By that time, a movement opposing these rulings and seeking to overturn them was underway.[30]

Roe merits attention here not merely because it is the centerpiece of debate on abortion, but also because it is a prime example of the struggle between fixed-originalism and fluid-living constitutionalism, one of several reasons that it engenders so much passion and vitriol. Particularly when it comes to passionate supporters on each side, they seem to live in different worlds from one another. Analytical patterns that surfaced in *Roe* reappeared in *Dobbs* five decades later, arguably in a magnified form.

Roe is based in large part on privacy, a right that, in his opinion for the Court, Justice Harry Blackmun acknowledged is not explicitly mentioned in the Constitution. He quickly added, however, that the Court had previously "recognized that a right of personal privacy, or a guarantee of certain areas or zones of privacy, does exist under the Constitution."[31] His *Roe* opinion cites several precedents to illustrate that the right of privacy "is broad enough to encompass a woman's decision whether or not to terminate her pregnancy."[32] This approach of interpreting a text by concluding that it contains implications not specifically present in the words represents prototypical living constitutionalism. Though the Court had previously recognized privacy as stemming from the Constitution—each occasion, an act of living constitutionalism—its application to any right to abortion was unprecedented, though firmly established with this ruling.

In his dissenting opinion, Justice William Rehnquist followed the originalist school of thought, rejecting the applicability of privacy. Though he acknowledged previous privacy applications, and thus the establishment of the right, Rehnquist wrote, "I have difficulty in concluding, as the Court does, that the right of 'privacy' is involved in this case."[33] Strongly playing the fixed-originalist/textualist card, the future Chief Justice questioned whether one constitutional source of privacy claimed by the Court actually contains any shred of privacy: "To reach its result, the Court necessarily has had to find within the scope of the Fourteenth Amendment a right that was apparently completely unknown to the drafters of the Amendment."[34]

While the *Roe* opinions contain depth and complexity not examined here, the battle lines that have been carried forward for generations were drawn, taking America to a place where "Roe has become nearly synonymous with political conflict."[35] Within that environment of conflict, the Court chose to hear two abortion-related cases during its 2021–2022 term. Though the first of those had less of a culture-changing impact than what followed, it is important for several reasons, including the signals the Court's majority sent about its feelings toward abortion, its regulation and precedent. *Whole Woman's Health v. Jackson*[36] stemmed from a Texas law that restricted any abortion after about six weeks of pregnancy. According to some observers, that law was purposefully structured to ultimately reduce, if not eliminate, the involvement of federal courts from the realm of abortion rights.[37] In part, that accounts for the case's intricate journey through the courts, both in Texas and in the federal system. For the purposes of this analysis, that history will be abbreviated, focusing on the role of the U.S. Supreme Court.

In responding to an emergency petition, the Court initially refused to preempt the law's enforcement. As expected, dissents were passionate and further illustrated the Court's polarization. "The Court's order is stunning," wrote Justice Sonia Sotomayor in dissent, likely addressing not only the majority in this decision but also anticipating a second abortion case on the horizon at that time. "Presented with an application to enjoin a flagrantly unconstitutional law engineered to prohibit women from exercising their constitutional rights and evade judicial scrutiny," she continued, "a majority of Justices have opted to bury their heads in the sand."[38] The following year, after the Court allowed a challenge to the law to move forward but within narrow boundaries,[39] another emergency petition was denied by the Court's majority. In dissent, Sotomayor characterized the Texas law as a "scheme [that] employs technical entanglements specifically to smother the federal right to choose."[40] Her conclusion: "This case is a disaster for the rule of law and a grave disservice to women in Texas."[41] In another example of fixed-originalists failing to see beyond text—in this case, the words of a state law—the Supreme Court majority enabled Texas courts and the state supreme court to effectively shut down any additional challenges in federal court.[42] The law stood.

Also during the 2021–2022 term, the Court chose to hear *Dobbs v. Jackson Women's Health Organization*.[43] Its path to the Court's docket is instructive. In 2018, Mississippi passed a law called the "Gestational Age Act" which with few exceptions, prohibits all abortions after the fifteenth week of pregnancy. The law's co-sponsor acknowledged it was intended to trigger a test case to challenge *Roe v. Wade* and was timed to coincide with changes in the U.S. Supreme Court's membership.[44] Jackson Women's Health Organization, the only licensed abortion facility in Mississippi, and one of its doctors filed a lawsuit in federal district court challenging the law and requesting an emergency temporary restraining order.

A district court granted the clinic's motion for summary judgment and enjoined Mississippi from enforcing the law, finding that the state had not provided evidence that a fetus would be viable at fifteen weeks. Supreme Court precedent prohibited states from banning abortions prior to viability.[45] The U.S. Court of Appeals for the Fifth Circuit affirmed.[46]

Mississippi filed an appeal to the U.S. Supreme Court in June 2020, but it took almost a year before the Court agreed to hear it. Why the delay? Why did it take more than a year for at least four justices to choose to hear the case? The change in the Court's membership—Justice Barrett taking what had been Justice Ginsburg's seat on the bench. As Christian Farias profoundly observed in noting the Court's three newest members, by the time it agreed to hear the case, "the Supreme Court was no longer the Roberts court, but the Trump court."[47] The case, according to Greenhouse, offered "a vehicle [that] the newly empowered anti-abortion supermajority was waiting for."[48]

Oral arguments were revealing, including Justice Sotomayor's headline-garnering question: "Will this institution survive the stench that this creates in the public perception that the Constitution and its reading are just political acts?"[49] In the aftermath of oral arguments, attention understandably focused on that question, but it is important to also view it in context. Sotomayor was engaging Mississippi Solicitor General Scott Stewart, questioning the validity of the state's claim given that, in the opinion of many, the law surrounding abortion had been settled with both *Roe* and *Casey* as precedents.[50] According to Stewart, though, nothing had been settled given ongoing public turmoil regarding the abortion issue. Sotomayor then pried open the Pandora's Box of Supreme Court politics, not just within the building, but also related to how those approaching the Court framed their cases. She pointed out that when the Mississippi bill at issue was introduced in that state's legislature, its sponsors conceded their strategic timing: "[B]ecause we have new justices" on the Supreme Court.[51] That is, the bill was passed with the acknowledgment not only that it would be challenged, but also that the time was right given the new members of the Court who very likely would be favorable to their cause.

After her "stench" comment, Sotomayor offered the valuable perspective that the Court's "watershed decisions"[52] seem to attract challenges based not so much on constitutional issues, but instead with the goal of reaching specific political ends. The Court's legitimacy hangs in the balance. "If people actually believe that it's all political, how will we survive?" she asked. "How will the Court survive?"[53] In addition to citing watershed decisions, Justice Sotomayor created her own watershed moment in Supreme Court history, pulling back the curtain on a process—and an institution—that too often is used as a political weapon.

The Court's 6–3 ruling served to confirm this notion. Written by Justice Samuel Alito,[54] and together with a concurring opinion by Justice Clarence Thomas, *Dobbs* may epitomize the fixed worldview tenet of returning the law and nation to a previous era. Rather than approaching both the issue and his reading of the Constitution objectively, Alito brought a history of partiality to his authorship. "A slow-burning hostility to constitutional abortion rights runs through the career of the author of the Supreme Court opinion overturning them,"[55] wrote Charlie Savage.

Alito's views were molded when he was a first-year law student at Yale in 1973, not coincidentally, the year of the *Roe* ruling. Later as a 35-year-old lawyer in the Justice Department, he advised the Reagan administration how to approach an effort to overturn *Roe*—cautiously and with patience. For many years, the Court lacked the votes. "With Justice Ruth Bader Ginsburg still on the bench, there were not five votes to overturn Roe," Savage wrote. By 2021, however, "there was no longer need for a restrained, slower-burning approach."[56] Indeed, the Court's majority approached *Dobbs* with "the swaggering confidence of a bloc that knows it has the votes to do whatever it wants."[57]

That is what the supermajority did—what it wanted to do, another power play of flexing judicial muscle.[58] Five of its members chose to de-constitutionalize the right to choose by detaching it from the Constitution. Despite a plea by Chief Justice Roberts to apply judicial restraint by ruling only on the Mississippi law at the root of *Dobbs*,[59] Alito led the gang of five in rejecting and overturning *Roe*. They did so with a textbook example of fixed worldview originalism.

Alito's view is embedded in a literal, textual approach to the Constitution—a document which, he emphasized, makes no mention of abortion.[60] The *Dobbs* dissenters—Justices Breyer, Sotomayor and Kagan, who wrote a joint opinion—are direct and clear in bottom-lining the flaws in the majority's unyielding and narrow view that not only relies on history, but is also a perspective that regards laws, constitutional amendments and court rulings as being fixed from the time they were written. As Harvard law professor Noah Feldman wrote, "In place of the living Constitution that protects liberty and equality from the tyranny of the majority, the court . . . announced a Constitution that only protects rights that already existed in the distant past."[61]

The majority's reliance on history in *Dobbs* especially includes its rejection of any Fourteenth Amendment application to abortion rights under the due process and equal protection clauses.[62] "That provision has been held to guarantee some rights that are not mentioned in the Constitution," Alito acknowledged, "but any such right must be 'deeply rooted in this Nation's history and tradition' and 'implicit in the concept of ordered liberty.' The right to abortion does not fall within this category."[63]

Instead, the fluid worldview dissenters asserted, "applications of liberty and equality can evolve while remaining grounded in constitutional principles, constitutional history, and constitutional precedents."[64] That is, they advocated for, and provided a lesson in, living constitutionalism: "The majority's core legal postulate, then, is that we in the 21st century must read the Fourteenth Amendment just as its ratifiers did. And that is indeed what the majority emphasizes over and over again."[65] Those who passed the Fourteenth Amendment in 1868 did not represent "We the People" but rather only a portion of them given that its authors were white men who "were not perfectly attuned to the importance of reproductive rights for women's liberty, or for their capacity to participate as equal members of our Nation."[66]

Alito's view of history's influence on the possible application of Constitutional rights was not limited to the Fourteenth Amendment. Whether a right is "deeply rooted" in the nation's history and tradition, he wrote, "is essential to our Nation's 'scheme of ordered liberty.'"[67] Because it was not until the latter part of the twentieth century that support for a constitutional right to obtain an abortion occurred, Alito concluded that any claim to any such right does not meet the standard of being deeply rooted in American history and tradition.

The Court's opinion relies on standards established by works hundreds of years old, some dating to the thirteenth century,[68] and observes that abortion was a crime in those eras,[69] in part because of the risk to mothers.[70] Herein lies one of originalism's pitfalls: Over-reliance on the past, such as the majority's examination of colonial America's abortion practices and laws,[71] yields a very narrow view and discounts a variety of advancements across many fields since those periods—in medical practice and technology, for example. Utilizing his lawyerly skills, Alito marshals and arranges facts to create what on the surface seems to be a compelling argument. Historical inquiries, he writes, are essential when determining, for example, whether a new component of liberty is covered by the Fourteenth Amendment.[72] However, evaluating any issue by selective cherry picking and ignoring contemporary conditions—apparently two prerequisites of fixed-originalism—is myopic.[73] Moreover, as the dissent points out, this kind of narrow approach yields problematic results: "When the majority says that we must read our foundational charter as viewed at the time of ratification (except that we may also check it against the Dark Ages), it consigns women to second-class citizenship."[74]

Alito relied on a pro-democracy rationale in *Dobbs*: Remove the abortion issue from the national level. Send it to the states where citizens can vote for officials whose lawmaking will echo their wishes. The problem is, thanks in part to Alito's own view in the voting rights cases described above—*Shelby*

County (where he joined the opinion of the Court) and *Brnovich* (for which he delivered the opinion of the Court)—democratic values are more difficult to achieve given that the power of the collective vote has been diminished because fewer people *can* vote. This provides evidence and fuels claims of a methodical right-wing revolution that initially focused on the Supreme Court and has spread to various parts of the nation.[75] As the *Dobbs* dissenters pointed out, the ruling harms, not helps, democracy.[76]

In rationalizing its ruling, the polarized Supreme Court blamed *Roe* for contributing to American polarization and turmoil.[77] In turn, the Court implied that by doing away with the divisive *Roe* doctrine, unification, at least on the abortion issue, would follow. Instead, chaos ensued in the immediate aftermath,[78] inflaming the kinds of national divisions described in chapter 1. While, as noted above, Alito claimed that dismantling a national standard and allowing states to autonomously regulate abortion is democracy at work through "ordered liberty,"[79] *Dobbs* created anything but order. By depriving thousands of women a once-federally protected right and by default creating a two-tiered scheme, confusion escalated.[80] As articulated in "The New Abortion Battleground," the absence of *Roe* creates "a novel world of complicated, interjurisdictional legal conflicts over abortion. Instead of creating stability and certainty, it will lead to profound confusion because advocates on all sides of the abortion controversy will not stop at state borders in their efforts to apply their policies as broadly as possible."[81]

Not surprisingly, to further justify its decision, the Court was highly critical of *Roe*. In addition to referring to it as a "bad decision" and as one that "halted a political process,"[82] it was also "wrongly decided,"[83] "plainly incorrect,"[84] an "exercise in raw judicial power,"[85] "egregiously wrong from the start,"[86] contained exceptionally weak reasoning,[87] "had damaging consequences,"[88] lacked "grounding in the constitutional text, history, or precedent,"[89] and contained a "constitutionally irrelevant"[90] analysis.

The *Roe* decision was 7–2. That means that every member of the seven-person majority—Justices Blackmun, Burger, Douglas, Brennan, Stewart, Marshall, and Powell—not to mention those who subscribed to its doctrine since, apparently lacked reason and failed in their interpretations of the Constitution. In *Dobbs*, "Justice Alito and his majority," wrote Linda Greenhouse, "are necessarily saying that these predecessors, joining the court over a period of four decades, didn't know enough, or care enough, to use the right methodology and reach the right decision. The arrogance and unapologetic nature of the [*Dobbs*] opinion are breathtaking."[91]

The Court's disregard for public opinion that supported *Roe* and what it stands for[92] is also on display in *Dobbs*. As Justice Thomas said weeks before the official release of the decision, "We can't be an institution that can be 'bullied' into giving you the outcomes you want."[93] Indeed, the Court *should* make decisions regardless of public opinion and perception. That is sometimes necessary to arrive at a constitutionally sound decision. But decisions consistently out of step with both public opinion *and* the Constitution are problematic. Moreover, the Court's indifference to public sentiment is a symptom of the nation's polarization, according to Mary Ziegler: "That the conservative majority could make such an argument—that it could believe such an idea—is a product of America's grievous polarization. This majority knows that it will be celebrated by the conservative legal movement and the leaders of the Republican Party."[94] Thus, not only is the nation divided, but its polarization also fuels the behavior and decision making of some of the Court's members. Reflecting that polarization, *Dobbs* was, in fact, hailed in some circles.[95]

Another issue the *Dobbs* majority was forced to confront was abandoning a precedent—that is, *stare decisis*. "When one of our constitutional decisions goes astray," Alito wrote, referring to *Roe*, "the country is usually stuck with a bad decision unless we correct our own mistake . . . [W]e must be willing to reconsider and, if necessary, overrule constitutional decisions."[96] Further justifying the Court's opinion, Alito notes that some of the Court's most important constitutional decisions have overruled precedents. Many examples were cited,[97] but unlike *Dobbs*, in none of them had the Court rescinded a constitutionally based right. This was a first.[98]

Stare decisis, the *Dobbs* majority held, "does not compel unending adherence to *Roe*'s abuse of judicial authority."[99] The dissenters referred to the Court's rejection of precedent as "cavalier,"[100] in turn taking the majority to school: "*Stare decisis* is the Latin phrase for a foundation stone of the rule of law: that things decided should stay decided unless there is a very good reason for change. It is a doctrine of judicial modesty and humility. Those qualities are not evident in today's opinion."[101] The primary change since 1973's *Roe* decision had nothing to do with its constitutionality, but instead it was the Court's membership. As the dissent stated, "The majority has overruled *Roe* and *Casey* for one and only one reason: because it has always despised them, and now it has the votes to discard them. The majority thereby substitutes a rule by judges for the rule of law."[102]

Practices such as those that apply to *stare decisis* seem to be in the rearview mirror, at least when abandoning them enhances an opportunity to achieve a political goal. As Ezra Klein wrote shortly after *Dobbs* was issued, "Under the norms that have governed the court for decades, Roe should have been safe, not because the majority agrees with it today, but because the Supreme Court does not upend settled law based on what the majority believes today."[103] Because *stare decisis* was a norm and not a law, however, the *Dobbs* majority simply dismissed it. Other norms on the Court had kept it from being largely nonpartisan but, Klein added, "those days are long gone."[104] It is little wonder that the dissenters described the ruling as "catastrophic."[105]

Many aspects of the *Dobbs* ruling were expected, particularly after the leak of its draft opinion nearly two months beforehand. Less anticipated, however, was the conservative majority's denunciation of one of its own, Chief Justice Roberts. Though he agreed with the Court's judgment, his concurring opinion reads more like a dissent across many of its passages.[106] Reflecting the moderation and concern for public opinion that Chief Justices often demonstrate,[107] Roberts advocated for "a more measured course"[108] than the one that overturned *Roe*. For him, that meant exercising judicial restraint by upholding the constitutionality of the Mississippi law at issue, but no more: "If it is not necessary to decide more to dispose of a case, then it is necessary *not* to decide more," Robert wrote. "Perhaps we are not always perfect in following that command, and certainly there are cases that warrant an exception. But this is not one of them."[109] While describing the Court's opinion as "thoughtful and thorough," Roberts added, "those virtues cannot compensate for the fact that its dramatic and consequential ruling is unnecessary to decide the case before us."[110] In short, Roberts believed overturning *Roe* was wrong.[111]

The jousting between the Chief Justice and Alito—for example, the latter characterizing Roberts's opinion as having "serious problems" and for "its failure to offer any principled basis for its approach"[112]—is noteworthy for at least two reasons. First, it becomes all the clearer that some members of the Court relished this opportunity to eviscerate *Roe* and were not going to let it slip through their fingers. Second, it reveals polarization not only on the Court, but also within its conservative wing. (Contrast that with the solidarity displayed by the dissenters who authored their opinion collectively.) Roberts is known for playing the long game, patiently and incrementally advancing his agendas. Life tenure means there is no rush. This approach, however, frustrates his conservative colleagues,[113] particularly now given their numbers. Having a supermajority means that the other five no longer need to wait for the Chief Justice.[114] In *Dobbs*, they didn't.[115]

In addition to joining the Opinion of the Court, Justice Brett Kavanaugh wrote his own concurring opinion. In doing so, he joined the chorus that attempted to justify the majority's decision. The Court's neutrality on abortion was essential, he claimed, playing the originalist card: "Because the Constitution is neutral on the issue of abortion, this court also must be scrupulously neutral."[116] The dissent responded: "[W]hen it comes to rights, the court does not act 'neutrally' when it leaves everything up to the states. Rather, the court acts neutrally when it protects the right against all comers."[117]

In asking how the *Dobbs* ruling could happen, the dissenters answered their own question: "[T]he majority's pinched view of how to read our Constitution."[118] In providing a lesson on living constitutionalism, they wrote that the Constitution's authors "knew they were writing a document designed to apply to ever-changing circumstances over centuries."[119] They quoted Chief Justice John Marshall who in 1819 had said the Constitution is "intended to endure for ages to come," and must adapt itself to a future "seen dimly," if at all.[120] The dissent continued:

> The Framers (both in 1788 and 1868) understood that the world changes. So they did not define rights by reference to the specific practices existing at the time. Instead, the Framers defined rights in general terms, to permit future evolution in their scope and meaning. And over the course of our history, this Court has taken up the Framers' invitation. It has kept true to the Framers' principles by applying them in new ways, responsive to new societal understandings and conditions.[121]

That is, until June 2022.

NOTES

1. *Buck v. Bell*, 274 U.S. 200 (1927).
2. Ibid., 207.
3. Ibid., 205.
4. Erwin Chemerinsky, *The Case Against the Supreme Court* (New York: Penguin Books, 2014), 4.
5. Ibid., 4–5.
6. *Dobbs v. Jackson Women's Health Organization*, 142 S. Ct. 2228, 2318 (2022) (The Court's majority "says that from the very moment of fertilization, a woman has no rights to speak of. A State can force her to bring a pregnancy to term, even at the steepest personal and familial costs")(Breyer, Sotomayor and Kagan, JJ., dissenting). See Ibid. ("As of today, this Court holds, a State can always force a woman to give birth, prohibiting even the earliest abortions. A State can thus transform what, when freely undertaken, is a wonder into what, when forced, may be a nightmare").
7. Margaret Atwood, "I Invented Gilead. The Supreme Court is Making it Real," *Atlantic*, May 13, 2022, https://www.theatlantic.com/ideas/archive/2022/05/supreme-court-roe-handmaids-tale-abortion-margaret-atwood/629833/.
8. Linda Greenhouse, Justice on the Brink: *The Death of Ruth Bader Ginsburg, the Rise of Amy Coney Barrett, and Twelve Months That Transformed the Supreme Court* (New York: Random House, 2021), 185.
9. See Katherine Stewart, "Eighty-One Percent of White Evangelicals Voted for Donald Trump. Why?" *Nation*, November 17, 2016, https://www.thenation.com/article/archive/eighty-one-percent-of-white-evangelicals-voted-for-donald-trump-why/ (attributing Donald Trump's 2016 election to his vow to "flip the Supreme Court" and to his disclosure during the campaign of a list of his potential Supreme Court nominees with the exclamation, "These judges are all pro-life!").

10. See David Karol, "Abortion Will Remain a National Issue No Matter What the Supreme Court Does," *Washington Post*, December 20, 2021, https://www .washingtonpost.com/outlook/2021/12/20/abortion-will-remain-national-issue-no -matter-what-supreme-court-does/ ("The antiabortion activists never gave up hope over five decades, even though the Supreme Court voted 7 to 2 against them in 1973. Over nearly half a century, they succeeded in shifting the court's balance").

11. 142 S. Ct. 2228 (2022).

12. 410 U.S. 113 (1973).

13. 505 U.S. 833 (1992).

14. Jesse Wegman, "The Supreme Court Is Out of Step with Most Americans," *New York Times*, May 3, 2022, https://www-nytimes-com.ezproxy1.lib.asu.edu/2022 /05/03/opinion/supreme-court-roe-wade.html.

15. See *Dobbs*, 2240 ("Abortion presents a profound moral issue on which Americans hold sharply conflicting views").

16. Mary Ziegler, *Abortion and the Law in America: Roe v. Wade to the Present* (Cambridge: Cambridge University Press, 2020), 212.

17. See David A. Kaplan, *The Most Dangerous Branch: Inside the Supreme Court in the Age of Trump* (New York: Broadway Books, 2018), 247 ("For justices like Scalia and Thomas, the ruling epitomized the sins of an activist Court, adrift from its constitutional moorings").

18. See, for example, Mary Ziegler, "Grassroots Originalism: Judicial Activism Arguments, the Abortion Debate, and the Politics of Judicial Philosophy," *University of Louisville Law Review* 51 (2013): 212 ("By the mid- to late 1970s . . . the Religious Right had become a political force—a grassroots movement with a highly structured and professional leadership"). See also Stephen T. Pfeffer, "Hostile Takeover: The New Right Insurgent Movement, Ronald Reagan, and the Republican Party, 1977–1984" (PhD dissertation, Ohio University, 2012), http://rave.ohiolink.edu/etdc /view?acc_num=ohiou1345147645 (asserting the New Right met with some success in the late 1970s over social issues such as abortion and school prayer. Along with the Moral Majority, they were instrumental in attaching social and cultural issues to the Republican Party platform).

19. Zielger, "Grassroots Originalism," 238.

20. Ibid. See also Adam Serwer, "The Constitution Is Whatever the Right Wing Says It Is," *Atlantic*, June 25, 2022, https://www.theatlantic.com/ideas/archive/2022 /06/roe-overturned-supreme-court-samuel-alito-opinion/661386/ (writing that the *Dobbs* ruling that over turned *Roe v. Wade* was "the result of decades of right-wing political advocacy, organizing, and electoral victory").

21. Ziegler, *Abortion and the Law in America,* 212.

22. Ibid., 5.

23. Rickie Sollinger (ed.), *Abortion Wars: A Half-Century of Struggle, 1950–2000* (Berkeley: University of California Press 1998), 1.

24. See Stewart, "Eighty-One Percent of White Evangelicals Voted for Donald Trump. Why?" (attributing the emergence of abortion as a significant social issue, in part, to "the emergence of a cadre of religious conservative leaders who, alarmed

by the rapid social changes of the 1960s and 1970s, shared a strong desire to form a political coalition").

25. Jamal Greene, "Let's Talk About How Truly Bizarre Our Supreme Court Is," interview by Ezra Klein, "The Ezra Klein Show," *New York Times* podcast, February 4, 2022, audio 5:47, https://www.nytimes.com/2022/02/04/opinion/ezra-klein -podcast-jamal-greene.amp.html.

26. Ibid., audio 41:45. See also Stewart, "Eighty-One Percent of White Evangelicals Voted for Donald Trump. Why?" ("Republicans realized that by turning abortion into a matter of 'family values,' they could make the cause of switching party affiliation attractive, especially to their white working-class base").

27. Greenhouse, *Justice on the Brink,* 43.

28. 505 U.S. 833 (1992) (upholding *Roe* but altering the standard for analyzing restrictions on that right, crafting an "undue burden standard" for abortion restrictions—stating a legislature cannot make a particular law that is too burdensome or restrictive of one's fundamental rights).

29. 505 U.S. 833, 1000–01 (1992) (Scalia, J., dissenting in part).

30. See Michael Scherer, Josh Dawsey, Caroline Kitchener and Rachel Roubein, "A 49-Year Crusade: Inside the Movement to Overturn Roe v. Wade," *Washington Post*, May 7, 2022, https://www.washingtonpost.com/politics/2022/05/07/abortion -movement-roe-wade/ (detailing a five-decade movement to overturn Roe). See also Marc Ramirez, "Conservatives Spent Decades Pushing to Upend Roe v. Wade. And 'It's Only the Beginning,'" *USA Today,* May 4, 2022, https://www.usatoday.com/ story/news/nation/2022/05/04/supreme-court-ruling-could-victory-anti-abortion-rights-groups/9632605002/?gnt-cfr=1.

31. *Roe v. Wade*, 410 U.S. 113, 152 (1973).

32. Ibid., 153. The citations noted by Blackmun are linked to the First, Fourth, Fifth, Ninth, and Fourteenth Amendments, as well as writing that privacy exists "in the penumbras of the Bill of Rights." Ibid.

33. Ibid., 172 (Rehnquist, J., dissenting).

34. Ibid., 174.

35. Linda Greenhouse and Reva B. Siegel, "Before (and After) Roe v. Wade: New Questions About Backlash," *Yale Law Journal* 120 (June 2011): 2030.

36. *Whole Woman's Health v. Jackson*, 141 S. Ct. 2494, 2498 (2021). See also *Whole Woman's Health v. Jackson*, 642 S.W.3d 569 (Tex. 2022) (Texas Supreme Court effectively shutting down any federal challenge to the state's law restricting abortions after six weeks of pregnancy).

37. See, for example, Kate Zernike and Adam Liptak, "Texas Supreme Court Shuts Down Final Challenge to Abortion Law," *New York Times*, March 11, 2022, https:// www.nytimes.com/2022/03/11/us/texas-abortion-law.html ("By empowering everyday people and expressly banning enforcement by state officials, the law . . . was designed to escape judicial review in federal court"). See also *In re Whole Women's Health v. Jackson*, 142 S. Ct. 701, 705 (2022):

[T]he state legislature enacted a convoluted law that instills terror in those who assist women exercising their rights between 6 and 24 weeks. State officials knew that the fear and confusion caused by this legal-procedural labyrinth would restrict citizens from accessing constitutionally protected medical care, providers from offering it, and federal courts from restoring it. The dilatory tactics to which this Court accedes today are consistent with, and part of, this scheme (Sotomayor, J., dissenting).

38. *Whole Woman's Health v. Jackson*, 141 S. Ct. 2494, 2498 (2021) (Sotomayor, J., dissenting).

39. *Whole Woman's Health v. Jackson II*, 142 S. Ct. 522 (2021) (ruling that opponents of the law could file suit against Texas medical licensing officials, who might discipline abortion providers who violate the law).

40. *In re Whole Woman's Health v. Jackson*, 142 S. Ct. 701, 705 (2022) (Sotomayor, J., dissenting).

41. Ibid.

42. *Whole Woman's Health v. Jackson*, 642 S.W.3d 569 (Tex. 2022).

43. *Dobbs v. Jackson Women's Health Organization*, 142 S. Ct. 2228 (2022).

44. Ashton Pittman, "Southern 'Defiance': The Fight for Roe Rages in Mississippi," *Jackson* (MS) *Free Press,* May 29, 2019, https://www.jacksonfreepress.com/news/2019/may/29/southern-defiance-fight-roe-rages-mississippi (quoting Sen. Joey Fillingane: "With a fifth conservative taking the seat of Justice Kennedy, who was considered a moderate on the court, I think a lot of people thought, finally, we have five conservative justices and so now would be a good time to start testing the limits of Roe").

45. See *Planned Parenthood v. Casey*, 505 U.S. 833, 845 (1992) (reaffirming *Roe v. Wade*'s holding of the right of a woman to choose to have an abortion before the fetus is viable and to obtain it without undue interference from the State).

46. *Dobbs v. Jackson Women's Health Organization*, 945 F.3d 265 (5th Cir. 2019).

47. Christian Farias, "'Power, Not Reason': The Fall of *Roe* and the Rise of Republican Orthodoxy at the Supreme Court," *Vanity Fair*, June 24, 2022, https://www.vanityfair.com/news/2022/06/fall-of-roe-rise-of-republican-orthodoxy-at-supreme-court (referring to the fact that the Court now contained three Trump nominees). See also *Payne v. Tennessee*, 501 U.S. 808, 843–45 (1991) (Marshall, J., dissenting) (expressing regret over shifts in Court personnel resulting in the abandonment of liberties previously established).

48. Linda Greenhouse, "The Supreme Court, Weaponized," *New York Times*, December 16, 2021, https://www.nytimes.com/2021/12/16/opinion/supreme-court-trump.html. See also Mary Ziegler, "The End of Roe Is Coming, and It Is Coming Soon," *New York Times*, December 1, 2021, https://www.nytimes.com/2021/12/01/opinion/supreme-court-abortion-mississippi-law.html ("The only real question is how the justices will rationalize their decision to side with Mississippi") (emphasis in original).

49. Transcript of Oral Argument, at 15:9–12, *Dobbs v. Jackson Women's Health Organization* 142 S. Ct. 2228 (2022).

50. See Becky Sullivan, "What Conservative Justices Said—and Didn't Say—About Roe at Their Confirmations," NPR, May 3, 2022, https://www.npr.org/2022/05/03/1096108319/roe-v-wade-alito-conservative-justices-confirmation-hearings ("[M]

uch was made of a private meeting between Kavanaugh and Sen. Susan Collins, R-Maine, who said the nominee had told her he considered *Roe* to be settled law").

51. Transcript of Oral Argument, 14:23, *Dobbs v. Jackson Women's Health Organization*, 142 S. Ct. 2228 (2022).

52. Ibid., 15:10 (mentioning *Brown v. Board of Education, New York Times v. Sullivan* and Second Amendment cases).

53. Ibid., 15:25–27.

54. It is worth noting that Alito's seat on the Court came about after political maneuverings. When the nomination of Harriet Miers seemed doomed, President George W. Bush replaced her with Alito. See, for example, Alex Markels, "Why Miers Withdrew As Supreme Court Nominee," NPR, October 27, 2005, https://www.npr.org/2005 /10/27/4976787/why-miers-withdrew-as-supreme-court-nominee (reporting that her nomination "faced opposition almost from the moment it was announced").

55. Charlie Savage, "Decades Ago, Alito Laid Out Methodical Strategy to Eventually Overrule Roe," *New York Times*, June 25, 2022, https://www.nytimes.com/2022 /06/25/us/politics/samuel-alito-abortion.html.

56. Ibid.

57. Wegman, "The Supreme Court Is Out of Step with Most Americans." See also Linda Greenhouse, "Requiem for the Supreme Court," *New York Times*, June 24, 2022, https://www.nytimes.com/2022/06/24/opinion/roe-v-wade-dobbs-decision .html (writing of *Dobbs*, "they did it because they could. It was as simple as that"); Paul Waldman, "The Supreme Court's EPA Ruling Says: We'll Do Whatever We Want," *Washington Post*, June 30, 2022, https://www.washingtonpost.com/opinions /2022/06/30/supreme-court-epa-climate-change-conservative-message/.

58. See *Dobbs*, 2348 ("Power, not reason, is the new currency of this Court's decisionmaking") (Breyer, Sotomayor, and Kagan, JJ., dissenting) (internal citation omitted).

59. Ibid., 2311 (Roberts, C.J., concurring in the judgment) ("If it is not necessary to decide more to dispose of a case, then it is necessary *not* to decide more. Perhaps we are not always perfect in following that command, and certainly there are cases that warrant an exception. But this is not one of them") (emphasis in original). See also Jessica Levinson, "Justice Elena Kagan Has a Prescription for an Ailing Court," MSNBC, August 2, 2022, https://www.msnbc.com/opinion/msnbc-opinion/kagan -roberts-know-supreme-court-burning-n1297556 ("Roberts tried desperately to find a middle ground to prevent the Supreme Court from overturning *Roe v. Wade*").

60. *Dobbs*, 2240. See also *West Virginia v. Environmental Protection Agency,* 142 S. Ct. 2587, 2641 (2022) (Kagan, J., dissenting) ("Some years ago, I remarked that '[w]e're all textualists now.' It seems I was wrong. The current Court is textualist only when being so suits it") (internal citation omitted).

61. Noah Feldman, "Ending *Roe* Is Institutional Suicide for the Supreme Court," *Baltimore Sun*, June 26, 2022, https://www.baltimoresun.com/opinion/op-ed/bs-ed -op-0626-ending-roe-institutional-suicide-20220626-55anw5pgszb77oeutqa264zkiu -story.html ("The majority considered it irrelevant that the people who ratified the original constitutional provisions did not include women, whose rights are at issue in

Dobbs and whose equality is derogated by the decision. According to the majority, the dead hand of the past rules our constitutional future").

62. See Charlie Savage, "Abortion Ruling Poses New Questions About How Far Supreme Court Will Go," *New York Times*, June 24, 2022, https://www.nytimes.com /2022/06/25/us/supreme-court-abortion-contraception-same-sex-marriage.html:

> The heart of Justice Alito's majority opinion is that the 14th Amendment protects only unwritten rights that were already understood to exist in 1868, when it was adopted. Many states then banned abortion, so it was wrong for the Supreme Court, in 1973's *Roe v. Wade*, to interpret the 14th Amendment as encompassing a right to abortion, he reasoned.

63. *Dobbs*, 2242 (internal citation omitted).
64. Ibid., 2326 (Breyer, Sotomayor and Kagan, JJ., dissenting).
65. Ibid, 2324.
66. Ibid. See also Feldman, "Ending *Roe* is Institutional Suicide for the Supreme Court":

> The right to an abortion was based on the principle of a living Constitution that evolves to expand liberty and equality . . . It is the same principle that undergirds dozens of other decisions establishing rights we today consider fundamental, from sexual freedom to stop and seizure, that were not considered similarly basic in 1791 when the Bill of Rights was ratified or in 1868 when the 14th Amendment was.

67. *Dobbs,* 2246 (internal citation omitted).
68. Ibid., 2323–34 ("it is not clear what relevance such early history should have, even to the majority").
69. See, for example, Ibid., 2249 ("Sir Edward Coke's 17th-century treatise likewise asserted that abortion of a quick child was murder").
70. Ibid., 2251 ("Manuals for justices of the peace printed in the Colonies in the 18th century typically restated the common-law rule on abortion . . . that anyone who prescribed medication 'unlawfully to destroy the child' would be guilty of murder if the woman died").
71. Ibid.
72. Ibid., 2252–54.
73. See Erwin Chemerinsky, *Worse Than Nothing: The Dangerous Fallacy of Originalism* (New Haven: Yale University Press, 2022), 9 ("Being governed by the views and values that prevailed in 1787 or 1791 or 1868 leads to results that rightly would be deemed unacceptable in our very different world. Moreover, there are many constitutional issues on which originalism is utterly unable to provide guidance adequate for our complex technological time").
74. *Dobbs*, 2325 (Breyer, Sotomayor, and Kagan, JJ., dissenting).
75. See, for example, Stephen M. Teles, *The Rise of the Conservative Legal Movement: The Battle for Control of the Law* (Princeton, NJ: Princeton University Press, 2010). See also Jackie Calmes, *Dissent: The Radicalization of the Republican Party and Its Capture of the Court* (New York: Twelve, 2021).

76. *Dobbs*, 2331, n.7. The majority contends that the *Roe* Court "short-circuited the democratic process by closing it to those who disagreed." Ibid., 9. See also Ezra Klein, "Dobbs Is Not the Only Reason to Question the Legitimacy of the Supreme Court," *New York Times*, June 30, 2022, https://www.nytimes.com/2022/06/30/opinion/dobbs-mcconnell-supreme-court.html ("the Supreme Court has gone from being undemocratic to being anti-democratic" and "makes a mockery of the public will").

77. See Greenhouse, "Requiem for the Supreme Court" ("the only turmoil that was caused by Roe and Casey was due to the refusal of activists, politicians and Republican-appointed judges to accept the validity of the precedents").

78. See Michelle Goldberg, "America's Post-*Roe* Chaos Is Here," *New York Times*, July 1, 2022, https://www.nytimes.com/2022/07/01/opinion/post-roe-chaos.html.

79. *Dobbs*, 2242, 2244.

80. See, for example, Patricia Mazzei, "Florida Judge Will Temporarily Block 15-Week Abortion Ban," *New York Times*, June 30, 2022, https://www.nytimes.com/2022/06/30/us/florida-abortion-ban-blocked.html. See also Mary Jo Pitzl, "Brnovich: 1864 Ban on Abortions in AZ is Law," *Arizona Republic*, June 30, 2022, A1; Ariana Eunjung Cha, "Physicians Face Confusion and Fear in Post-*Roe* World," *Washington Post*, June 28, 2022, https://www.washingtonpost.com/health/2022/06/28/abortion-ban-roe-doctors-confusion/.

81. David S. Cohen, Greer Donely, and Rachel Rebouché, "The New Abortion Battleground" (draft version), *Columbia Law Review* 122 (2023): 2.

82. *Dobbs*, 2279.

83. Ibid., 2224.

84. Ibid., 2240.

85. Ibid., 2241(quoting Roe, 410 U. S., 222, White., J., dissenting).

86. Ibid., 2243.

87. Ibid.

88. Ibid.

89. Ibid., 2266.

90. Ibid., 2240.

91. Greenhouse, "Requiem for the Supreme Court."

92. See Hannah Hartig, "About Six-in-Ten Americans Say Abortion Should Be Legal in All or Most Cases," Pew Research Center, June 13, 2022, https://www.pewresearch.org/fact-tank/2022/06/13/about-six-in-ten-americans-say-abortion-should-be-legal-in-all-or-most-cases-2/ (revealing the results of a poll taken shortly before the release of the *Dobbs* decision showing that 61 percent of U.S. adults believe abortion should be legal in all or most cases).

93. Rina Torchinsky, "After the Leaked Roe Opinion, Justice Thomas Says the Supreme Court Can't Be Bullied," NPR, May 7, 2022, ttps://www.npr.org/2022/05/07/1097382507/supreme-court-abortion-clarence-thomas-bullied-roe-v-wade.

94. Mary Ziegler, "The Conservatives Aren't Just Ending Roe—They're Delighting in It," *Atlantic*, May 3, 2022, https://www.theatlantic.com/ideas/archive/2022/05/supreme-court-leak-overturn-roe-polarization/629743/.

95. See, for example, Veronica Stracqualursi, "'Pro-Mom, Pro-Baby, Pro-Life': People at Anti-Abortion Convention Celebrate Roe's Downfall and Focus on 'Long Battle Ahead,'" CNN, June 24, 2022, https://www.cnn.com/2022/06/24/politics/national-right-to-life-supreme-court-dobbs-decision/index.html.

96. *Dobbs*, 2262.

97. See, for example, *Brown v. Board of Education*, 347 U. S. 483 (1954); *Plessy v. Ferguson*, 163 U. S. 537 (1896); *West Coast Hotel Co. v. Parrish*, 300 U. S. 379 (1937); *West Virginia Bd. of Ed. v. Barnette*, 319 U. S. 624 (1943).

98. See Christian Farias, "Samuel Alito's Roe Message Is Clear: This Supreme Court Is Ready to Burn It All Down," *Vanity Fair*, May 3, 2022, https://www.vanityfair.com/news/2022/05/samuel-alitos-roe-message-is-clear ("This is unprecedented in American history: The Supreme Court has never recognized such a fundamental right for the entire nation and then, with the flip of a switch, determined that, actually, the right is not a right, but a political issue that politicians must decide on a piecemeal, case-by-case basis") (emphasis in original). See also Wegman, "The Supreme Court Is Out of Step with Most Americans" (describing the first-time development as "an astonishing moment").

99. *Dobbs*, 2243.

100. Ibid., 2319 (Breyer, Sotomayor, and Kagan, JJ., dissenting).

101. Ibid.

102. Ibid., 2335. See also Ruth Marcus, "The Radical Conservative Majority's Damage to the Supreme Court Cannot Be Undone," *Washington Post,* June 24, 2022, https://www.washingtonpost.com/opinions/2022/06/24/supreme-court-conservative-majority-rule-of-law ("This radical conservative majority . . . has proven itself unmoored from the rule of law, and therefore unworthy of the public esteem that can be its only source of enduring authority").

103. Klein, "Dobbs Is Not the Only Reason to Question the Legitimacy of the Supreme Court."

104. Ibid.

105. *Dobbs*, 2333 (Breyer, Sotomayor, and Kagan, JJ., dissenting).

106. See Marcus, "The Radical Conservative Majority's Damage to the Supreme Court Cannot Be Undone" ("There is no better proof of the radical nature of the majority's actions than the concurring opinion by Chief Justice John G. Roberts Jr.").

107. See, for example, C.L. Ostberg and Matthew E. Wetstein, "Strategic Behaviour and Leadership Patterns of Modern Chief Justices," *Osgoode Hall Law Journal* 55 (Spring 2018): 487 ("chief justices may moderate their own policy preferences in order to foster greater agreement and thereby strengthen court legitimacy"). See also Michael Scherer, "Supreme Court Goes Against Public Opinion in Rulings on Abortion, Guns," *Washington Post*, June 24, 2022, https://www.washingtonpost.com/politics/2022/06/24/supreme-court-goes-against-public-opinion-rulings-abortion-guns/:

Concern over losing the public trust has repeatedly been voiced by Chief Justice John G. Roberts Jr., a Republican appointee who often shaped the court's approach before Ginsburg's death. In a 2007 interview with the Atlantic, he spoke of the "high priority to keep any kind of partisan divide out of the judiciary." He said it was important to shore up the court's "legitimacy as an institution." Ibid.

108. *Dobbs*, 2310 (Roberts, C.J., concurring).

109. Ibid., 2311 (emphasis in original).

110. Ibid.

111. Ibid., 2313 ("None of this, however, requires that we also take the dramatic step of altogether eliminating the abortion right first recognized in *Roe*. Mississippi itself previously argued as much to this Court in this litigation") (Roberts, C.J., concurring).

112. Ibid., 2281.

113. See Greenhouse, *Justice on the Brink*, 164 (writing of "John Roberts's isolation on the court"). See also Ibid., 167 (writing of the "fissure between Roberts and the justices to his right").

114. See Adam Liptak, "June 24, 2022: The Day Chief Justice Roberts Lost His Court," *New York Times*, June 24, 2022, https://www.nytimes.com/2022/06/24/us/abortion-supreme-court-roberts.html ("Outflanked by five impatient and ambitious justices to his right, the chief justice has become powerless to pursue his incremental approach").

115. See Maureen Dowd, "Marilyn Monroe v. Samuel Alito," *New York Times,* May 7, 2022, https://www.nytimes.com/2022/05/07/opinion/abortion-supreme-court-puritanism.html (referring to how Alito's *Dobbs* draft opinion "brought to the fore how radical the majority on the court is, willing to make women fit with their zealous world view—a view most Americans reject").

116. *Dobbs*, 2305 (Kavanaugh, J., concurring).

117. Ibid., 2328 (Breyer, Sotomayor, and Kagan, JJ., dissenting).

118. Ibid., 2325.

119. Ibid.

120. *McCulloch v. Maryland*, 4 Wheat. 316, 415 (1819).

121. *Dobbs*, 2325.

PART 3

Principles and Processes

Chapter 7

"Equal Justice Under Law"

Within one week in June 2022, the Supreme Court issued four rulings that changed the face of America. It was a turning point. Analyzed in the four previous chapters, each one was a 6–3 ruling, all with the same six justices in the majority and the same three in dissent. Individually, these decisions are significant. However, the whole is greater than the sum of the parts. Their collective weight is cataclysmic.

Forecasts that an agenda-fueled Supreme Court would transform law with a narrow view of the Constitution once seemed far-fetched and overly fearful. Today they are real. In that seven-day span in 2022, the Court twice chipped away at church-state separation, expanded the right to carry firearms in public places and—by employing the Orwellian practice of disappearing freedoms—drove a stake into the heart of the 49-year-old constitutional right of women to choose whether to continue or terminate their pregnancy. By focusing on the past and consistent with its fixed worldview, the Court's majority succeeded in returning the nation to a previous era and in the eyes of many, helped to make America great again.[1]

By the end of its 2021–2022 term, it was clear that the Court had been weaponized by the political right. Moreover, the Court's majority *was* the political right. It was no longer merely a victim of America's polarization; it was a purveyor of the divide.[2] At its conclusion, and relying on objective data analysis, the term was characterized as the Court's most conservative in almost a century,[3] "relentlessly" shifting to the right in a way that "will transform American life."[4] Thanks to its Supreme Court, the nation that Americans woke up to after that week in June was much different from the one that existed beforehand.

The U.S. Supreme Court is a political institution. That conclusion is reached not only in these pages, but it was also a belief supported by law professor Mary Ziegler in the immediate aftermath of the Court's release of the *Dobbs* abortion case decision: "[I]t's clear that over the years the Supreme Court has become yet another partisan institution—and one that's unaccountable to the

American people. In that light, it's hard to see the court's aggressive moves to remake American constitutional law as anything but anti-democratic."[5]

To be sure, the concept of a political Court—for example, as a cog within the machinery of a political system,[6] or its role at the top of one branch of American government[7]—has been explored in the past. These pages, however, have revealed that this predicament can be brought into sharper focus by looking at it through the lens of worldview. Unlike the past when the Court was merely a player within a political system, it is now political in every sense of the word,[8] molded for the purpose of moving both the law and nation in a specific political direction.[9] This, too, has been the subject of analysis. As noted herein, for example, the Court led by Chief Justice Earl Warren, 1953–1969, is a frequent target.[10] That Court provided a set of rulings that reverberated in ways that may be characterized as "political." There is an important distinction, however, between then and now. Through a view of the Constitution less tied to its text, those Warren Court decisions *expanded* rights, especially for those in minority groups and those lacking power. In the current era, by contrast, decisions whether to hear cases, and then how to rule on them, are often motivated by the political goals of sitting justices. Typically, as examined in these pages, those rulings tend to *constrain* rights, sometimes stripping away liberties previously granted by the Court after years of struggle to secure them.

The Court's legitimacy hangs in the balance. As its politicization swells, particularly in ways that consistently bulldoze preferences of majorities and rights of minorities, its credibility wanes.[11] Absent public acceptance, and coupled with specious reasoning, its institutional authority crumbles. As law professor Stephen Vladeck writes, "The proliferation of principle-free decisions affecting more and more Americans—and with a clear, troubling tendency of favoring Republicans over Democrats—calls [the Court's] legitimacy into increasingly serious question."[12] In contrast, Vladeck recalls when, in 1992, justices insisted that "the Court's legitimacy depends on making legally principled decisions under circumstances in which their principled character is sufficiently plausible to be accepted by the nation."[13]

The Court is now an institution dominated by fixed worldview originalists determined to strategically carry out a conservative agenda, returning the nation to a prior period by overturning its own precedents that had expanded civil rights to growing numbers of people.[14] This transformation from the principles of neutrality and independence, advocated by people like Justice Stephen Breyer up to his 2022 retirement, to the political reality of today was driven by several factors. Worldview is among the most relevant, providing a unique perspective to probe, reveal, and explain how and why the polarization that occurs in groups, big and small, also afflicts our justices and their institution. The analysis yields the conclusion that the Court is now an overwhelmingly political institution. That said, so what? And what to do about it?

To answer these questions, this concluding chapter looks at the unacceptability and inevitability of the Supreme Court as a political institution. The Court's guardrails have not only been lost, they were dismantled both from within and by political forces outside its building.[15] Particularly with a supermajority armed with fixed-originalist worldviews bent on turning back the clock,[16] the lack of checks on its power is especially problematic given its stated aspiration of achieving "Equal Justice Under Law."

That some justices occasionally try to convince the public that the Court is independent, neutral, and apolitical does not occur in a vacuum. They are responding to public perception based in fact.[17] There is a record, after all—primarily, the justices' opinions, sometimes abetted by the Court's oral arguments—on which the public may base its views. Those opinions, moreover, often reveal sharp conflict in which the weaknesses of opposing views are called out.[18] The public-targeted proclamations of harmony and objectivity seem more like attempts to dissuade—the kind fittingly common in political advertising designed to create image contrary to reality. Justice Sonia Sotomayor's 2021 rebuke that the Court's reading of the Constitution is a political act[19] was by no means the dawn of this phenomenon. Instead, it was a call to arms about an ongoing and critical situation, one that threatens the stability of not only the institution, but also the republic—a fragile republic, to paraphrase Benjamin Franklin, that is ours to keep only if we can do the necessary work.[20]

It is not surprising that the Supreme Court has become a political institution given that the tenure of each member begins with a highly political process, one that is controlled by politicians.[21] The infusion of politics into the nomination and confirmation processes is not without precedent.[22] The practice has especially escalated since the 1980s,[23] and rose to new levels in the twenty-first century.[24] For example, it is now not uncommon for members of the Senate's Judiciary Committee—the body that conducts the confirmation hearings—to use them to make political points unrelated to the nominee, including relitigating previous hearings,[25] fighting culture wars or launching their own presidential campaigns.[26] That the process is predictably political was demonstrated in 2022 when *before* a nominee was selected to succeed Justice Breyer, columnist Jamelle Bouie wrote, "A new vacancy on the Supreme Court means a new round of political theater over the beliefs and qualifications of the president's eventual nominee."[27]

To no one's surprise, the prediction was accurate. With Judge Ketanji Brown Jackson in place as the nominee, the Judiciary Committee hearings in March 2022 frequently devolved into little more than melodramatic bombast. Law professor Melissa Murray, for example, said, "Judge Jackson's confirmation hearings have merely provided a forum for this form of political theater."[28]

This downward spiral in the character of confirmation hearings has drawn widespread criticism,[29] including from members of the current Court. First, within a period of relative harmony and goodwill in hearings, Elena Kagan in 1995 described the process as a "vapid and hollow charade."[30] As if to substantiate this description, the confirmation process came to be known for some nominees avoiding candor in their testimony.[31] Second, a decade-and-a-half before joining the Court, Neil Gorsuch suggested that both major political parties needed a "wake-up call" to remind them that their "responsibility in picking judges is to help the nation find objectively excellent public servants."[32] Instead, he lamented, the process had become "an ideological food fight."[33] Third and more recently, Chief Justice Roberts noted how the public partisanship on display at confirmation hearings can only hurt the Court's credibility. "When you have a sharply political, divisive hearing process," he said in 2016, "it increases the danger that whoever comes out of it will be viewed in those terms."[34]

The 2022 Jackson confirmation process demonstrated not only politics at work, but also the fixed-originalist/fluid-living constitutionalist divide. Judge Jackson, for example, faced many questions about how she, as a trial judge, had sentenced guilty criminal defendants. Her Senate questioners, clearly seeking to portray concern about safety and keeping dangerous people off the streets, strongly suggested that her sentences were overly lenient and did not comport with various guidelines. Judge Jackson's responses embraced nuance: "Sentencing is a discretionary act of a judge, but it's not a numbers game."[35] While other issues were factors in these exchanges—for example, power and authority—this was a classic example of the uneasiness that fixed-originalists find with discretion and choice that they believe strays outside of static (i.e., fixed) boundaries and their desire to eliminate it (or, at the least, to make political points about it).

Presidents are often transparent in their plans to use the federal courts, particularly the Supreme Court, to achieve political/ideological goals.[36] During his 2016 campaign, for example, Donald Trump promised to "flip the Court" by nominating jurists who opposed abortion rights. He shared a list of potential nominees to demonstrate his allegiance to that cause.[37] According to some, that was his primary path to electoral victory.[38] His plan to flip the Court, as described by Ian Milhiser, was executed "with the accuracy of a drone strike."[39] Due to a combination of unforeseen circumstances and political maneuverings, in a single presidential term Trump installed three justices, all of whom met his standards.[40] With some help from the Mitch McConnell–led Republican-controlled Senate, the three "are doing exactly what they were sent to the court to do."[41]

McConnell's manipulations are noteworthy given the high-stakes politics—and "power grabs"[42]—that they embodied. Justice Antonin Scalia's unexpected death in February 2016 left a vacancy on the Court, more than eight months prior to that year's November election and the end of President Barack Obama's second term the next January. Even before Obama nominated Judge Merrick Garland to succeed Scalia, however, then–Senate majority leader McConnell announced that any appointment by the sitting president was null and void. Without precedent,[43] and with unwavering support from within his political party, the "McConnell blockade" held strong.[44] A hearing and vote on Garland never occurred. Denying Obama the Supreme Court nominee—ostensibly because "the American people should have a say in the court's direction" with their votes for the next president[45]—left the door open to the possibility that Scalia's seat could be filled with a like-minded jurist rather than by Garland, a moderate. Ultimately, Trump's election resulted in Neil Gorsuch filling the vacancy, the first of three fixed-originalist Trump nominees.[46]

When a potentially similar situation surfaced more than four years later, the same "principle" was rejected by McConnell. Though Justice Ruth Bader Ginsburg died much closer to a presidential election than had Justice Scalia, McConnell did not apply the Garland rationale then.[47] In a process firmly directed by McConnell from the outset,[48] Amy Coney Barrett was nominated 11 days after Ginsburg's September 18, 2020, death and confirmed on October 26, eight days prior to the presidential election. Why the difference? Led by Senator McConnell, whose "reshaping of the courts was the result of a strategic plan by a man who became obsessed with the Senate's role in filling the federal judiciary during his early days as a staff aide during the Nixon administration,"[49] the answer is politics.

The politics that permeated the selection of all the Trump nominees was palpable. Not only was political cunning inherent in each, then-Judges Gorsuch, Kavanaugh, and Barrett all had pre–Supreme Court records that opposed government regulations protecting the environment, a woman's right to choose, same-sex marriage, and that favored narrow (i.e., originalist) interpretations of the Second Amendment.[50] As noted in this book's introduction, nominees do not suddenly abandon their views when they arrive at the Court.[51] To the contrary, in fact, they are selected *because* of their views, not in spite of them,[52] and with the expectation that those views will manifest themselves on the Court.[53] As Millhiser wrote, "Say what you will about Trump's justices, but before they got on the Court, they were quite open about just how eager they are to abolish foundational principles of American law."[54]

This politically infused new normal of selecting Supreme Court justices is, according to Justice Sotomayor, highly problematic: "The emphasis to pick nominees with extensive writings and publicly expressed views on precedents of the court can be viewed as a way—and can be viewed by the public as ways—to control a judge from changing his or her mind."[55] This comment was viewed as a (not so) veiled reference to groups like the conservative Federalist Society, which has exerted its influence in seeking ideological uniformity in nominees.[56] Echoing her previous "stench" comment and alluding to the notion that at least some rulings are preordained, Sotomayor continued: "We have an obligation to keep open minds, that we are willing to change with time and experience. If we don't show it, people will believe—perhaps wrongly—that we are just political creatures and not independent judges."[57]

The solution to this oil-and-water dynamic is simple and is directly addressed by the 2021 Presidential Commission on the Supreme Court of the United States: "Judges should not be partisans."[58] It is a basic tenet of the American judiciary, yet it is a standard that has been allowed, even encouraged, to deteriorate. The Commission continued:

> Other government officials, depending on their positions, might legitimately set out to promote the interests of the political party with which they are associated; one requirement of judicial independence is that judges not do that. And, importantly—because federal judges are appointed and confirmed *by political actors*—the belief that the judiciary is independent can be undermined if judges are perceived to be "playing on the team" of one party or another.[59]

Though unsurprising, this statement captured much of the current problem—the politics common to other branches has seeped into and poisoned the judiciary.

Concern about the Court's lack of independence has grown in proportion to its tilt to the political right that is driven by conservative fixed-originalists.[60] The Court is now described as a body that not only "has taken a hard right turn with Trump's appointments, it is also increasingly seen as composed of clashing ideologues, both liberal and conservative, rather than independent jurists."[61] In the era of the post-Trump presidency, the battle of ideologues is one-sided, with the fixed worldview supermajority intent on reshaping the landscape of American rights.[62]

Just as it is not surprising that the nomination process for would-be Supreme Court justices has become so political, it is not unexpected that it has caught the attention of current members. Justice Sotomayor, for example, believes that as the norms of the nomination and confirmation process are broken, the Court's credibility problems grow: "The more partisan the voting becomes, the less belief that the public is likely to have that Congress is making a merit-based or qualifications-based assessment of judicial nominees."[63] Any hope that this process's outlook contains the possibility of reduced partisanship was put to rest by the Presidential Commission on the Supreme Court.

It reported that "the struggles over the confirmation process appear likely to persist, if not intensify," with the possibility that future Senate majorities may "decline to take up any nomination from a President of the opposing party at any time at all, not just in the last year of the President's term."[64] To that point, McConnell suggested in 2021 that if his party regained a Senate majority, blocking any nominee of President Joe Biden was possible.[65]

The trend in the Senate's confirmation (or rejection) votes of Supreme Court nominees since 1981 is telling (see table 7.1).

Table 7.1. Trend in Senate Confirmation Votes of Supreme Court Nominees Since 1981.

Year	Nominee	Vote
1981	Sandra Day O'Connor	99–0
1986	William Rehnquist	65–33
1986	Antonin Scalia	98–0
1987	Robert Bork	42–58
1988	Anthony Kennedy	97–0
1990	David Souter	90–9
1991	Clarence Thomas	52–48
1993	Ruth Bader Ginsburg	96–3
1994	Stephen Breyer	87–9
2005	John Roberts	78–22
2006	Samuel Alito	58–42
2009	Sonia Sotomayor	68–31
2010	Elena Kagan	63–37
2017	Neil Gorsuch	55–45
2018	Brett Kavanaugh	50–48
2020	Amy Coney Barrett	52–48
2022	Ketanji Brown Jackson	53–47

Source: "Supreme Court Nominations (1789–present)," United States Senate, accessed June 30, 2022, https://www.senate.gov/legislative/nominations/SupremeCourtNominations1789present.htm.

The margins that by and large decreased over time did so in proportion to intense partisan politics being thrust into the confirmation process, with Senate votes now overwhelmingly in line with party politics.

The Presidential Commission on the Supreme Court corroborated this assessment, reporting that the recent history of confirmation votes reveals "escalating partisanship."[66] Commission witnesses testified about the "'confirmation hardball' played by Republicans since 2016."[67] One of those witnesses was Harvard law professor Vicki Jackson:

It is an unstable situation for a party supported by a minority of the population to be able to control the Senate, frequently the presidency, and the Supreme

Court . . . If citizens cannot look to elections, nor to the Courts, nor to the amending process, to achieve a federal government that is in broad terms responsive to democratic views, what remains are methods that should trouble all who believe in the rule of law.[68]

Senator Susan Collins is among those who concurs: "No matter where you fall on the ideological spectrum," she stated in 2022, "anyone who has watched several of the last Supreme Court confirmation hearings would reach the conclusion that the process is broken."[69] She added that there has been a "disturbing trend of politicizing the judicial nomination process."[70] Another senator, Chris Murphy, echoed those sentiments:

The Merrick Garland debacle was the point of no return. Once McConnell stole that seat from Obama, I didn't think there was any way to depoliticize this process. Something fundamentally broke in this place when Sen. McConnell chose not to give even a hearing to Merrick Garland . . . [T]he consequence of McConnell's decision will be an eventual constitutional crisis.[71]

As noted, it should not be surprising that an institution becomes political when its members join through a process that is predicated on politics that may be described accurately as blatant, unashamed, and sometimes brawling. The stakes rose in proportion to the recognition of both the power and influence of lifetime appointments granted to justices, and of how that power was wielded—*political* power.[72] That is, justices began ruling—on certain cases, particularly—in precisely the ways they were expected to when nominated. On the surface it appears that nonpoliticians are doing the work that politicians cannot or will not; in reality, politicians *are* doing the work. These politicians, however, reside not in the legislative or executive branches, but in the judiciary.

It is unacceptable that politics has become such an integral part of virtually every aspect of the Supreme Court. In considering any approach to the law—for example, fluid-living constitutionalism or fixed-originalism—it is imperative for any court to remind itself of its purpose.[73] A starting place for the Supreme Court is the "Equal Justice Under Law" inscription above the front entrance to its own building. While the Court's guardrails may be lost, they and their substance may be rediscovered in the nation's founding. James Madison, for example, recognized not only the danger of factionalism—not dissimilar to the tribalism described in chapter 1—but also that its innate character is "sown into the nature of man."[74] This sentiment was echoed by George Washington who called factionalism "inseparable from our nature."[75] He added that it is the worst enemy of popular governments, and warned of "the alternate domination of one faction over another, sharpened by the spirit of revenge."[76] In settings within which deeply seated views are held, a "tyranny of the majority" may emerge.[77] Philosopher John Stuart Mill wrote that it is necessary to protect against the "tyranny of the prevailing opinion and feeling; against the tendency of society to impose . . . its own ideas and practices as rules of conduct on those who dissent from them."[78] Just as in society, majorities within institutions can wield power, and in ways that may be regarded as especially toxic to democracy when they represent minority interests.

One more lesson from Madison, and that is from one his most famous proclamations: "If men were angels, no government would be necessary. If angels were to govern men, neither external nor internal controls on government would be necessary."[79] Just as he noted the importance of human nature in his analysis of factions, Madison saw that the potential for self-interest and thirst for power can be destructive.[80] He recognized that if left unresolved, clashes between factions can fester into open conflict or "convulse the society."[81]

To combat these dangers, Madison envisioned a system of checks and balances to inhibit self-interested factional tyranny.[82] The federal government was structured to check majority factions and, according to law professor Samuel Olken, "to protect individual rights from the tyranny of popular majorities that were controlled by factions eager to promote their own interests at the expense of the public good."[83] Unless majorities could be controlled, Madison said, they would oppress minorities. He warned that once a majority is motivated and united, restraining it can be difficult.[84] This is especially applicable when considering a majority faction in the Supreme Court. Granted, even with a supermajority on the Court, the minority provides a checking function. Checking absent balancing, however, provides only half the benefit. Dissenting opinions remain important, continuing to plant seeds for another day.[85] A supermajority earns that label for a reason, however: Because of the disparity in group size—in this case, 6–3—it is often bulletproof from its minority counterpart even on those occasions when a member of the majority strays.

Checking power, particularly that of a majority, was an ongoing dilemma for the Founders, and one that persists to the present. Of the Constitution, historian Robert Tracy McKenzie writes, "Its genius lay in how it held in tension two seemingly incompatible beliefs: first, that the majority must generally prevail; and second, that the majority is predisposed to seek personal advantage above the common good."[86] While probably not having the Supreme Court in mind, McKenzie's words certainly apply. Majorities, including those within relatively small groups, can abuse their power, and in ways that harm the common good.

As David Brooks has observed, America's "founders were aware that majorities are easily led by ambitious demagogues. So our founders built a system that respected popular opinion and majority rule while trying to build guardrails to check popular passion and prejudice."[87] The majorities that concerned the Founders were primarily those of citizens, less so factions within government institutions. Nevertheless, they provided guardrails for the judiciary, not only in the Constitution's Article III, but also in what is now referred to as the *Federalist Papers*. In Federalist No. 78, Alexander Hamilton wrote, "there is no liberty if the power of judging be not separated from the legislative and executive powers," adding that liberty has "every thing [*sic*] to fear" from the union of the judiciary with either of the other branches.[88] As factions of both the Court and Congress unite today, Hamilton's assessment of the judiciary as the weakest and "least dangerous"[89] branch of government has arguably diminished. Rather than checking judicial power, as Hamilton prescribed,[90] political power has been conferred to and shared with the Court.

Today's Supreme Court majority—a "carefully constructed conservative supermajority"[91]—is not merely wielding its power, but its tyranny is used to diminish the rights and quality of life of large segments of the American citizenry.[92] With its *Dobbs* ruling, the Court put an end not only to *Roe* rights, but also to modern constitutional law, according to Noah Feldman: "The tyranny of the majority won the day."[93] The rights and opportunities in place are being reduced if not rescinded, and sometimes by a Court breaking with its own precedents. When we consider governments globally doing the same to their citizens, we find that unacceptable. When it happens domestically, it should be no less tolerable.

As a nation, as much as we lean on our founders and what they built—often with good reason—Ezra Klein writes that there sometimes is a tendency to think it is "somehow heretical to question" the "creaking, cracking structure of American government."[94] But diving into the history of Court reform, Klein asserts—as the 2021 Presidential Commission did—"is to be reminded that the Supreme Court was imagined by human minds, and made and remade by human hands. We honor the idea of the American experiment, but we have lost the spirit of experimentation that made it work."[95] It is time to recapture that spirit.

Efforts should be directed at depoliticizing the Court as much as possible. Yes, some politics and ideology on the Supreme Court are unavoidable. As explained throughout this volume, all people have ideas, ideas that are shaped by various factors including worldview. Moreover, we want our judges and Supreme Court justices to be thinking people. To be clear, unanimity on the bench—any bench—is not the goal. Quite the contrary. Our democracy depends on viewpoint diversity. It is also a reasonable expectation, however, for the Court to consist of justices who are clear-eyed and view every case with the independence and neutrality that they claim to possess. Instead, we have a Court where many rulings are predictable, justice-by-justice, given their transparent ideologies.[96] Rather, a bit of unpredictability rooted in apolitical, impartial approaches would be both welcomed and beneficial.

Too often the people being nominated to the Supreme Court have records in which their ideologies are apparent. While the recommendation here is not for nominees with blank slates, their records should exhibit neutrality and independence rather than being screeds that are attractive to one side of the aisle, abhorrent to the other.

The selection, nomination, and confirmation processes for the Supreme Court are flawed. As noted, this begins with the fact that they are controlled completely by politicians. Recent history reveals a highly political series of procedures that—if depoliticization of the Court is the goal—are doomed to fail. With the tenure of a justice beginning with such fault-riddled methods, it is virtually inevitable that the problems explored here surface when the Court conducts its business.

While the political nature of how the Court has operated and ruled may be the catalyst of any plan to enlarge the size of the Court or to rework how it operates, a chosen plan should strive to be as apolitical as possible.[97] That is, unlike how nominees are selected currently—with future rulings front of mind—new requirements should not be approached with the idea of exacting any specific results other than creating a Court that operates with clear-eyed neutrality.

Solutions are complex and require heavy lifting. Because there are multiple options to remedy the various ailments described in these pages, none of them in isolation is necessarily vital. That said, however, in combination, their remedial effects grow exponentially. It should be noted that the recommendations herein are general. That is, it is acknowledged that working out details remains on the table. Most importantly, the recommendations here are secondary to the importance of first recognizing the overarching problem: the Court has lost its way and is now a full-fledged political institution that jeopardizes America's democratic republic.

As noted, rather than being above politics, the Court has come to resemble and reflect—and sometimes cause—the divided politics found in the nation at large, including the politics in other parts of the government. That begins with the process of the White House selecting nominees. To be sure, it is a requirement established in the Constitution's Article II: The President "shall nominate, and by and with the Advice and Consent of the Senate . . . judges of the supreme Court."[98] It is suggested here to establish a bipartisan (admitting that nonpartisan is pure fantasy) Presidential Commission, not unlike the body assembled in 2021 that evaluated the Court. It would assume responsibilities similar to those of "headhunters" in the business world. Such a commission could be ad hoc, assembled each time a vacancy occurs on the Court; or it could be a "permanent" commission to be established with members who have finite terms (not unlike, for example, the Federal Communications Commission). A permanent commission could have responsibilities assigned to it in addition to those related to the Supreme Court—for example, the entirety of the federal judiciary. A public report would be required for each of its recommendations. Thus, rather than the nomination process being directed solely by a President's political appointees and inner circle, this would occur outside the White House. While the President retains the power to nominate—consistent with the Constitution—it is possible that this pre-nomination step will acquire public credibility to the extent that rejecting the commission's recommendation(s) could create political fallout. The hope is that this would result in prioritizing the selection of outstanding jurists rather than judges with agendas who are only too happy to execute them.

In addition to reforming the nominee selection process, the subsequent confirmation procedures require attention. As described herein, in recent history they have been highly flawed, replete with partisanship and rancor. Absent addressing this setting in which the character and temperament most starkly revealed are too often not those of the nominees but those of the senators who confront them, the toxic atmosphere is likely to worsen.[99]

Despite the predictability of these hearings going off the rails[100]—and while several analyses have been conducted[101]—the status quo remains in place, enabling the conduct that is now common yet generally unwanted. Reform is overdue. The hearings are being abused, primarily by senators, not the nominees. Nevertheless, that abuse colors not only the process but, echoing the previously noted concern by Chief Justice Roberts,[102] sometimes also negatively influences the careers on the bench that follow.

The first confirmation hearing of a Supreme Court nominee to be televised live was Sandra Day O'Connor's in 1981.[103] Not coincidentally, America's media landscape began a significant transformation at about the same time. Cable television and its myriad viewing options took root then. As the decades unfolded, additional technological evolution resulted in new media with more platforms where, particularly on social media, content could not only be seen and heard, but now published by anyone. "Likes" became a new currency. These platforms became outlets for those seeking attention, including politicians.[104] Accordingly, it is not inconceivable that in efforts to attract the spotlight in a universe of attention seekers, behavior is orchestrated to stand out.

Confirmation hearings are not immune from this phenomenon. "[S]enators treat the confirmation hearings as their own public forums," writes Paul Vaglica.[105] In 2022, brusque behavior by several senators unsurprisingly attracted media attention. Video segments of the hearings were played on evening newscasts, and the surly-by-day senators transformed into gentlemen-by-night when they appeared on cable news channels, with praise from compliant hosts.[106]

One Judiciary Committee member, Senator Ben Sasse, suggested that the "jackassery" on display during 2022's Jackson hearing was a conscious effort by "people mugging for short-term camera opportunities" and "trying to get on cable that night or get a viral video."[107] In part defending the Supreme Court's no-cameras policy during oral arguments, Sasse continued: "Cameras change human behavior."[108] Perhaps unwittingly, he also provided a pseudo-endorsement for what others have recommended and which is echoed here: Eliminate cameras from the Judiciary Committee's hearings of Supreme Court nominees.

It is documented that awareness of being observed affects behavior. While that may increase productivity in some settings,[109] it can also fuel attention-starved politicians who, for various reasons, have concluded that outrage, whether genuine or contrived, is a path to success.[110] Apparently believing P.T. Barnum's mantra that there is no such thing as bad publicity, they transformed what should be a solemn occasion into a circus. The process and the Court itself are degraded.

While several factors are responsible, a correlation between the presence of cameras in the hearing room—together with the growth of media platforms—and the escalation of contentious behavior is unmistakable. The cameras became triggers for grandstanding that is only enhanced with politicians' knowledge that specific behaviors will very likely be rewarded with the exposure they seek.

Though a democracy requires transparency, it is suggested here that removing cameras from confirmation hearings would eliminate the instruments that seem to compel politicians' grandstanding. This proposal is meant to punish neither the media nor citizens. Instead, it is meant to help preserve democracy by improving the process. This is not to suggest that Americans should be insulated from frank talk. Tough questions to nominees should be part of the confirmation hearings. Such questions, however, are not dependent on the presence of cameras. Thus, this recommendation should not be construed as a suggestion to prevent coverage of the process by the news media. Rather than shielding the dialogue, whatever form it may take, the intent of this proposal is to encourage it, particularly in a meaningful way. The goal is to elevate the process—and in turn, the Court itself—by depoliticizing it, with the possibility of civility emerging. The prediction here is that absent cameras—regrettably, instruments that trigger rancor in this setting—nominees will be provided better opportunities to take their seats absent the political stench that too often shadows them onto the bench.

Next, though the size of the Supreme Court has remained at nine members since 1869—or is it *because* of that fact?—the issue of Court expansion surfaces periodically.[111] Typically, aside from any direct benefits or liabilities, it is an issue considered largely in isolation. Here, expanding the permanent membership of the Supreme Court is concurrent with another suggestion, part of a two-step process. The Supreme Court is the only federal court where every case is heard by every judge/justice on staff (aside from the rare recusal). That should change. It is proposed here to first expand the Court through legislation. One option considered by the 2021 Presidential Commission on the Supreme Court was to allow an "extra" justice to be nominated during each of the next several four-year presidential terms. The suggestion here is to utilize that recommendation, ultimately bringing the number of Supreme Court justices to thirteen.

The critical second step of this transformation is then for the Court to adopt a new internal procedure where from the pool of thirteen, nine justices are chosen to hear each case. A specific selection process would be implemented, most likely a random rotation not unlike what is typically employed in the federal courts of appeal.

This dual-pronged proposal steers clear of any constitutional challenge under Article III's requirement that there be "one Supreme Court."[112] It is not necessary to create a second Court; all thirteen justices would be members of the one and only Supreme Court. Lastly, for historical purposes, because every case would continue to be subject to nine votes, the ability to compare outcomes over time remains intact. In addition, this could create the possibility of increasing the Court's overall caseload without increasing the workload of any given justice.[113]

The 2021 Presidential Commission reported that some proponents of Court expansion believe that it could help to restore political/ideological (and thus, worldview) balance "that was disrupted by significant norm violations in the confirmation process."[114] While balance is valued here, it should not be the immediate goal, but instead a residual outcome. That is, through a revised nomination procedure that depoliticizes that process and ultimately the Court and its rulings, balance will likely result organically. The problem at hand on the Court is much less that rulings sometimes occur in favor of one political cause or another. That is inevitable. Instead, it is problematic when those rulings regularly appear to be predetermined *because of* the political/ideological inclinations of some justices. Simply stated, by depoliticizing the Court, particularly beginning with nominations and confirmation, the Court's business and rulings will become less political in both perception and reality. Those factors alone will help to bring about a sense of balance.

An additional benefit is pointed by, among others, Jamal Greene. By spreading the burden across members of a larger group, he points out, the focus on individuals decreases. That reverberates to the nomination and confirmation process where the stakes would change. That is, knowing that a particular nominee, even if confirmed, would not hear and decide every case "lowers the political temperature" of that procedure.[115]

Lastly, term limits are recommended here. Lifetime appointments were intended to insulate the justices from politics. Instead, they have become a catalyst of the Court's politicization. "You can think of term limits as a kind of healthy politicization of the court," according to Klein, "one meant to counter the unhealthy politicization of the court."[116]

Term limits should be implemented by staggering them across the Court's membership and set at some determined length; 18-year terms are often mentioned.[117] Several factors are relevant to this issue. First, life tenure is virtually exclusive to the American federal judiciary. The United States is the only major constitutional democracy in the world that has neither a retirement age nor a fixed term limit for its high court justices.[118] Among the world's democracies, at least twenty-seven have term limits for their constitutional courts.[119] Domestically, almost all states also establish fixed terms for high court justices, ranging from six to 15 years. Though some states allow for term renewal, with potential reappointment in others, mandatory retirement applies in most of these systems.[120] Rhode Island is the only state that has neither term limits nor a mandatory retirement age for its supreme court justices.[121] While exclusivity is not necessarily a liability, one has to wonder why all courts aside from U.S. federal courts have concluded that limiting time on the bench is better than not doing so. In evaluating pros and cons of term limits,[122] the advantages win the day overall.

Two additional factors surface within this discussion, one at each end of a justice's tenure on the Court. First, in recent history especially, nominees are often selected according to their relative youth. That is, it is often paramount whether the nominee will be able to remain on the Court and exert influence for decades. Term limits would significantly diminish the importance of this factor, expanding the pool of candidates to those who can serve 13 years, not necessarily 30 or more. Second, term limits would largely eliminate the possibility of "strategic retirements" and, just as importantly, the perception that justices retire for strategic reasons. Reportedly, for example, Justice Anthony Kennedy was persuaded to retire in 2018, in part so that a younger replacement could sustain his legacy.[123]

The recommendations outlined immediately above are based on the conclusions derived from the information presented in the preceding pages. Worldview is ever present. Recognizing its presence and dynamics helps to explain human behavior. Those who possess fixed and fluid worldviews will forever be divided, driving polarization in any group. In many respects, those people live in different worlds. In the judiciary, divergent constitutional approaches are yet additional polarizers that, by definition, drive opposing conclusions and rulings. As demonstrated above, each approach attaches to a corresponding worldview category: fixed-originalism and fluid-living constitutionalism. While probability suggests that groups will consist of people on both sides of these benchmarks, these factors do not ensure group dysfunctionality or other unmanageable problems. The addition of politics and political agendas into an already volatile mix, however, is a lighted match onto an already flammable situation.

As suggested, the solution is straightforward, though not easily accomplished: depoliticization. When politics is not only allowed, but also encouraged, the Court becomes not merely a political institution, but one that loses its way, straying from its purpose. Under a regime of politics, worldview and constitutional approach are magnified, with their various traits forced to the surface. Faustian bargains are made with politicians in robes who, from their nominations onward, are expected to bring about specific results and, in some cases, are happy to fulfill those expectations. The Supreme Court may retain the moniker of "court of last resort," but for growing numbers of people that signifies despair, not hope. The story of twentieth-century American constitutional law was one of bringing people who were previously excluded into the fold. It was always known that the movement had its dissidents. Now it seems that while still a minority of American society, they are a majority on the nation's highest court.

As the fixed worldview originalism dominates the current Court and many of its rulings, too many people are being deprived of rights and opportunities that are integral to the democracy.[124] The dissenters in *Dobbs* warned this will get worse before it gets better: "The Constitution will, today's majority holds, provide no shield, despite its guarantees of liberty and equality for all. And no one should be confident that this majority is done with its work."[125] This concern is intensified given the supermajority's reliance on originalism. "We should be very afraid of where originalism will lead the Court," writes Erwin Chemerinsky, "and afraid for the future of constitutional rights and equality."[126]

In the aftermath of the 2022 Uvalde, Texas, mass shooting, the *New York Times* opined that "as currently structured," one American institution "is fundamentally unresponsive to the needs of its most vulnerable citizens and has been corrupted by powerful interest groups."[127] Though referring to Congress, the editorial easily could have been describing the Supreme Court. An emphasis on the common good is missing from our law today, writes Harvard law professor Adrian Vermeule, an absence that is "keenly felt."[128] Perhaps nowhere was it felt more than in the 2022 *Dobbs* abortion rights ruling. Justice Brett Kavanaugh eschewed a responsibility that many believe to be basic to the Court—protecting individual rights—claiming that "taking sides" on the issue by the *Roe v. Wade* majority was improper then and continues to be inappropriate.[129] Instead, the dissent protested, "When the Court decimates a right women have held for 50 years," it *did* take sides "against women who wish to exercise the right."[130]

Rather than expanding on what has been an American tradition of extending freedom to ever-wider circles of people, decisions like *Dobbs* repudiate and reverse that practice.[131] As a *Washington Post* editorial asserted, by betraying this legacy, the Supreme Court's majority justices "would appear to be not fair-minded jurists but reckless ideologues who are dangerously out of touch and hostile to a core American ethic."[132] We the People need and deserve—and must demand—a Supreme Court that embraces a commitment to the rights and welfare of *all* the people, with justices who realize that Equal Justice Under Law is more than a hollow catchphrase engraved into the building where they work, but that it is also a binding job description.

NOTES

1. See Christian Farias, "Samuel Alito's Roe Message Is Clear: This Supreme Court Is Ready to Burn It All Down," *Vanity Fair*, May 3, 2022, https://www.vanityfair.com /news/2022/05/samuel-alitos-roe-message-is-clear (writing that the *Dobbs* opinion "does everything social conservatives, religious activists, and Republican officials and voters have demanded of a Supreme Court they've worked hard to reshape in their image").

2. See Jonathan Weisman, "Spurred by the Supreme Court, a Nation Divides Along a Red-Blue Axis," *New York Times*, July 2, 2022, https://www.nytimes.com/2022/07/02/us/politics/us-divided-political-party.html ("Pressed by Supreme Court decisions diminishing rights that liberals hold dear and expanding those cherished by conservatives, the United States appears to be drifting apart into separate nations, with diametrically opposed social, environmental and health policies"). See also Robert Barnes, "With Sweep and Speed, Supreme Court Conservatives Ignite a New Era," *Washington Post*, July 2, 2022, https:// www.washingtonpost.com/politics/2022/07/02/supreme-court-conservative-majority ("The avalanche of change achieved by the Supreme Court's conservative majority this term spans the breadth of American life").

3. Adam Liptak, "A Transformative Term at the Most Conservative Supreme Court in Nearly a Century," *New York Times*, July 1, 2022, https://www.nytimes.com/2022/07/01/us/supreme-court-term-roe-guns-epa-decisions .html (utilizing data from the Supreme Court Database, http://scdb.wustl.edu/).

4. Ibid.

5. Mary Ziegler, "Roe's Death Will Change American Democracy," *New York Times*, June 24, 2022, https://www.nytimes.com/2022/06/24/opinion/roe-v-wade -dobbs-democracy.html. See also Jamelle Bouie, "Let's Bring the Supreme Court Back Down to Earth," *New York Times*, February 1, 2022, https://www.nytimes.com /2022/02/01/opinion/biden-breyer-supreme-court.html ("The Supreme Court does not exist outside of ordinary politics").

6. See, for example, Richard Posner, "The Supreme Court, 2004 Term—Foreword: A Political Court," *Harvard Law Review* 119 (November 2005): 40 (concluding the Supreme Court, "when it is deciding constitutional cases, is political in the sense of having and exercising discretionary power as capacious as a legislature's"). See also Robert A. Dahl, "Decision-Making in a Democracy: The Supreme Court as a National Policy-Maker," *Emory Law Journal* 50 (2001): 565 (concluding that the Court is compelled to be a policymaking political institution in part because of the vagueness on the Constitution, but also noting that Justices' personal policy preference can also lead the Court into the political realm).

7. Gerald N. Rosenberg, "The Road Taken: Robert A. Dahl's Decision-Making in a Democracy: The Supreme Court as a National Policy-Maker," *Emory Law Journal* 50 (Spring 2001): 619 ("To consider the Supreme Court of the United States strictly as a legal institution is to underestimate its significance in the American political system").

8. To be clear, the charge here of being political is confined to the Court as an institution and justices' work within it. But see Danny Hakim and Jo Becker, "The Long Crusade of Clarence and Ginni Thomas," *New York Times Magazine*, February 22, 2022, https://www.nytimes.com/2022/02/22/magazine/clarence-thomas-ginni -thomas.html:

> Because Supreme Court justices do not want to be perceived as partisan, they tend to avoid political events and entanglements, and their spouses often keep low profiles. But the Thomases have defied such norms. Since the founding of the nation, no spouse of a sitting Supreme Court justice has been as overt a political activist as Ginni Thomas . . . For the three decades he has sat on the Supreme Court, they have worked in tandem from the bench and the political trenches to take aim at targets like *Roe v. Wade* and affirmative action.

9. See, for example, Margaret Talbot, "Amy Coney Barrett's Long Game," *New Yorker*, February 7, 2022, https://www.newyorker.com/magazine/2022/02/14/amy -coney-barretts-long-game/amp. See also "The Republican Party's Supreme Court," *New York Times*, October 26, 2020, https://www.nytimes.com/2020/10/26/opinion/ amy-coney-barrett-supreme-court.html (writing that Justice Barrett's confirmation "represent[s] the culmination of a four-decade crusade by conservatives to fill the federal courts with reliably Republican judges who will serve for decades as a barricade against an ever more progressive nation"); Hakim and Becker, "The Long Crusade of Clarence and Ginni Thomas" (reporting that Justice Thomas tells his clerks their work is "not about winning and losing at the court. It is about the entire country and the idea of this country"); Coral Davenport, "Republican Drive to Tilt Courts Against Climate Action Reaches a Crucial Moment," *New York Times*, June 19, 2022, https: //www.nytimes.com/2022/06/19/climate/supreme-court-climate-epa.html (reporting that "a coordinated, multiyear strategy by Republican attorneys general and conservative allies" resulted in the Court hearing cases designed to limit enforcement of environmental regulations).

10. See Geoffrey R. Stone and David A. Strauss, *Democracy and Equality: The Enduring Constitutional Vision of the Warren Court* (New York: Oxford University

Press, 2020), 2 (writing of the Warren Court, "conservative critics attack it—now as they did then—as 'lawless'").

11. This is not to suggest that the U.S. Supreme Court's rulings should rubber stamp public opinion. Its strength and value have always rested on its independence to decide cases consistent with the Constitution even when inconsistent with public views. See, for example, Michael Vitiello, "How Imperial Is the Supreme Court? An Analysis of Supreme Court Abortion Doctrine and Popular Will," *University of San Francisco Law Review* 34 (Fall 1999): 89:

Comparing public opinion with Supreme Court decisions tells only part of the story. When the Court's critics attack the Court as elitist or as antimajoritarian, they compare the Court with the ideology of the political branches of government. However, if one compares the Court's holding in a case like Roe with positions taken by the "representative" branches of government, the Court's performance looks closer to public opinion than does that of many elected officials.

12. Stephen I. Vladeck, "Roberts Has Lost Control of the Supreme Court," *New York Times*, April 13, 2022, https://www.nytimes.com/2022/04/13/opinion/john-roberts-supreme-court.html.

13. *Planned Parenthood v. Casey*, 505 U.S. 833, 866 (1992) (O'Connor, Kennedy, and Souter, JJ.).

14. See, for example, Mark Joseph Stern, "Republicans Don't Need to Win Elections. They Already Won the Supreme Court," *Slate*, January 24, 2022, https://slate.com/news-and-politics/2022/01/supreme-court-affirmative-action-republican-policy.amp (writing that an expected ruling on affirmative action "will reverse 44 years of precedent, affect thousands of schools across the country, and upend the admissions process for millions of students"). See also Elizabeth Warren, "Expand the Court," *Boston Globe*, December 15, 2021, https://www.bostonglobe.com/2021/12/15/opinion/expand-supreme-court/ ("I believe in an independent judiciary. I also believe in a judiciary that upholds the rule of law—not one that ignores it to promote a deeply unpopular and partisan agenda at odds with the Constitution and the settled rights of our citizens").

15. See Steven Levitsky and Daniel Ziblatt, *How Democracies Die* (New York: Broadway Books, 2018), 146 ("As our soft guardrails have weakened, we have grown increasingly vulnerable to antidemocratic leaders").

16. See Jamelle Bouie, "It's Not Looking Too Good for Government of the People, by the People and for the People," *New York Times*, May 27, 2022, https://www.nytimes.com/2022/05/27/opinion/uvalde-senate-gun-control.html (writing of the "capture of America's political institutions by an unrepresentative minority whose outright refusal to compromise is pushing the entire system to a breaking point").

17. See, for example, Jeffrey M. Jones, "Approval of U.S. Supreme Court Down to 40%, a New Low," Gallup.com, September 23, 2021, https://news.gallup.com/poll/354908/approval-supreme-court-down-new-low.aspx.

18. See, for example, Ariana de Vogue, "Supreme Court Justices Insist All Is Well, But Their Caustic Written Opinions Say Otherwise," CNN, February 10, 2022, https://www.cnn.com/2022/02/10/politics/supreme-court-justices-opinions/index.html ("what the country is taking note of is what the justices are actually saying on paper,

where the veneer of civility has worn thin as the liberals' criticism of conservative opinions—and the conservatives' responses—have extended beyond usual disagreements centered on judicial ideology").

19. Transcript of Oral Argument, 15:3–6, *Dobbs v. Jackson Women's Health Organization* (No. 19–1392), December 1, 2021 (decided June 24, 2022) ("Will this institution survive the stench that this creates in the public perception that the Constitution and its reading are just political acts?").

20. See Benjamin Franklin, quoted in Eric Metaxas, *If You Can Keep It: The Forgotten Promise of American Liberty* (New York: Penguin Books, 2017), 9. (Franklin responded to a question about whether the Founders had created a monarchy or a republic: "A republic, madam, if you can keep it").

21. See, for example, Jay Willis, "A Brief Guide to Supreme Court Confirmation Hearings, the Silliest Ritual In Washington," *Balls and Strikes*, March 15, 2022, https://ballsandstrikes.org/nominations/supreme-court-confirmation-hearings-brief-guide ("In practice, hearings typically consist of senators droning on about a constellation of topics that may or may not have anything to do with the nominee, the job, or even the law itself").

22. See, for example, Stephen L. Carter, *The Confirmation Mess: Cleaning Up the Federal Appointments Process* (New York: Basic Books, 1994). See also John S. Dzienkowski, "The Contributions of Louis Brandeis to the Law of Lawyering," *Touro Law Review* 33 (2017): 192 (writing of the 1916 Brandies hearings—the first time that confirmation hearings were made public: "Without doubt, the charges leveled against Louis Brandeis in the confirmation hearings were motivated by political hatred, antisemitism, and economic protectionism").

23. See, for example, Nina Totenberg, "Robert Bork's Supreme Court Nomination 'Changed Everything, Maybe Forever,'" NPR, December 19, 2012, https://www.npr.org/sections/itsallpolitics/2012/12/19/167645600/robert-borks-supreme-court-nomination-changed-everything-maybe-forever (writing about the 1987 nomination and confirmation hearing of Robert Bork, considered the beginning of the process being intensely politically influenced). See also Sarah Pruitt, "How Robert Bork's Failed Nomination Led To a Changed Supreme Court," History.com, September 21, 2018, https://www.history.com/news/robert-bork-ronald-reagan-supreme-court-nominations ("the outcome would have far-reaching consequences for the Court and the country").

24. Adam Liptak, "Confirmation Hearings, Once Focused on Law, Are Now Mired in Politics," *New York Times*, March 23, 2022, https://www.nytimes.com/2022/03/23/us/politics/ketanji-brown-jackson-confirmation-hearing.html (referring to the 1987 confirmation of Robert Bork: "His confirmation battle was a turning point in a process that has become increasingly politicized").

25. See, for example, Glenn Thrush, "As Republicans Prepare to Grill Jackson, They Are Re-Litigating Kavanaugh's Confirmation Battle," *New York Times*, March 21, 2022, https://www.nytimes.com/2022/03/21/us/politics/ketanji-brown-jackson-kavanaugh.html. See also Li Zhou, "Republicans Made Ketanji Brown Jackson's Confirmation Hearing About Brett Kavanaugh," *Vox*, March 21, 2022, https://www.vox.com/22990018/ketanji-brown-jackson-confirmation-hearing-brett-kavanaugh.

26. See, for example, Blake Hounshell and Leah Askarinam, "For These Republicans, Supreme Court Hearings Are an Irresistible Opportunity," *New York Times*, March 21, 2022, https://www.nytimes.com/2022/03/21/us/politics/republicans-judge-ketanji-brown-jackson.html ("For the supremely ambitious, a Supreme Court nomination battle is an irresistible opportunity. It's a chance to build email lists, rustle up campaign cash and impress base voters"). See also Michelle Cottle, "Oh, Josh & Marsha & Ted & Lindsey . . . Sorry, Judge Jackson," *New York Times*, April 7, 2022, https://www.nytimes.com/2022/04/07/opinion/jackson-cruz-scotus.html (the confirmations "double as prime opportunities for members of the Senate Judiciary Committee—especially those harboring presidential aspirations—to strut their stuff for a larger-than-usual audience . . . [and] to turn the proceedings into a circus. So much performative outrage. So little interest in reality").

27. Jamelle Bouie, "Let's Bring the Supreme Court Back Down to Earth," *New York Times*, February 1, 2022, https://www.nytimes.com/2022/02/01/opinion/biden-breyer-supreme-court.html.

28. Madeleine Carlisle, "On Day Two of Hearings, Republicans Accuse Ketanji Brown Jackson of Being Weak on Crime," *Time*, March 22, 2022, https://time.com/6159672/ketanji-brown-jackson-hearings-day-two/ (quoting Professor Murray: "It seems more like the Republicans are laying soundbite breadcrumbs that they will reprise in the 2022 midterm elections and the 2024 general elections to brand the Democrats and the Biden Administration as soft on crime—the kind of soundbites that play well with suburban swing voters, as well as the GOP base"). See also Kristyn Burtt, "Ketanji Brown Jackson Faced Some Astonishingly Stupid Questions About Racism from Ted Cruz," *Yahoo*, March 23, 2022, https://finance.yahoo.com/news/ketanji-brown-jackson-faced-astonishingly-174346125.html ("Judge Ketanji Brown Jackson's second day of questioning from the Senate Judiciary Committee was filled with political theater from several Republicans").

29. See Nancy Pelosi and Chuck Schumer, "Pelosi, Schumer Joint Statement on Reported Draft Supreme Court Decision to Overturn Roe v. Wade," Office of the Speaker of the House, May 2, 2022, https://www.speaker.gov/newsroom/5222-2 ("Several of these conservative Justices, who are in no way accountable to the American people, have lied to the U.S. Senate, ripped up the Constitution and defiled both precedent and the Supreme Court's reputation").

30. Elena Kagan, "Confirmation Messes, Old and New," review of *The Confirmation Mess*, by Stephen L. Carter, *University of Chicago Law Review* 62 (Spring 1995): 941.

31. See, for example, Alison Durkee, "Did Supreme Court Justices Lie by Claiming They Wouldn't Overturn *Roe v. Wade*? Here's What They Actually Said," *Forbes*, June 28, 2022, https://www.forbes.com/sites/alisondurkee/2022/06/28/did-supreme-court-justices-lie-by-claiming-they-wouldnt-overturn-roe-v-wade-heres-what-they-actually-said/?sh=34cccebf5420.

32. Neil Gorsuch, "Justice White and Judicial Excellence," UPI, May 4, 2002, https://www.upi.com/Top_News/2002/05/04/Justice-White-and-judicial-excellence/72651020510343/.

33. Ibid.

34. "Inside the Supreme Court," C-SPAN, February 3, 2016, https://www.c-span.org/video/?404131-1/discussion-chief-justice-john-roberts.

35. Barbara Sprunt, "Judge Ketanji Brown Jackson Confirmation Hearings: What Happened Tuesday," NPR, March 22, 2022, https://www.npr.org/2022/03/22/1087967982/judge-ketanji-brown-jackson-confirmation-hearings-what-happened-on-tuesday.

36. See Erwin Chemerinsky and Jeffrey Abramson, "What Do We Teach Law Students When We Have No Faith in the Supreme Court?" *Los Angeles Times*, January 16, 2022, https://www.latimes.com/opinion/story/2022-01-16/supreme-court-conservatives-ideology-precedent-law-schools ("the entrenched partisan Senate confirmation process now guarantees that a Supreme Court nominee will be chosen to carry out political and ideological aims").

37. Janet Hook and Beth Reinhard, "Donald Trump Reaches Out to Evangelicals, Promising Antiabortion Judicial Nominees," *Wall Street Journal*, June 10, 2016, https://www.wsj.com/articles/donald-trump-reaches-out-to-evangelicals-promising-antiabortion-judicial-nominees-1465588284.

38. See Katherine Stewart, "Eighty-One Percent of White Evangelicals Voted for Donald Trump. Why?" *Nation*, November 17, 2016, https://www.thenation.com/article/archive/eighty-one-percent-of-white-evangelicals-voted-for-donald-trump-why/ (Trump "did not simply check the box opposing abortion, as Republican politicians have traditionally done. He backed up his newfound anti-abortion conviction with a promise to flip the Supreme Court . . . [O]ne out of every four Trump voters voted with the Supreme Court in mind"). See also Dan Mangan, "Trump: I'll Appoint Supreme Court Justices to Overturn Roe v. Wade Abortion Case," CNBC, October 19, 2016, https://www.cnbc.com/2016/10/19/trump-ill-appoint-supreme-court-justices-to-overturn-roe-v-wade-abortion-case.html.

39. Ian Millhiser, "Why Democrats Can't Get a Fair Shake in the Supreme Court, In One Chart," *Vox*, February 14, 2022, https://www.vox.com/2022/2/14/22925457/supreme-court-senate-confirmation-ketanji-brown-jackson-leondra-kruger-michelle-childs.

40. See Jackie Calmes, *Dissent: The Radicalization of the Republican Party and Its Capture of the Court* (New York: Twelve, 2021), x (writing "of three arch-conservatives that Republicans forced onto the Supreme Court. In the process, it was roiled by the hyper-partisanship plaguing the U.S. government more broadly. The dynamic on the court shifted after Kavanaugh's arrival and then again after Amy Coney Barrett's").

41. Millhiser, "Why Democrats Can't Get a Fair Shake in the Supreme Court, In One Chart." See also Jesse Wegman, "Ginni and Clarence Thomas Have Done Enough Damage," *New York Times*, March 25, 2022, https://www.nytimes.com/2022/03/25/opinion/ginni-clarence-thomas-trump.html (writing of the " the crippling assaults on the court that Mitch McConnell and his Senate Republicans have carried out over the past six years in order to secure a right-wing supermajority that often resembles a judicial policy arm of the Republican Party").

42. "Ketanji Brown Jackson Won't Be Able to Change a Radical Court. Yet," *New York Times*, February 27, 2022, SR8 (describing the current Court, "whose

conservative supermajority was manufactured over the past several years in a series of power grabs by Senator Mitch McConnell and his Republican caucus").

43. Robin Bradley Kar and Jason Mazzone, "The Garland Affair: What History and the Constitution Really Say About President Obama's Powers to Appoint a Replacement for Justice Scalia," *New York University Law Review Online* 91 (May 2016): 60:

> There have been 103 prior cases in which—like the case of President Obama's nomination of Judge Garland—an elected President has faced an actual vacancy on the Supreme Court and began an appointment process prior to the election of a successor. In all 103 cases, the President was able to both nominate and appoint a replacement Justice, by and with the advice and consent of the Senate. This is true even of all eight such cases where the nomination process began during an election year.

44. Ron Elving, "What Happened With Merrick Garland In 2016 And Why It Matters Now," NPR, June 29, 2018, https://www.npr.org/2018/06/29/624467256/what-happened-with-merrick-garland-in-2016-and-why-it-matters-now.

45. Ibid. (quoting Mitch McConnell).

46. See *Bostock v. Clayton Cty.*, 140 S. Ct. 1731 (2020) (Gorsuch adhering to a textualist/originalist approach despite it resulting in a proprogressive outcome that Title VII protects employees against discrimination when they are gay or transgender).

47. See Carl Hulse, "How Mitch McConnell Delivered Justice Amy Coney Barrett's Rapid Confirmation," *New York Times*, October 27, 2020, https://www.nytimes.com/2020/10/27/us/mcconnell-barrett-confirmation.html ("Ignoring cries of blatant hypocrisy, the Senate leader pushed through pre-election approval, capping off his reshaping of the judiciary").

48. See Linda Greenhouse, *Justice on the Brink: The Death of Ruth Bader Ginsburg, the Rise of Amy Coney Barrett, and Twelve Months That Transformed the Supreme Court* (New York: Random House, 2021), xv (describing a phone call by McConnell shortly after Ginsburg's death in which he told Donald Trump, "You've gotta nominate Amy Coney Barrett").

49. See Hulse, "How Mitch McConnell Delivered Justice Amy Coney Barrett's Rapid Confirmation."

50. Ian Millhiser, "Why Democrats Can't Get a Fair Shake in the Supreme Court, In One Chart."

51. Adam Cohen, "Justice Breyer's Legacy-Defining Decision," *Atlantic*, June 12, 2021, https://www.theatlantic.com/ideas/archive/2021/06/stephen-breyer-legacy-retirement/619168/. See also Adam Serwer, "The Lie About the Supreme Court Everyone Pretends to Believe," *Atlantic*, September 28, 2021, https://www.theatlantic.com/ideas/archive/2021/09/lie-about-supreme-court-everyone-pretends-believe/620198/:

> I take exception to . . . the demand from judges and justices that the public acquiesce to their self-delusion that they are wise sages who hold themselves above the vulgarities of partisan politics, even as they deliver sweeping victories to a conservative movement and Republican Party that have worked for half a century to achieve those victories.

See also David Orentlicher, "Politics and the Supreme Court: The Need for Ideological Balance," *University of Pittsburgh Law Review* 79 (Spring 2018): 413 (noting "of course, a Justice's political philosophy does matter. Otherwise, Republican Senators would have considered Merrick Garland's nomination to the Supreme Court in 2016, and other nominations also would not fail because of partisan opposition") (footnotes omitted).

52. See Calmes, *Dissent*, 30–31 (writing that all six conservative members of the Court as of 2021 were members of the influential Federalist Society, and all but Barrett had served in Republican administrations).

53. See Talbot, "Amy Coney Barrett's Long Game" (writing of Justice Barrett, "[H]er background and her demeanor suggested to social conservatives that, if placed on the Court, she would deliver what they wanted, expanding gun rights and religious liberties, and dumping Roe").

54. Millhiser, "Why Democrats Can't Get a Fair Shake in the Supreme Court, In One Chart." See also "The Republican Party's Supreme Court":

> [T]oday's conservative majority is among the most activist in the court's history, striking down long-established precedents and concocting new judicial theories on the fly, virtually all of which align with Republican policy preferences . . . [T]hese three Supreme Court choices were part of the project to turn the courts from a counter-majoritarian shield that protects the rights of minorities to an antidemocratic sword to wield against popular progressive legislation.

55. Devin Dwyer, "Justice Sotomayor Sees 'Unprecedented' Threat to Supreme Court in Confirmation Battles," ABC News, February 10, 2022, https://abcnews.go.com/Politics/justice-sotomayor-sees-unprecedented-threat-scotus-confirmation-battles/story?id=82798225.

56. See, for example, Dylan Matthews and Byrd Pinkerton, "The Incredible Influence of the Federalist Society, Explained," *Vox,* June 3 2019, https://www.vox.com/future-perfect/2019/6/3/18632438/federalist-society-leonard-leo-brett-kavanaugh:

> The most visible impact of Federalist Society has had on American life is through appointments to the Supreme Court. Every administration has a network that they turn to when they're looking to identify potential judicial candidates. What's happened, though, is that on the right, the Federalist Society has a monopoly on that process.

See also Laurence Baum and Neal Devins, "Federalist Court: How the Federalist Society Became the De Facto Selector of Republican Supreme Court Justices," *Slate*, January 31, 2017, https://slate.com/news-and-politics/2017/01/how-the-federalist-society-became-the-de-facto-selector-of-republican-supreme-court-justices.html. See also Sheldon Whitehouse, "Sen. Whitehouse: Three New Supreme Court Justices Being Told What to Do by Donor Front Groups," interview by Joy Reid, *The Reidout,* MSNBC, March 23, 2022, audio 2:05, https://www.msnbc.com/the-reidout/watch/sen-whitehouse-speaks-about-dark-money-at-ketanji-brown-jackson-s-supreme-court-hearing-136040005543 (stating that "dark money" funneled through organizations like the Federalist Society controls not only the nomination of some Supreme Court justices, but also influences their behavior on the Court once confirmed).

57. Dwyer, "Justice Sotomayor Sees 'Unprecedented' Threat to Supreme Court in Confirmation Battles."

58. Presidential Commission on the Supreme Court of the United States, December 7, 2021, 24, https://www.whitehouse.gov/wp-content/uploads/2021/12/SCOTUS-Report-Final-12.8.21-1.pdf.

59. Ibid. (emphasis added). See also "Confirmation Hearing on the Nomination of John G. Roberts, Jr. to Be Chief Justice of the United States," Hearings before the Committee on the Judiciary, United States Senate, 109th Congress, September 12–15, 2005, 56, https://www.judiciary.senate.gov/imo/media/doc/GPO-CHRG-ROBERTS.pdf (Roberts: "I will remember that it's my job to call balls and strikes, and not to pitch or bat").

60. See Sahil Kapur and Frank Thorp V, "Is the Supreme Court Confirmation Process Irreparably Broken? Some Senators Say Yes," NBC News, April 2, 2022, https://www.nbcnews.com/politics/supreme-court/supreme-court-confirmation-process-irreparably-broken-senators-say-yes-rcna22608 ("Many [Republican Senators] insist that any nominee embrace 'originalism,' a framework of narrow constitutional interpretation popular on the right").

61. Hakim and Becker, "The Long Crusade of Clarence and Ginni Thomas." See also "Ketanji Brown Jackson Won't Be Able to Change a Radical Court. Yet," *New York Times*, February 27, 2022, SR8 ("the current court . . . is now the most right-wing it has been in a century, even as the country as a whole has moved left").

62. See Kapur and Thorp, "Is the Supreme Court Confirmation Process Irreparably Broken?" (describing GOP efforts "to engineer the most conservative Supreme Court in a century—a 6–3 majority poised to reshape U.S. law").

63. Dwyer, "Justice Sotomayor Sees 'Unprecedented' Threat to Supreme Court in Confirmation Battles."

64. Presidential Commission, 22. See also Kapur and Thorp, "Is the Supreme Court Confirmation Process Irreparably Broken?" (writing of the "ongoing disintegration of the Supreme Court confirmation process, which some senators fear is irreparably broken").

65. Carl Hulse, "McConnell Suggests He Would Block a Biden Nominee for the Supreme Court in 2024," *New York Times*, June 14, 2021, https://www.nytimes.com/2021/06/14/us/politics/mcconnell-biden-supreme-court.html.

66. Presidential Commission, 16.

67. Ibid., 77. See also Kapur and Thorp, "Is the Supreme Court Confirmation Process Irreparably Broken?" ("GOP [confirmation hearing] tactics reveal a party that remains hungry for confrontation").

68. Vicki C. Jackson, "Submission to the Presidential Commission on the Supreme Court of the United States, July 16, 2021," 22, https://www.whitehouse.gov/wp-content/uploads/2021/07/Jackson-Testimony.pdf.

69. Susan Collins, "Senator Collins' Statement on Judge Jackson's Nomination to the U.S. Supreme Court," March 30, 2022, https://www.collins.senate.gov/newsroom/senator-collins-statement-on-judge-jacksons-nomination-to-the-us-supreme-court.

70. Ibid. See also Ruth Marcus, "The Supreme Court Is Broken. So Is the System That Confirms Its Justices," *Washington Post*, April 8, 2022, https://www.washingtonpost.com/opinions/2022/04/08/supreme-court-broken-jackson-kagan-bork:

> The result is a fiercely partisan process that demeans the Senate and politicizes the court, rendering it a creature of political will and power . . . Judicial philosophy is now aligned with political party as never before in the court's history. So it is no surprise to witness the same phenomenon—the raw exercise of power overtaking normal processes—unfolding on the court itself.

71. Kapur and Thorp, "Is the Supreme Court Confirmation Process Irreparably Broken?"
72. See Jamelle Bouie, "You May Not Find Many Friends on This Power-Hungry Supreme Court," *New York Times*, April 8, 2022, https://www.nytimes.com/2022/04/08/opinion/ketanji-brown-jackson-supreme-court.html.
73. See Adrian Vermeule, "Supreme Court Justices Have Forgotten What the Law Is For," *New York Times*, February 3, 2022, https://www.nytimes.com/2022/02/03/opinion/us-supreme-court-nomonation.html:

> The great promise of our legal system as understood by many modern theorists—that law can create a framework to reconcile plural interests in a diverse society—has manifestly failed. Instead the law has become ever more politically contested and bitterly divisive; the tolerance celebrated by the proponents of liberalism appears to be more science fiction than fact. Something has gone badly wrong: It is unclear . . . what the point of the law is, what higher ends it should strive to attain.

74. James Madison, "The Federalist No. 10," in *The Federalist Papers*, ed. Clinton Rossiter (New York: Penguin Books, 1961), 79. See also Cass R. Sunstein, "Interest Groups in American Public Law," *Stanford Law Review* 38 (November 1985): 40 ("Madison viewed the recent history as sufficient evidence that sound governance could not rely on traditional conceptions of civic virtue and public education to guard against factional tyranny. Such devices would be unable to overcome the natural self-interest of men and women, even in their capacity as political actors").
75. George Washington, "Farewell Address," September 19, 1796, Senate Document No. 106–21, 16, https://www.govinfo.gov/content/pkg/GPO-CDOC-106sdoc21/pdf/GPO-CDOC-106sdoc21.pdf.
76. Ibid.
77. See Alexis de Tocqueville, *Democracy in America*, trans. Harvey C. Mansfield and Delba Winthrop (Chicago: University of Chicago Press, 2000), 241 ("what is most repugnant to me in America . . . is the lack of a guarantee against tyranny").
78. John Stuart Mill, *On Liberty and Other Writings*, ed. Stefan Collini (Cambridge: Cambridge University Press, 1989), 8 (1859). See also Ibid., 20 ("If all mankind minus one were of one opinion, and only one person were of the contrary opinion, mankind would be no more justified in silencing that one person, than he, if he had the power, would be justified in silencing mankind").

79. James Madison, "The Federalist No. 51," in *The Federalist Papers*, ed. Clinton Rossiter (New York: Penguin Books, 1961), 322.

80. See Daniel Lambright, "Man, Morality, and the United States Constitution," *University of Pennsylvania Journal of Constitutional Law* 17 (May 2015): 1501 (analyzing Madison's statements about men, angels, and government).

81. Madison, "The Federalist No. 10," 80. See also Jonathan Haidt, "After Babel: How Social Media Dissolved the Mortar of Society and Made America Stupid," *Atlantic*, May 2022, 58:

> The Framers of the Constitution were excellent social psychologists . . . The key to designing a sustainable republic, therefore, was to build in mechanisms to slow things down, cool passions, require compromise, and give leaders some insulation from the mania of the moment while still holding them accountable to the people periodically, on Election Day.

82. See Madison, "The Federalist No. 10," 79 (observing that people are so susceptible to factionalism that "the most frivolous and fanciful distinctions have been sufficient to kindle their unfriendly passions and excite their most violent conflicts").

83. Samuel R. Olken, "Justice George Sutherland and Economic Liberty: Constitutional Conservatism and the Problem of Factions," *William and Mary Bill of Rights Journal* 6 (Winter 1997): 13.

84. Colleen A. Sheehan, "The Measure and Elegance of Freedom: James Madison and the Bill of Rights," *Georgetown Journal of Law and Public Policy* 15 (Summer 2017): 519 ("Once a majority faction is actuated and united, Madison warned, there is no court of higher appeal in popular government").

85. Charles Evans Hughes, *The Supreme Court of the United States* (New York: Columbia University Press, 1928), 68 (1928) ("A dissent in a Court of last resort is an appeal . . . to the intelligence of a future day, when a later decision may possibly correct the error into which the dissenting judge believes the court to have been betrayed").

86. Robert Tracy McKenzie, *We the Fallen People: The Founders and the Future of American Democracy* (Westmont, IL: IVP Academic, 2021), xx.

87. David Brooks, "The Dark Century," *New York Times*, February 17, 2022, https://nytimes.com/2022/02/17/opinion/liberalism-democracy-russia-ukraine.amp.html.

88. Alexander Hamilton, "The Federalist No. 78," in *The Federalist Papers*, ed. Clinton Rossiter (New York: Penguin Books, 1961), 466.

89. Ibid., 465.

90. Ibid., 467 ("the courts were designed to be an intermediate body between the people and the legislature" and "keep the latter within the limits assigned to their authority").

91. Linda Greenhouse, "What Kind of Story Will Ketanji Brown Jackson Tell Her Fellow Justices?" *New York Times*, March 4, 2022, https://www.nytimes.com/2022/03/04/opinion/supreme-court-biden-jackson.html.

92. See Eric Holder, "It's Time to Reform the Supreme Court," National Democratic Redistricting Committee, June 24, 2022, https://democraticredistricting.com/eric-holder-its-time-to-reform-the-supreme-court/ ("The Supreme Court must be

reformed in order to ensure that the Court serves the interests of the people instead of the interests of an extreme, minority faction").

93. Noah Feldman, "Ending *Roe* is Institutional Suicide for the Supreme Court," *Baltimore Sun*, June 26, 2022, https://www.baltimoresun.com/opinion/op-ed/bs-ed -op-0626-ending-roe-institutional-suicide-20220626-55anw5pgszb77oeutqa264zkiu -story.html (calling *Dobbs* "a catastrophe for all Americans—and for people all over the world who have built their own modern constitutional courts on the U.S. model").

94. Ezra Klein, "What a Reckoning at the Supreme Court Could Look Like," *New York Times*, July 10, 2022, https://www.nytimes.com/2022/07/10/opinion/supreme -court-biden-reform.html.

95. Ibid.

96. See, for example, *Dobbs v. Jackson Women's Health Organization,* 142 S. Ct. 2228 (2022); *New York State Rifle & Pistol Association, Inc. v. Bruen*, 142 S. Ct. 2111 (2022); *Kennedy v. Bremerton School District*, 142 S. Ct. 2407 (2022); *Carson v. Makin*, 142 S. Ct. 1987 (2022).

97. See, for example, Alex Badas, "Policy Disagreement and Judicial Legitimacy: Evidence from the 1937 Court-Packing Plan," *Journal of Legal Studies* 48 (June 2019): 393 (writing of FDR's politically motivated plan to enlarge the Court's membership, "the assumption was that Roosevelt and New Deal supporters would be able to achieve their desired policy outcomes by placing new justices on the Court who would vote in favor of New Deal policies. This is because justices tend to support the policies of the president who appointed them") (internal citation omitted).

98. U.S. Const., art II.

99. See Paul Kane, "Graham: Judicial Confirmation Process Could Get Even More Toxic," *Washington Post*, March 26, 2022, https://www.washingtonpost.com/politics /2022/03/26/lindsey-graham-supreme-court ("[S]enior Republicans and Democrats agree with Graham that a judicial confirmation process that is already painfully partisan . . . could turn even more toxic").

100. See Bouie, "Let's Bring the Supreme Court Back Down to Earth."

101. See, for example, David M. O'Brien, "Judicial Roulette: Report of the Twentieth Century Fund Task Force on Judicial Selection," Twentieth Century Task Fund (New York: Priority Press Publications, 1988): 10 (suggesting that television cameras be banned from the hearings); Stephen L. Carter, "The Confirmation Mess, Revisited," 84 *Northwestern University Law Review* 84 (1990): 962–75; Robert Post and Reva Siegel, "Questioning Justice: Law and Politics in Judicial Confirmation Hearings," *Yale Law Journal Pocket Part* 115 (January 2006): 38–51; Lori A. Ringhand, "In Defense of Ideology: A Principled Approach to the Supreme Court Confirmation Process," *William and Mary Bill of Rights Journal* 18 (October 2009): 131–71.

102. "Inside the Supreme Court," C-SPAN, February 3, 2016, https://www.c-span .org/video/?404131-1/discussion-chief-justice-john-roberts.

103. See, for example, Charles W. "Rocky" Rhodes, "Navigating the Path of the Supreme Court Appointment," *Florida State University Law Review* 38 (Spring 2011): 565. See also Paul M. Collins Jr. and Lori A. Ringhand, "The Institutionalization of Supreme Court Confirmation Hearings," *Law and Social Inquiry* 41 (Winter 2016): 129 ("gavel-to-gavel television coverage of the hearings beginning in 1981

enhanced the ability of senators to use the hearings to convey information to their constituents").

104. Joel Mathis, "Ted Cruz Checked His Twitter Mentions and a Little Bit of Our Democracy Died," *Yahoo*, March 24, 2022, https://www.yahoo.com/lifestyle/ted-cruz -checked-twitter-mentions-154452447.html.

105. Paul E. Vaglica, "Step Aside, Mr. Senator: A Request for Members of the Senate Judiciary Committee to Give Up Their Mics," *Indiana Law Journal* 87 (Fall 2012): 1823 ("this problem will be alleviated (if not eliminated) by banning the existence of cameras from the room entirely"). See also Ibid. at 1823–24 (quoting Elena Kagan, "Confirmation Messes, Old and New," review of *The Confirmation Mess*, by Stephen L. Carter, *University of Chicago Law Review* 62 (Spring 1995): 919–42:

> [I]t is not surprising that the current confirmation process provides an ample opportunity for senators to speak to their constituents via national television. Members of the Senate Judiciary Committee have taken full advantage of the opportunity. Throughout confirmation hearings, senators make multiple statements that they hope will resonate with their constituents at the expense of scrutinizing Supreme Court nominees to the highest degree . . . Without reform, confirmation hearings of Supreme Court justices will continue to be "vapid and hollow" and "reinforce cynicism that citizens often glean from the government."

106. See, for example, Tom Cotton, "Sen. Cotton Joins the Ingraham Angle," interview by Laura Ingraham, *The Ingraham Angle*, Fox News Channel, March 23, 2022, audio:34, https://www.cotton.senate.gov/news/videos/watch/march-23-2022 -senator-cotton-joins-the-ingraham-angle; Ted Cruz, "Sen. Ted Cruz: Ketanji Brown Jackson Didn't Want to Answer Questions About Critical Race Theory," interview by Sean Hannity, *Hannity*, Fox News Channel, March 22, 2022, audio 0:00, https:// www.foxnews.com/transcript/hannity-on-ketanji-brown-jackson-ukraine-war; Lindsay Graham, "Lindsey Graham: Ketanji Brown Jackson Was Top Choice of 'Every Nutjob Liberal Group,'" interview by Jeanine Pirro, *The Ingraham Angle*, Fox News Channel, March 23, 2022, audio 1:05, https://www.foxnews.com/media/ketanji -brown-jackson-lindsey-graham-ingraham-angle-reaction.

107. "Sasse Cites 'Jackassery' in Warning Against Cameras in Supreme Court," *Wall Street Journal*, March 23, 2022, https://www.wsj.com/livecoverage/supreme -court-confirmation-hearings-ketanji-brown-jackson-2022-03-23/card/sasse-cites -jackassery-in-warning-against-cameras-in-supreme-court-sviheOZfF674JOwo1dLc. (Demonstrating political tribalism, Sasse voted against the confirmation of Ketanji Brown Jackson despite his criticism of the process.)

108. Ibid.

109. See, for example, Philip Sedgwick, "The Hawthorne Effect," *British Medical Journal* 344 (2011): 1468; Frank Merrett, "Reflections on the Hawthorne Effect," *Educational Psychology* 26, no. 1 (2006): 143. Stemming from a study in an electric plant, the Hawthorne effect suggests that people alter their behavior, either consciously or unconsciously, when they know they are being observed.

110. See Carter, *The Confirmation* Mess, 194 ("The presence of television cameras probably makes everyone behave worse").

111. See, for example, Warren, "Expand the Court" ("Without reform, the Supreme Court's 6–3 conservative supermajority will continue to threaten basic liberties for decades to come").

112. U.S. Const., art. III ("[T]he judicial Power of the United States, shall be vested in one supreme Court, and in such inferior Courts as the Congress may from time to time ordain and establish").

113. See, for example, "Caseloads: Supreme Court of the United States, Method of Disposition, 1970–2016," Federal Judicial Center, https://www.fjc.gov/history/courts/caseloads-supreme-court-united-states-method-disposition-1970-2016 (showing a consistent decline in the number of cases argued at the Supreme Court since 1970–151—to 2016–71. The most cases argued over the years encompassed in the database utilized here occurred twice in the 1980s, 184. The fewest was in the last term of the database, 2016, 71).

114. Presidential Commission, 76. See also Levitsky and Ziblatt, *How Democracies Die*, 146 (writing that the Merrick Garland nomination incident was "an extraordinary instance of norm breaking").

115. Jamal Greene, "Let's Talk About How Truly Bizarre Our Supreme Court Is," interview by Ezra Klein, *The Ezra Klein Show*, New York Times podcast, February 4, 2022, audio 1:00:45, https://www.nytimes.com/2022/02/04/opinion/ezra-klein-podcast-jamal-greene.amp.html.

116. Klein, "What a Reckoning at the Supreme Court Could Look Like."

117. See, for example, Seung Min Kim and Robert Barnes, "Supreme Court Term Limits Seem to Be Popular—and Appear to Be Going Nowhere," *Washington Post*, December 28, 2021, https://www.washingtonpost.com/nation/2021/12/28/supreme-court-term-limits/.

118. Presidential Commission, 112.

119. Ibid.

120. Ibid.

121. Ibid.

122. See, for example, Ibid., 111–51. See also "Should Supreme Court Justices Have Term Limits? Pro/Con," *Philadelphia Enquirer*, September 24, 2020, https://www.inquirer.com/opinion/commentary/supreme-court-term-limits-lifetime-appointment-ruth-bader-ginsburg-20200924.html.

123. See, for example, Abigail Tracy, "Donald Trump Made Justice Kennedy an Offer He Couldn't Refuse," *Vanity Fair*, June 29, 2018, https://www.vanityfair.com/news/2018/06/donald-trump-justice-anthony-kennedy-retirement ("Behind the scenes, the president worked for months to assure Kennedy his legacy would be in good hands"). See also Julian Borger, "Book Reveals Trump Effort to Persuade Justice Kennedy to Step Aside for Kavanaugh," *Guardian*, February 4, 2020, https://www.theguardian.com/us-news/2020/feb/04/trump-family-anthony-kennedy-brett-kavanaugh-dark-towers.

124. See Levitsky and Ziblatt, *How Democracies Die*, 146 ("The traditions underpinning America's democratic institutions are unraveling, opening up a disconcerting gap between how our political system works and long-standing expectations about how it *ought* to work") (emphasis in original).

125. *Dobbs*, 2319 (2022) (Breyer, Sotomayor, and Kagan, JJ., dissenting). See also Kevin Boyle, "We Are Living in Richard Nixon's America. Escaping It Won't Be Easy," *New York Times*, July 31, 2022, https://www.nytimes.com/2022/07/31/opinion/richard-nixon-america-trump.html ("The court's supermajority [in 2022] handed down the first of what could be at least a decade of rulings eviscerating liberal precedents").

126. Erwin Chemerinsky, *Worse Than Nothing: The Dangerous Fallacy of Originalism* (New Haven: Yale University Press, 2022), 10.

127. "A Heartbroken Nation," *New York Times,* May 29, 2022, SR8.

128. Vermeule, "Supreme Court Justices Have Forgotten What the Law Is For" ("The common good is no abstract idea . . . In the past few decades, Americans have discovered that individuals and families cannot flourish if the whole community is fundamentally unhealthy, torn apart by conflict, lawlessness, poverty, pollution, sickness, and despair").

129. *Dobbs,* 2306 (Kavanaugh, J., concurring). The *Dobbs* dissenters were highly critical of Kavanaugh's rationale—a need to remain neutral, writing that "the Court acts neutrally when it *protects* the right against all comers." Ibid., 2328 (Breyer, Sotomayor, Kagan, JJ., dissenting) (emphasis added).

130. Ibid., 2328.

131. See Noah Feldman, "Ending *Roe* is Institutional Suicide for the Supreme Court" ("When the Supreme Court overturned *Roe v. Wade* and *Casey v. Planned Parenthood*, it repudiated the very idea that America's highest court exists to protect people's fundamental liberties from legislative majorities that would infringe on them").

132. "The Supreme Court Might Never Recover from Overturning Roe v. Wade," *Washington Post,* May 3, 2022, https://www.washingtonpost.com/opinions/2022/05/03/supreme-court-might-never-recover-overturning-roe-v-wade/.

Bibliography

"12 Questions That Would Actually Tell Us Something About Ketanji Brown Jackson." *Politico*, March 22, 2022, https://www.politico.com/news/magazine /2022/03/22/senate-confirmation-questions-ketanji-brown-jackson-00018982.

303 Creative LLC v. Elenis, 142 S. Ct. 1106 (2022), No. 21–476, Petition for a Writ of Certiorari.

Abrams v. United States, 250 U.S. 616 (1919).

Abramson, Jill. "This Justice Is Taking Over the Supreme Court, and He Won't Be Alone." *New York Times*, October 15, 2021, https://www.nytimes.com/2021/10/15 /opinion/clarence-thomas-supreme-court.amp.html.

Ackerman, Bruce. "2006 Oliver Wendell Holmes Lecture: The Living Constitution." *Harvard Law Review* 120 (May 2007): 1737–1812.

Adams, Arlin M., and Charles J. Emmerich. "A Heritage of Religious Liberty." *University of Pennsylvania Law Review* 137 (May 1989): 1559–1671.

Addicott, Jeffrey F. "Reshaping American Jurisprudence in the Trump Era: The Rise of 'Originalist' Judges." *California Western Law Review* 55 (Spring 2019): 341–62.

Alicke, Mark. "Willful Ignorance and Self-Deception." *Psychology Today*, September 10, 2017, https://www.psychologytoday.com/us/blog/why-we-blame/201709/ willful-ignorance-and-self-deception.

Alito, Samuel. "Keynote Address." 2022 Religious Liberty Summit, Rome, July 28, 2022. Audio 5:00–41:34. https://www.youtube.com/watch?v=uci4uni608E&t =826s.

Alter, Alexandra, and Elizabeth A. Harris. "Dr. Seuss Books Are Pulled, and a 'Cancel Culture' Controversy Erupts." *New York Times*, March 4, 2021, https://www -nytimes-com/2021/03/04/books/dr-seuss-books.html.

Altheide, David L. *Terrorism and the Politics of Fear*. Lanham, MD: Rowman & Littlefield, 2006.

"Amy Coney Barrett Senate Confirmation Hearing Day 2 Transcript," October 13, 2020, https://www.rev.com/blog/transcripts/amy-coney-barrett-senate -confirmation-hearing-day-2-transcript.

Anders, David B. "Justices Harlan and Black Revisited: The Emerging Dispute Between Justice O'Connor and Justice Scalia Over Enumerated Fundamental Rights." *Fordham Law Review* 61 (March 1993): 895–933.

Applebaum, Anne, and Peter Pomerantsev. "How To Put Out Democracy's Dumpster Fire." *Atlantic*, April 2021, https://www.theatlantic.com/magazine/archive/2021/04/the-internet-doesnt-have-to-be-awful/618079/.

Ariz. Rev. Stat. Ann. § 16–542 (D).

Ariz. Rev. Stat. Ann. § 16–584 (Cum. Supp. 2020).

Arizona State Legislature v. Arizona Independent Redistricting Commission, 576 U.S. 787 (2015).

Arnold, Craig Anthony. "The Reconstitution of Property: Property as a Web of Interests." *Harvard Environmental Law Review* 26 (2002): 281–364.

Arroyo, Kaiya M. "Originalism and Constitutional Construction: A Shelby County Case Study." 18 *University of Pennsylvania Journal of Constitutional Law Online* (April 2016): 1–27.

Atwood, Margaret. "I Invented Gilead. The Supreme Court Is Making It Real." *Atlantic*, May 13, 2022, https://www.theatlantic.com/ideas/archive/2022/05/supreme-court-roe-handmaids-tale-abortion-margaret-atwood/629833/.

Badas, Alex. "Policy Disagreement and Judicial Legitimacy: Evidence from the 1937 Court-Packing Plan." *Journal of Legal Studies* 48 (June 2019): 377–408.

Baker, Peter. "Battle Over Abortion threatens to Deepen America's Divide." *New York Times,* May 6, 2022, http://www.nytimes.com/2022/05/06/us/politics/abortion-rights-supreme-court-roe-v-wade.html.

Balkin, Jack M. "Constitutional Interpretation and Change in the United States: The Official and the Unofficial. *Jus Politicum*, accessed July 15, 2022, http://juspoliticum.com/article/Constitutional-Interpretation-and-Change-in-the-United-States-The-Official-and-the-Unofficial-1088.html.

———. "Jack Balkin's Constitutional Text and Principle: Nine Perspectives on Living Originalism." *University of Illinois Law Review* (2012): 815–77.

———. *Living Originalism*. Cambridge: Harvard University Press, 2011.

———. "The Roots of the Living Constitution." *Boston University Law Review* 92 (July 2012): 1129–60.

———. "Balkinization." June 27, 2008, http://balkin.blogspot.com/2008/06/this-decision-will-cost-american-lives.html.

Barnes, Robert. "Supreme Court to Hear Case of High School Football Coach Who Lost Job After Praying with Players." *Washington Post*, January 14, 2022, https://www.washingtonpost.com/politics/courts_law/supreme-court-football-coach-joseph-kennedy/2022/01/14/d9a98630-7585-11ec-8b0a-bcfab800c430_story.html.

———. "With Sweep and Speed, Supreme Court Conservatives Ignite a New Era." *Washington Post*, July 2, 2022, https://www.washingtonpost.com/politics/2022/07/02/supreme-court-conservative-majority.

———, Carol D. Leonnig, and Ann E. Marimow. "How the Future of Roe Is Testing Roberts on the Supreme Court." *Washington Post*, May 7, 2022, https://www.washingtonpost.com/politics/2022/05/07/supreme-court-abortion-roe-roberts-alito/.

Barrett, Amy Coney. "Originalism and Stare Decisis." *Notre Dame Law Review* 92 (May 2017): 1921–43.

Bassett, Laura. "Samuel Alito Gloats About Abortion Ruling, Says Boris Johnson 'Paid the Price' for Condemning It." *Jezebel*, July 28, 2022, https://jezebel.com/samuel-alito-gloats-about-abortion-ruling-says-boris-j-1849345843/amp.

Baum, Laurence, and Neal Devins. "Federalist Court: How the Federalist Society Became the De Facto Selector of Republican Supreme Court Justices." *Slate*, January 31, 2017, https://slate.com/news-and-politics/2017/01/how-the-federalist-society-became-the-de-facto-selector-of-republican-supreme-court-justices.html.

Bayer, Peter Brandon. "Deontological Originalism: Moral Truth, Liberty, and Constitutional 'Due Process': Part I—Originalism and Deontology." *Thurgood Marshall Law Review* (Fall 2019): 1–164.

Bd. of County Comm'rs v. Umbehr, 518 U.S. 668 (1996).

Beck, Julie. "This Article Won't Change Your Mind." *Atlantic*, March 13, 2017, https://www.theatlantic.com/science/archive/2017/03/this-article-wont-change-your-mind/519093.

Bendroth, Margaret. "Christian Fundamentalism in America." *Oxford Research Encyclopedias*, February 27, 2017, https://oxfordre.com/religion/view/10.1093/acrefore/9780199340378.001.0001/acrefore-9780199340378-e-419.

Berardino, Mike, and Ann E. Marimow. "Justice Thomas Defends the Supreme Court's Independence and Warns of 'Destroying Our Institutions.'" *Washington Post,* September 16, 2021, https://www.washingtonpost.com/politics/courts_law/justice-clarence-thomas/2021/09/16/d2ddc1ba-1714-11ec-a5e5-ceecb895922f_story.html.

Bergengruen, Vera. "The Antivax Movement Is Taking Over the Right." *Time*, February 14/21, 2022, 16–17.

Berman, Mitchell N. "Originalism Is Bunk." *New York University Law Review* 84 (April 2009): 1–96.

Bishop, Bill. *The Big Sort: Why the Clustering of Like-Minded America Is Tearing Us Apart*. Boston: Houghton Mifflin Harcourt, 2008.

Biskupic, Joan. "John Roberts' Argument for Saving Obamacare Helping Power Legal Challenge." CNN, July 10, 2019, https://www.cnn.com/2019/07/10/politics/john-roberts-affordable-care-act-5th-circuit/index.html.

———. "The Inside Story of How John Roberts Failed to Save Abortion Rights." CNN, July 26, 2022, https://www.cnn.com/2022/07/26/politics/supreme-court-john-roberts-abortion-dobbs/index.html.

Blackburn, Marsha. "Blackburn Raises Concerns Over Judge Ketanji Brown Jackson's Judicial Record." March 21, 2022, https://www.blackburn.senate.gov/2022/3/blackburn-raises-concerns-over-judge-ketanji-brown-jackson-s-judicial-record.

Blackburn, Simon. *On Truth*. Oxford: Oxford University Press, 2018.

Blake, Aaron. "The Supreme Court Reform Whose Time Has Come?" *Washington Post*, December 20, 2021, https://www.washingtonpost.com/politics/2021/10/20/supreme-court-reform-whose-time-has-come.

Blasi, Vincent. "Holmes and the Marketplace of Ideas." *Supreme Court Review* (2004): 1–46.

Bloom, Lackland H., Jr. "The Legacy of Griswold." *Ohio Northern University Law Review* 16, no. 3 (1989): 511–44.

Blow, Charles M. "The American Killing Fields." *New York Times*, May 25, 2022, https://www.nytimes.com/2022/05/25/opinion/uvalde-shooting-republicans.html.

———. "Anti-Vax Insanity." *New York Times*, August 8, 2021, https://www.nytimes.com/2021/08/08/opinion/anti-vaccine-america.html.

———. "Seven Steps to Destroy a Democracy." *New York Times*, March 13, 2022, https://www.nytimes/2022/03/13/opinion/republicans-democracy.html.

———. "The Supreme Court as an Instrument of Oppression." *New York Times*, May 8, 2022, https://www.nytimes.com/2022/05/08/opinion/supreme-court-oppression.html.

Blumenson, Eric. "The Challenge of a Global Standard of Justice: Peace, Pluralism, and Punishment at the International Criminal Court." *Columbia Journal of Transnational Law* 44 (2006): 801–74.

Blumenthal, Richard. "The Nomination of Ketanji Brown Jackson to be an Associate Justice on the Supreme Court of the United States." Senate Judiciary Committee, March 21, 2022. Audio, 2:26:48. https://www.judiciary.senate.gov/meetings/the-nomination-of-ketanji-brown-jackson-to-be-an-associate-justice-of-the-supreme-court-of-the-united-states.

Bond, Michael. "Trump's Volatile Crowds Not an Accident." *USA Today*, March 23, 2016, 7A.

Borger, Julian. "Book Reveals Trump Effort to Persuade Justice Kennedy to Step Aside for Kavanaugh." *Guardian*, February 4, 2020, https://www.theguardian.com/us-news/2020/feb/04/trump-family-anthony-kennedy-brett-kavanaugh-dark-towers.

Bork, Robert H. "Neutral Principles and Some First Amendment Problems." *Indiana Law Journal* 47 (Fall 1971): 1–35.

Bostock v. Clayton County, 140 S. Ct. 1731 (2020).

Bouie, Jamelle. "It's Not Looking Too Good for Government of the People, by the People and for the People." *New York Times*, May 27, 2022, https://www.nytimes.com/2022/05/27/opinion/uvalde-senate-gun-control.html.

———. "Let's Bring the Supreme Court Back Down to Earth." *New York Times*, February 1, 2022, https://www.nytimes.com/2022/02/01/opinion/biden-breyer-supreme-court.html.

———. "The Supreme Court Did the Right Thing. Still, I'm Worried." *New York Times*, March 11, 2022, https://www.nytimes.com/2022/03/11/opinion/north-carolina-pennsylvania-gerrymandering.html.

———. "The Supreme Court Is Just Doing What the Supreme Court Does." *New York Times*, February 11, 2022, https://www.nytimes.com/2022/02/11/opinion/supreme-court-alabama-maps.amp.html.

———. "Why We Are Not Facing the Prospect of a Second Civil War." *New York Times*, February 15, 2022, https://www.nytimes.com/2022/02/15/opinion/second-civil-war.html.

———. "You May Not Find Many Friends on This Power-Hungry Supreme Court." *New York Times*, April 8, 2022, https://www.nytimes.com /2022/04/08/opinion/ketanji-brown-jackson-supreme-court.html.

Bowie, Nikolas. "Presidential Commission on the Supreme Court of the United States: The Contemporary Debate Over Supreme Court Reform: Origins and Perspectives." Written testimony, June 30, 2021, https://www.whitehouse.gov/wp -content/uploads/2021/06/Bowie-SCOTUS-Testimony-1.pdf.

Boyd, Lillian, Stacey Barchenger, and Ray Stern. "Court Protest Boils Over in Phoenix." *Arizona Republic*, June 26, 2022, A1.

Boylan, Jennifer Finney. "The Radical Normalcy of a Trans 'Jeopardy!' Winner." *New York Times*, January 7, 2022, https://www.nytimes.com/2022/01/07/opinion/ culture/jeopardy-trans-amy-schneider.html.

Boyle, Kevin. "We Are Living in Richard Nixon's America. Escaping It Won't Be Easy." *New York Times*, July 31, 2022, https://www.nytimes.com/2022/07/31/ opinion/richard-nixon-america-trump.html.

Brandenburg v. Ohio, 395 U.S. 444 (1969).

Brewster, Jack. "Republican Confidence In Science Drops Nearly 30 Points Since 1975, Poll Finds," *Forbes*, July 16, 2021, https://www.forbes.com/sites/ jackbrewster/2021/07/16/republican-confidence-in-science-drops-nearly-30-points -since-1975-poll-finds.

Breyer, Stephen. *The Authority of the Court and the Peril of Politics*. Cambridge: Harvard University Press, 2021.

Brnovich v. Democratic Nat'l Committee, 141 S. Ct. 2321 (2021).

Brnovich v. Democratic Nat'l Committee, 141 S. Ct. 2321 (2021) (No. 19–1257), Transcript of Oral Argument, March 2, 2021, 1–120.

Brooks, David. "The Retreat to Tribalism." *New York Times*, January 1, 2018, https:// www.nytimes.com/2018/01/01/opinion/the-retreat-to-tribalism.html.

———. "America Is Falling Apart at the Seams." *New York Times*, January 13, 2022, https://www.nytimes.com/2022/01/13/opinion/america-falling-apart.html.

———. "Joe Biden Is Succeeding." *New York Times*, November 18, 2021, https:// www.nytimes.com/2021/11/18/opinion/biden-infrasturcture-stimulus-bill.html.

———. "The Dark Century." *New York Times*, February 17, 2022, https://nytimes .com/2022/02/17/opinion/liberalism-democracy-russia-ukraine.amp.html.

Brown, Chelsea. "Not Your Mother's Remedy: A Civil Action Response to the Westboro Baptist Church's Military Funeral Demonstrations." *West Virginia Law Review* 112 (Fall 2009): 207–40.

Brown, Rebecca L. "Activism Is Not a Four-Letter Word." *University of Colorado Law Review* 73 (Fall 2002): 1257–73.

Brown v. Board of Education, 347 U.S. 483 (1954).

Brownstein, Ronald. "The Real Reason America Doesn't Have Gun Control." *Atlantic*, May 25, 2022, https://www.theatlantic.com/politics/archive/2022/05/ senate-state-bias-filibuster-blocking-gun-control-legislation/638425/.

Buck v. Bell, 274 U.S. 200 (1927).

Bump, Philip. "Fox News Didn't Just Ignore the Jan. 6 Hearing. It Did Something Worse." *Washington Post*, June 10, 2022, https://www.washingtonpost.com/politics /2022/06/10/fox-news-didnt-just-ignore-jan-6-hearing-it-did-something-worse.

Burger, Warren. "PBS News Hour." Interview by Charlayne Hunter-Gault. PBS, December 16, 1991, https://www.youtube.com/watch?v=Eya_k4P-iEo.

Burton, Robert A. *On Being Certain: Believing You Are Right Even When You're Not*. New York: St. Martin's Griffin, 2008.

Burtt, Kristyn. "Ketanji Brown Jackson Faced Some Astonishingly Stupid Questions About Racism from Ted Cruz." *Yahoo*, March 23, 2022, https://finance.yahoo.com /news/ketanji-brown-jackson-faced-astonishingly-174346125.html.

Calmes, Jackie. *Dissent: The Radicalization of the Republican Party and Its Capture of the Court*. New York: Twelve, 2021.

Calvert, John H. "Kitzmiller's Error: Defining 'Religion' Exclusively Rather Than Inclusively." *Liberty University Law Review* 3 (Spring 2009): 213–328.

Cárdenas, Hector H., Jr. "United States v. Alvarez-Machain: Result Oriented Jurisprudence." *Houston Journal of International Law* 16 (Fall 1993): 101–37.

Carlisle, Madeleine. "On Day Two of Hearings, Republicans Accuse Ketanji Brown Jackson of Being Weak on Crime." *Time*, March 22, 2022, https://time.com /6159672/ketanji-brown-jackson-hearings-day-two/.

Carson v. Makin, 979 F. 3d (2020 1st Cir.).

Carson v. Makin, 141 S. Ct. 2883, cert. granted (U.S. July 2, 2021).

Carson v. Makin, 142 S. Ct. 1987 (2022).

Carter, Jimmy. "I Fear for Our Democracy." *New York Times*, January 9, 2022, SR4.

Carter, Stephen L. "The Confirmation Mess, Revisited." *Northwestern University Law Review* 84 (1990): 962–75.

———. *The Confirmation Mess: Cleaning Up the Federal Appointments Process*. New York: Basic Books, 1994.

———. "The Supreme Court Has Always Been Political." *Washington Post*, May 10, 2022, https://www.washingtonpost.com/business/the-supreme-court-has-always -been-political/2022/05/05/6d85e418-cc91-11ec-b7ee-74f09d827ca6_story.html.

"Caseloads: Supreme Court of the United States, Method of Disposition, 1970–2016." Federal Judicial Center, https://www.fjc.gov/history/courts/caseloads-supreme -court-united-states-method-disposition-1970-2016.

Cave, Damien. "How Australia Saved Thousands of Lives While Covid Killed a Million Americans." *New York Times*, May 15, 2022, https://www.nytimes.com /2022/05/15/world/australia/covid-deaths.html.

Chait, Jonathan. "Why Liberals Like Compromise and Conservatives Hate It." *New Republic*, March 2, 2011, https://newrepublic.com/article/84630/why-liberals -compromise-and-conservatives-hate-it.

Charles, Guy-Uriel, and Luis Fuentes-Rohwer. "The Court's Voting-Rights Decision Was Worse Than People Think." *Atlantic*, July 8, 2021, https://www.theatlantic .com/ideas/archive/2021/07/brnovich-vra-scotus-decision-arizona-voting-right /619330/.

Chemerinsky, Erwin. "The Brazenly Political Supreme Court Shows It Will Strike Down Abortion Rights." *Los Angeles Times*, May 2, 2022, https://www.latimes

.com/opinion/story/2022-05-02/roe-wade-overruled-supreme-court-politico-draft
-opinion.

————. *The Case Against the Supreme Court.* New York: Penguin Books, 2014.

————. *The Conservative Assault on the Constitution.* New York: Simon & Schuster, 2010.

————. *Worse Than Nothing: The Dangerous Fallacy of Originalism.* New Haven: Yale University Press, 2022.

Chemerinsky, Erwin, and Jeffrey Abramson. "What Do We Teach Law Students When We Have No Faith in the Supreme Court?" *Los Angeles Times*, January 16, 2022, https://www.latimes.com/opinion/story/2022-01-16/supreme-court-conservatives -ideology-precedent-law-schools.

"Cherry Picking: When People Ignore Evidence that They Dislike." *Effectiviology,* accessed June 25, 2022, https://effectiviology.com/cherry-picking/.

Chua, Amy. *Political Tribes: Group Instinct and the Fate of Nations.* New York: Penguin Books, 2018.

Cleveland, Garrett. "Shooting America Straight: Why the Time Is Now for the Supreme Court to Fortify Gun Rights in America Post-Heller." *Texas A&M Law Review Arguendo* 7 (February 2020): 13–34.

"Coach Kennedy Case." *First Liberty,* accessed June 30, 2022, https://firstliberty.org /cases/coachkennedy/.

"Cognitive Dissonance." *Psychology Today*, accessed June 21, 2022, https://www .psychologytoday.com/us/basics/cognitive-dissonance.

Cohen, Adam. "Justice Breyer's Legacy-Defining Decision." *Atlantic*, June 12, 2021, https://www.theatlantic.com/ideas/archive/2021/06/stephen-breyer-legacy -retirement/619168/.

————. *Supreme Inequality: The Supreme Court's Fifty-Year Battle for a More Unjust America.* New York: Penguin Press, 2020.

Cohen, David S., Greer Donely, and Rachel Rebouché. "The New Abortion Battleground" (draft version). *Columbia Law Review* 122 (2023): 1–55.

Cohen, Michael A. "House Censure Vote Shows How the GOP Rarely Breaks Ranks." MSNBC, November 18, 2021, https://www.msnbc.com/opinion/house -censure-vote-paul-gosar-shows-how-rarely-gop-breaks-n1284070.

Cohen, Richard. "Trump Has Taught Me to Fear My Fellow Americans." *Washington Post*, May 31, 2016, A15.

Colby, Thomas B., and Peter J. Smith. "Living Originalism." *Duke Law Journal* 59 (November 2009): 239–307.

Cole, Devan. "New Poll: 54% of Americans Disapprove of Supreme Court Following Roe Draft Opinion Leak." CNN, May 25, 2022, https://www.cnn.com/2022/05/25/ politics/supreme-court-approval-rating-drop-roe-leak/index.html.

Collins, Paul M., Jr., and Lori A. Ringhand. "The Institutionalization of Supreme Court Confirmation Hearings." *Law and Social Inquiry* 41 (Winter 2016): 126–51.

Collins, Susan. "Senator Collins' Statement on Judge Jackson's Nomination to the U.S. Supreme Court." March 30, 2022, https://www.collins.senate.gov/newsroom/ senator-collins-statement-on-judge-jacksons-nomination-to-the-us-supreme-court.

"Confirmation Hearing on the Nomination of John G. Roberts, Jr. To Be Chief Justice of the United States." Hearings before the Committee on the Judiciary, United States Senate, 109th Congress, September 12–15, 2005, https://www.judiciary .senate.gov/imo/media/doc/GPO-CHRG-ROBERTS.pdf.

Connaughton, Aidan. "Americans See Stronger Societal Conflicts Than People in Other Advanced Economies." Pew Research Center, October 13, 2021, https: //www.pewresearch.org/fact-tank/2021/10/13/americans-see-stronger-societal -conflicts-than-people-in-other-advanced-economies.

"Constitutional Amendment Process," National Archives, Office of the Federal Register, accessed July 15, 2022, https://www.archives.gov/federal-register/ constitution.

Corasaniti, Nick. "Donald Trump, In First Ad, Plays to Fears on Immigration and ISIS." *New York Times*, January 5, 2016, www.nytimes.com/2016/01/05/us/politics /in-first-ad-donald-trump-plays-to-fears-on-immigration-and-isis.html.

Cornell, Saul. "The Supreme Court's Latest Gun Case Made a Mockery of Originalism." *Slate*, November 10, 2021, https://slate.com/news-and-politics/2021 /11/bruen-supreme-court-guns-mockery-originalism.html.

Cornyn, John. "Jackson Confirmation Hearing, Day 1." CSPAN, March 21, 2022. Audio 58:34. https://www.c-span.org/video/?518341-1/jackson-confirmation -hearing-day-1.

Coronado, Acacia, and Sara Burnett. "Beto O'Rourke Interrupts Briefing, Echoing US Debate on Guns." *Miami Herald*, May 26, 2022, https://www.miamiherald.com /news/article261791482.html.

Cottle, Michelle. "Oh, Josh & Marsha & Ted & Lindsey . . . Sorry, Judge Jackson." *New York Times*, April 7, 2022, https://www.nytimes.com/2022/04/07/opinion/ jackson-cruz-scotus.html.

Cotton, Tom. "Sen. Cotton Joins the Ingraham Angle." Interview by Laura Ingraham. *The Ingraham Angle*, Fox News Channel, March 23, 2022. Audio:34. https: //www.cotton.senate.gov/news/videos/watch/march-23-2022-senator-cotton-joins -the-ingraham-angle.

Coyle, Marcia. "Sotomayor Clashes with Kavanaugh, as Justices Feud About Following Precedent." Law.com, April 22, 2021, https://www.law.com/nationallawjournal /2021/04/22/sotomayor-clashes-with-kavanaugh-as-justices-feud-about-following -precedent/?slreturn=20220014132202.

Cruz, Ted. "Sen. Ted Cruz: Ketanji Brown Jackson Didn't Want to Answer Questions About Critical Race Theory." Interview by Sean Hannity, *Hannity*, Fox News Channel, March 22, 2022. Audio 0:00. https://www.foxnews.com/transcript/ hannity-on-ketanji-brown-jackson-ukraine-war.

Cummings, William. "US Does Have 'Obama Judges': Trump Responds to Supreme Court Justice John Roberts' Rebuke." *USA Today*, November 21, 2018, https:// www.usatoday.com/story/news/politics/2018/11/21/john-roberts-trump-statement /2080266002/.

D. C. Code §§ 7-2501.01(12), 7-2502.01(a), 7-2502.02(a)(4) (2001).

Dahl, Robert A. "Decision-Making in a Democracy: The Supreme Court as a National Policy-Maker." *Emory Law Journal* 50 (2001): 563–82.

Davenport, Coral. "Republican Drive to Tilt Courts Against Climate Action Reaches a Crucial Moment." *New York Times*, June 19, 2022, https://www.nytimes.com/2022/06/19/climate/supreme-court-climate-epa.html.

Decker, Jefferson. *The Other Rights Revolution: Conservative Lawyers and the Remaking of American Government*. New York: Oxford University Press, 2016.

DeGirolami, Marc O., and Kevin C. Walsh. "Judge Posner, Judge Wilkinson, and Judicial Critique of Constitutional Theory." *Notre Dame Law Review* 90 (December 2014): 633–89.

Democratic Nat'l Comm. v. Hobbs, 948 F.3d 989 (2021) (9th Cir.).

Denham, Hannah, and Andrew Ba Tran. "Fearing Violence and Political Uncertainty, Americans Are Buying Millions More Firearms." February 3, 2021, *Washington Post*, https://www.washingtonpost.com/business/2021/02/03/gun-sales-january-background-checks.

Denworth, Lydia. "Conservative and Liberal Brains Might Have Some Real Differences." *Scientific American*, October 26, 2020, https://www.scientificamerican.com/article/conservative-and-liberal-brains-might-have-some-real-differences/.

Devins, Neal, and Lawrence Baum. "Split Definitive: How Party Polarization Turned the Supreme Court into a Partisan Court." *Supreme Court Review* (2016): 301–65.

de Vogue, Ariana. "Breyer Defends State of Supreme Court in Interview with CNN's Fareed Zakaria." CNN, September 19, 2021, https://www.cnn.com/2021/09/19/politics/breyer-fareed-zakaria-gps/index.html.

———. "Justices Worry About the Future of the Supreme Court—and Point Fingers as to Who's to Blame." CNN, July 29, 2022, https://www.cnn.com/2022/07/29/politics/supreme-court-kagan-sotomayor-barrett-roberts-thomas/index.html.

———. "Samuel Alito Mocks Foreign Critics of Repealing *Roe v. Wade* in Rome Speech on Religious Liberty." CNN, July 29, 2022, https://amp.cnn.com/cnn/2022/07/28/politics/samuel-alito-religious-liberty-notre-dame-rome/index.html.

———. "Supreme Court Justices Insist All Is Well, But Their Caustic Written Opinions Say Otherwise." CNN, February 10, 2022, https://www.cnn.com/2022/02/10/politics/supreme-court-justices-opinions/index.html.

———. "The Year Supreme Court Conservatives Made Their Mark." CNN, December 28, 2021, https://www.cnn.com/2021/12/28/politics/the-year-supreme-court-conservatives-made-their-mark/index.html.

Dias, Elizabeth, and Ruth Graham. "The Growing Religious Fervor in the American Right: 'This Is a Jesus Movement.'" *New York Times*, April 6, 2022, https://www.nytimes.com/2022/04/06/us/christian-right-wing-politics.html.

District of Columbia v. Heller, 554 U.S. 570 (2008).

Dixon, Rosiland. "Why the Supreme Court Needs (Short) Term Limits." *New York Times*, December 31, 2021, https://www.nytimes.com/2021/12/31/opinion/supreme-court-term-limits.amp.html.

Dobbs v. Jackson Women's Health Organization, 142 S. Ct. 2228 (2022).

Dobbs v. Jackson Women's Health Organization, 142 S. Ct. 2228 (2022), Transcript of Oral Argument, December 1, 2021, 1–114.

Dobbs v. Jackson Women's Health Organization, 945 F.3d 265 (5th Cir. 2019).

Doolittle, Tara Trower. "Don't Let Trump, Others Who Hate, Speak for You," *Austin American-Statesman*, December 13, 2015, E4.

Dorfman, Lawrence. *The Snark Handbook: A Guide to Verbal Sparring*. New York: Skyhorse Illustrated, 2009.

Douglas, Joshua A. "Is the Right to Vote Really Fundamental?" *Cornell Journal of Law & Public Policy* 18, no. 1 (Fall 2008): 143–201.

Douthat, Ross. "Let's Not Invent a Civil War." *New York Times*, January 12, 2022, https://www.nytimes.com/2022/01/12/opinion/civil-war-america.html.

Dowd, Maureen. "Marylin Monroe v. Samuel Alito." *New York Times*, May 7, 2022, https://www.nytimes /2022/05/07/opinion/abortion-supreme-court-puritanism.html.

———. "Too Much Church in the State." *New York Times,* May 15, 2022, SR11.

Dunsmore, Nichole. "Justice Antonin Scalia Says Constitution Not Meant to Answer Moral Questions." *GW Hatchet*, September 6, 2013, https://www.gwhatchet.com /2013/09/16/justice-antonin-scalia-says-he-is-not-philosopher-king-cant-answer -moral-questions/.archett

Dunster, Chandelis. "Justice Amy Coney Barrett Says Supreme Court Is 'Not a Bunch of Partisan Hacks.'" CNN, September 13, 2021, https://www.cnn.com/2021/09/13/ politics/amy-coney-barrett-supreme-court-not-partisan/index.html.

Durkee, Alison. "Did Supreme Court Justices Lie by Claiming They Wouldn't Overturn *Roe v. Wade*? Here's What They Actually Said." *Forbes,* June 28, 2022, https://www.forbes.com/sites/alisondurkee/2022/06/28/did-supreme-court-justices -lie-by-claiming-they-wouldnt-overturn-roe-v-wade-heres-what-they-actually-said /?sh=34cccebf5420.

Dworkin, Ronald. *Justice in Robes*. Cambridge: Harvard University Press, 2006.

———. *Taking Rights Seriously*. Cambridge: Harvard University Press, 1977.

Dwyer, Devin. "Justice Sotomayor Sees 'Unprecedented' Threat to Supreme Court in Confirmation Battles." ABC News, February 10, 2022, https://abcnews.go.com /Politics/justice-sotomayor-sees-unprecedented-threat-scotus-confirmation-battles /story?id=82798225.

Dzienkowski, John S. "The Contributions of Louis Brandeis to the Law of Lawyering." *Touro Law Review* 33 (2017): 177–93.

Eaton, Paul D., Antonio M. Taguba, and Steven M. Anderson. "3 Retired Generals: The Military Must Prepare Now For a 2024 Insurrection." *Washington Post*, December 17, 2021, https://www.washingtonpost.com/opinions/2021/12/17/eaton -taguba-anderson-generals-military.

Edsall, Thomas B. "This Is What Made Covid the 'Almost Ideal Polarizing Crisis.'" *New York Times*, January 26, 2022, https://www.nytimes.com/2022/01/26/opinion/ covid-biden-trump-polarization.html.

———. "Trumpism Without Borders." *New York Times*, June 16, 2021, https://www .nytimes.com/2021/06/16/opinion/trump-global-populism.html.

Ehli, Nick, and Robert Barnes. "Kagan Says Questions of Legitimacy Risky for Supreme Court." *Washington Post*, July 21, 2022, https://www.washingtonpost .com/politics/2022/07/21/elena-kagan-supreme-court-legitimacy/.

Eisler, Kim Isaac. *A Justice for All: William J. Brennan Jr., and the Decisions that Transformed America*. New York: Simon and Schuster, 1993.

Elving, Ron. "What Happened with Merrick Garland in 2016 and Why It Matters Now." NPR, June 29, 2018, https://www.npr.org/2018/06/29/624467256/what-happened-with-merrick-garland-in-2016-and-why-it-matters-now.

Employment Division v. Smith, 494 U.S. 872 (1990).

Epstein, Lee, Andrew D. Martin, Kevin M. Quinn, and Jeffrey A. Segal. "Ideological Drift Among Supreme Court Justices: Who, When, and How Important?" *Northwestern University Law Review* 101 (Fall 2007): 1483–541.

Epstein, Lee, and Eric Posner. "How the Religious Right Has Transformed the Supreme Court." *New York Times*, September 22, 2020, https://www.nytimes.com/2020/09/22/opinion/supreme-court-religion.amp.html.

Eunjung Cha, Ariana. "Physicians Face Confusion and Fear in Post-*Roe* World." *Washington Post*, June 28, 2022, https://www.washingtonpost.com/health/2022/06/28/abortion-ban-roe-doctors-confusion/.

Everson v. Bd. of Education, 330 U.S. 1 (1947).

Exec. Order No. 14,023, 86 Fed. Reg. 19,569 (April 9, 2021).

Fandos, Nicholas, and Jesse McKinley. "N.Y. Republican Drops Re-Election Bid After Bucking Party on Guns." *New York Times*, June 3, 2022, https://www.nytimes.com/2022/06/03/nyregion/chris-jacobs-congress-guns.html.

Farias, Christian. "Post-*Roe*, the Supreme Court Is on a Collision Course with Democracy." *Vanity Fair*, August 25, 2022, https://www.vanityfair.com/news/2022/08/post-roe-scotus-is-on-a-collision-course-with-democracy.

———. "'Power, Not Reason': The Fall of *Roe* and the Rise of Republican Orthodoxy at the Supreme Court." *Vanity Fair*, June 24, 2022, https://www.vanityfair.com/news/2022/06/fall-of-roe-rise-of-republican-orthodoxy-at-supreme-court.

———. "Samuel Alito's Roe Message Is Clear: This Supreme Court Is Ready to Burn It All Down." *Vanity Fair*, May 3, 2022, https://www.vanityfair.com/news/2022/05/samuel-alitos-roe-message-is-clear.

Feldman, Noah. "Ending *Roe* Is Institutional Suicide for the Supreme Court." *Baltimore Sun*, June 26, 2022, https://www.baltimoresun.com/opinion/op-ed/bs-ed-op-0626-ending-roe-institutional-suicide-20220626-55anw5pgszb77oeutqa264zkiu-story.html.

Feldman, Stephen M. "Free Speech Jurisprudence and Its Interactions with Social Justice: Free-Speech Formalism and Social Injustice." *William and Mary Journal of Race, Gender and Social Justice* 26 (Fall 2019): 47–75.

Festinger, Leon. *A Theory of Cognitive Dissonance*. Stanford, CA: Stanford University Press, 1957.

Finley, Bruce. "People Side with Political Tribe Even When COVID Survival Plan Is Same, CU Experiment Finds." *Denver Post*, January 20, 2022, https://www.denverpost.com/2022/01/20/covid-19-psychology-experiment-university-colorado/.

Fischer, Louis. "When Courts Play School Board: Judicial Activism in Education," *Education Law Reporter,* 51, no. 3 (April 1989): 693–709.

Flores, Alexandra, Jennifer C. Cole, Stephan Dickert, and Leaf Van Boven. "Politicians Polarize and Experts Depolarize Public Support for COVID-19 Management Policies Across Countries." Proceedings of the National Academy of the United States of America, January 18, 2022, https://www.pnas.org/content/119 /3/e2117543119.

Folkenflik, David. "Only One Major Cable News Channel Did Not Carry the Jan. 6 Hearing Live: Fox News." NPR, June 11, 2022, https://www.npr.org/2022/06/10 /1104116455/fox-news-jan-6-hearing.

Ford, Matt. "Ginni Thomas Is Giving the Supreme Court a Bleeding Ulcer It Can't Cure." *New Republic*, March 25, 2022, https://newrepublic.com/article/165858/ ginni-thomas-january-6-texts.

Fox, Kara, Krystina Shveda, Natalie Croker, and Marco Chacon. "How US Gun Culture Stacks Up with the World." CNN, November 26, 2021, https://amp .cnn.com/cnn/2021/11/26/world/us-gun-culture-world-comparison-intl-cmd/index .html.

Frank, Jerome. *Law and the Modern Mind*. New York: Brentano's, 1930.

Franklin, Cary. "Living Textualism." 2020 *Supreme Court Review* (2020): 119–202.

Franklin, Charles. "New Marquette Law School Poll National Survey Finds Approval of the Supreme Court at New Lows, with Strong Partisan Differences Over Abortion and Gun Rights." Marquette University Law, July 20, 2022, https://law .marquette.edu/poll/2022/07/20/mlspsc09-court-press-release.

Fried, Charles. "The Artificial Reason of the Law or: What Lawyers Know." *Texas Law Review* 60, no. 1 (1981): 35–58.

———. "Not Conservative." *Harvard Law Review Blog*, July 3, 2018, https://blog .harvardlawreview.org/not-conservative.

Friedman v. City of Highland Park, 577 U.S. 1039 (2015).

Friedman, Barry. *The Will of the People: How Public Opinion Has Influenced the Supreme Court and Shaped the Meaning of the Constitution*. New York: Farrar, Straus and Giroux, 2009.

Friedman, Thomas L. "Make America Immune Again." *New York Times*, May 5, 2020, https://www.nytimes.com/2020/05/05/opinion/coronavirus-us-immunity.html.

Frum, David. "America's Gun Plague." *Atlantic*, May 14, 2022, https://www .theatlantic.com/ideas/archive/2022/05/buffalo-shooting-great-replacement -ideology/629870/.

Fulton v. City of Philadelphia, 141 S. Ct. 1868 (2021).

Gale, William G., and Darrell M. West. "Is the U.S. Headed for Another Civil War?" Brookings, September 16, 2021, https://www.brookings.edu/blog/fixgov/2021/09 /16/is-the-us-headed-for-another-civil-war/.

Galston, Miriam. "Polarization at the Supreme Court? Substantive Due Process Through the Prism of Legal Theory." *Washington University Jurisprudence Review* 11 (2019): 255–91.

Garry, Patrick M. "The Myth of Separation: America's Historical Experience with Church and States." *Hofstra Law Review* 33 (Winter 2004): 475–500.

Gerstein, Josh. "Alito Speaks Out on Texas Abortion Case and 'Shadow Docket.'" *Politico*, September 30, 2021, https://www.politico.com/news/2021/09/30/alito-on -texas-abortion-case-shadow-docket-514828.

Gerstmann, Evan. "Public Confidence in the Supreme Court Is at A Low Point." *Forbes*, July 29, 2021, https://www.forbes.com/sites/evangerstmann/2021/07/29/ public-confidence-in-the-supreme-court-is-at-a-low-point/.

Gessen, Masha. *Surviving Autocracy*. New York: Riverhead Books, 2020.

Gideon v. Wainwright, 372 U.S. 335 (1963).

Gillman, Howard, and Erwin Chemerinsky. *The Religion Clauses: The Case for Separating Church and State*. New York: Oxford University Press, 2020.

Goldberg, Michelle. "America May be Broken Beyond Repair." *New York Times*, May 27, 2022, https://www.nytimes.com/2022/05/27/opinion/uvalde-shooting.html.

———. "America's Post-*Roe* Chaos Is Here." *New York Times*, July 1, 2022, https:// www.nytimes.com/2022/07/01/opinion/post-roe-chaos.html.

———. "Are We Really Facing a Second Civil War?" *New York Times*, January 6, 2022, https://www.nytimes.com/2022/01/06/opinion/america-civil-war/html.

Golding, Martin P. "Principled Decision-Making and the Supreme Court." *Columbia Law Review* 63 (1963): 35–58.

Gore, Al. *The Assault on Reason*. New York: Penguin Books, 2007.

Gorsuch, Neil. *A Republic, If You Can Keep It*. New York: Crown Forum, 2020.

———. "Justice White and Judicial Excellence." *UPI*, May 4, 2002, https: //www.upi.com/Top_News/2002/05/04/Justice-White-and-judicial-excellence /72651020510343/.

Graber, Mark. "Clarence Thomas and the Perils of Amateur History." In *Rehnquist Justice: Understanding the Court Dynamic*. Edited by Earl M. Maltz 70–102. Lawrence, KS: University of Kansas Press, 2003.

Graglia, Lino A. "Some Comments on Posner." Review of *The Federal Judiciary: Strengths and Weaknesses*, by Richard Posner. *Texas Review of Law and Politics* 25 (Fall 2020): 149–58.

Graham, Lindsey. "Lindsey Graham: Ketanji Brown Jackson Was Top Choice of 'Every Nutjob Liberal Group.'" Interview by Jeanine Pirro. *The Ingraham Angle*, Fox News Channel, March 23, 2022. Audio 1:05. https://www.foxnews.com/media /ketanji-brown-jackson-lindsey-graham-ingraham-angle-reaction.

Grant, Adam. *Think Again*. New York: Viking, 2021.

Grassley, Chuck. "Grassley Opening Statement." Senate Judiciary Committee, March 21, 2022, https://www.judiciary.senate.gov/scotus_grassley-opening-statement.

Greene, Jamal. "Let's Talk About How Truly Bizarre Our Supreme Court Is." Interview by Ezra Klein. "The Ezra Klein Show," *New York Times* podcast, February 4, 2022. Audio 5:47. https://www.nytimes.com/2022/02/04/opinion/ezra -klein-podcast-jamal-greene.amp.html.

———. "Selling Originalism." *Georgetown Law Journal* 97 (March 2009): 657–720.

Greenhouse, Linda. *Justice on the Brink: The Death of Ruth Bader Ginsburg, the Rise of Amy Coney Barrett, and Twelve Months That Transformed the Supreme Court*. New York: Random House, 2021.

———. "On Voting Rights, Justice Alito Is Stuck in the 1980s." July 15, 2021, *New York Times*, https://www.nytimes.com/2021/07/15/opinion/Voting-rights-supreme -court.html.

————. "Requiem for the Supreme Court." *New York Times*, June 24, 2022, https://www.nytimes.com/2022/06/24/opinion/roe-v-wade-dobbs-decision.html.

————. "Religious Doctrine, Not the Constitution, Drove the Dobbs Decision." *New York Times*, July 22, 2022, https://www.nytimes.com/2022/07/22/opinion/abortion-religion-supreme-court.html.

————. "Stephen Breyer Was the Right Justice for the Wrong Age." *New York Times*, January 26, 2022, https://www.nytimes.com/2022/01/26/opinion/breyer-supreme-court-retirement.html.

————. "The Supreme Court Has Crossed the Rubicon." *New York Times*, February 9, 2022, https://www.nytimes.com/2022/02/09/opinion/supreme-court-voting-rights.html.

————. "The Supreme Court, Too, Is on the Brink." *New York Times*, June 4, 2020, https://www.nytimes.com/2020/06/04/opinion/sunday/supreme-court-religion-coronavirus.html.

————. "The Supreme Court, Weaponized." *New York Times*, December 16, 2021, https://www.nytimes.com/2021/12/16/opinion/supreme-court-trump.html.

————. "This Is What Judicial Activism Looks Like on the Supreme Court." *New York Times*, April 8, 2021, https://nytimes.com/2021/04/08/opinion/Supreme-Court-religion-activism.amp.html.

————. "What Kind of Story Will Ketanji Brown Jackson Tell Her Fellow Justices?" *New York Times*, March 4, 2022, https://www.nytimes.com/2022/03/04/opinion/supreme-court-biden-jackson.html.

Greenhouse, Linda, and Reva B. Siegel. "Before (and After) Roe v. Wade: New Questions About Backlash." *Yale Law Journal* 120 (June 2011): 2028–87.

Gresko, Jessica, and Emily Swanson. "AP-NORC Poll: Two-Thirds in US Favor Term Limits for Justices." AP, July 25, 2022, https://apnews.com/article/abortion-ketanji-brown-jackson-us-supreme-court-government-and-politics-only-on-ap-8adc9a08c9e8001c8ef0455906542a60.

Griswold v. Connecticut, 381 U.S. 479 (1965).

Gryboski, Michael. "Trump Meets Coach Kennedy: Suspension for Praying After Games 'Outrageous,' 'Very Sad.'" *Christian Post*, October 4, 2016, https://www.christianpost.com/news/donald-trump-meets-coach-kennedy-suspension-praying-football-games-outrageous-very-sad.html.

Guthrie, Chris, Jeffrey J. Rachlinski, and Andrew J. Wistrich. "Inside the Judicial Mind." *Cornell Law Review* 86 (May 2001): 777–830.

Haidt, Jonathan. "After Babel: How Social Media Dissolved the Mortar of Society and Made America Stupid." *Atlantic*, May 2022.

Hakim, Danny, and Jo Becker. "The Long Crusade of Clarence and Ginni Thomas." *New York Times Magazine*, February 22, 2022, https://www.nytimes.com/2022/02/22/magazine/clarence-thomas-ginni-thomas.html.

Hall, Harriet. "On Being Certain." *Science-Based Medicine*, May 6, 2008, https://sciencebasedmedicine.org/on-being-certain.

Hamilton, Alexander. "The Federalist No. 78." *The Federalist Papers*. Edited by Clinton Rossiter. New York: Penguin Books, 1961, 464–72.

Hamilton, Eric. "Politicizing the Supreme Court." *Stanford Law Review Online* 65 (August 2012): 35–40.

Harrington, Brooke. "The Anti-Vaccine Con Job Is Becoming Untenable." *Atlantic*, August 1, 2021, https://www.theatlantic.com/ideas/archive/2021/08/vaccine -refusers-dont-want-blue-americas-respect/619627/.

Harris, Elizabeth A., and Alexandra Alter. "Book Ban Efforts Spread Across the U.S." *New York Times*, January 30, 2022, http://nytimes.com/2022/01/30/books/book -ban-us-schools.html.

Hartig, Hannah. "About Six-in-Ten Americans Say Abortion Should Be Legal in All or Most Cases." Pew Research Center, June 13, 2022, https://www.pewresearch .org/fact-tank/2022/06/13/about-six-in-ten-americans-say-abortion-should-be -legal-in-all-or-most-cases-2/.

Hauser, Christine. "A Partial List of Mass Shootings in the United States in 2022." *New York Times*, May 23, 2022, https://www.nytimes.com/article/mass-shootings -2022.html.

Healy, Jack. "Why an Arizona County Turned Down $1.9 Million in Covid Relief," *New York Times*, February 11, 2022, https://www.nytimes.com/2022/02/11/us/ covid-relief-funds.html.

Healy, Melissa. "Psychologists Ask: What Makes Some Smart People So Skeptical of Science?" *Los Angeles Times*, January 21, 2017, https://www.latimes.com/science/ sciencenow/la-sci-sn-science-skepticism-psychology-20170120-story.html.

"A Heartbroken Nation." *New York Times*, May 29, 2022, SR8.

Heller v. District of Columbia, 670 F.3d 1244 (2011 D.C. Cir.).

Hendrickson, Mark W. "The U.S. Constitution: Living, Breathing Document or Dead Letter?" *Center For Vision and Values*, May 28, 2009, http://www.visionandvalues .org/2009/05/the-us-constitution-living-breathing-document-or-dead-letter/.

"Here's Every Word from the Seventh Jan. 6 Committee Hearing on Its Investigation." NPR, July 12, 2022, https://www.npr.org/2022/07/12/1111123258/jan-6-committee -hearing-transcript.

Herron, Andrew R. "Collegiality, Justice, and the Public Image: Why One Lawyer's Pleasure Is Another's Poison." *University of Miami Law Review* 44 (January 1990): 807–38.

Hetherington, Marc J., and Jonathan Weiler. *Prius or Pickup? How the Answers to Four Simple Questions Explain America's Great Divide*. Boston: Houghton Mifflin Harcourt, 2018.

Hibbing, John R., Kevin B. Smith, and John R. Alford. *Predisposed: Liberals, Conservatives, and the Biology of Political Differences*. New York: Routledge, 2013.

Hill, Jemele. "Chris Paul Bears the Brunt of Pro Sports' Vaccination Problem." *Atlantic*, June 18, 2021, https://www.theatlantic.com/ideas/archive/2021/06/chris -paul-pro-sports-vaccination-problem/619250/.

Hofstadter, Richard. *The Paranoid Style in American Politics, and Other Essays*. New York: Knopf, 1952.

———. *Anti-Intellectualism in American Life*. New York: Vintage Books, 1962.

Holder, Eric. "It's Time to Reform the Supreme Court." National Democratic Redistricting Committee, June 24, 2022, https://democraticredistricting.com/eric -holder-its-time-to-reform-the-supreme-court.

Hollis-Brusky, Amanda. *Ideas with Consequences: The Federalist Society and the Conservative Counterrevolution.* New York: Oxford University Press, 2015.

Holmes, Oliver Wendell. *The Common Law.* Boston: Little Brown, 1881.

———. "Natural Law." *Harvard Law Review* 32, no. 1 (1918): 40–44.

Homans, Charles. "Where Does American Democracy Go from Here?" *New York Times Magazine,* March 20, 2022, https://www.nytimes.com/interactive/2022/03 /17/magazine/democracy.html.

Hook, Janet, and Beth Reinhard. "Donald Trump Reaches Out to Evangelicals, Promising Antiabortion Judicial Nominees." *Wall Street Journal,* June 10, 2016, https://www.wsj.com/articles/donald-trump-reaches-out-to-evangelicals-promising -antiabortion-judicial-nominees-1465588284.

Hornfischer, Jim. "The Conscience of a Constitutionalist: A Recipe for Living? Review of *Living the Bill of Rights: How to Be an Authentic American*, by Nat Hentoff." *Texas Journal on Civil Liberties and Civil Rights* 5 (Summer/Fall 2000): 217–32.

Hounshell, Blake, and Leah Askarinam. "For These Republicans, Supreme Court Hearings Are an Irresistible Opportunity." *New York Times,* March 21, 2022, https://www.nytimes.com/2022/03/21/us/politics/republicans-judge-ketanji-brown -jackson.html.

"How Close Is the US to Civil War? Closer Than You Think, Study Says." CNN, December 20, 2021, https://www.cnn.com/videos/politics/2021/12/20/us-civil-war -study-barbara-walter-intvu-intl-ovn-vpx.cnn.

Hughes, Charles Evans. *The Supreme Court of the United States.* New York: Columbia University Press, 1928.

Hulse, Carl. "McConnell Suggests He Would Block a Biden Nominee for the Supreme Court in 2024." *New York Times,* June 14, 2021, https://www.nytimes .com/2021/06/14/us/politics/mcconnell-biden-supreme-court.html.

———. "Cloud of Supreme Court Confirmation Bitterness Hangs Over Coming Fight." *New York Times,* January 29, 2022, https://www.nytimes.com/2022/01/29/ us/politics/supreme-court-confirmation-battles.amp.html.

———. "How Mitch McConnell Delivered Justice: Amy Coney Barrett's Rapid Confirmation." *New York Times,* October 27, 2020, at https://www.nytimes.com /2020/10/27/us/mcconnell-barrett-confirmation.html.

In re *Women's Whole Health v. Jackson*, 142 S. Ct. 701 (2022).

"In U.S., Far More Support Than Oppose Separation of Church and State." Pew Research Center, October 28, 2021, https://www.pewresearch.org/religion/2021/10 /28/in-u-s-far-more-support-than-oppose-separation-of-church-and-state/.

"Inside the Supreme Court." C-SPAN, February 3, 2016, https://www.c-span.org/ video/?404131-1/discussion-chief-justice-john-roberts.

Jackson v. City & Cty. of San Francisco, 576 U.S. 1013 (2015).

Jackson, Vicki C. "Submission to the Presidential Commission on the Supreme Court of the United States." July 16, 2021, https://www.whitehouse.gov/wp-content/uploads/2021/07/Jackson-Testimony.pdf.

Jacoby, Susan. *The Age of American Unreason in a Culture of Lies*. New York: Vintage Books, 2018.

Jones, Jeffrey M. "Approval of U.S. Supreme Court Down to 40%, a New Low." Gallup.com, September 23, 2021, https://news.gallup.com/poll/354908/approval-supreme-court-down-new-low.aspx.

———. "Confidence in U.S. Supreme Court Sinks to Historic Low." Gallup.com, June 23, 2022, https://news.gallup.com/poll/394103/confidence-supreme-court-sinks-historic-low.aspx.

———. "Democratic, Republican Confidence in Science Diverges." Gallup.com, July 16, 2021, https://news.gallup.com/poll/352397/democratic-republican-confidence-science-diverges.aspx.

Jones v. Mississippi, 141 S. Ct. 1307 (2021).

"Justice Agreement—All Cases." ScotusBlog, accessed June 21, 2022, https://www.scotusblog.com/wp-content/uploads/2019/07/StatPack_OT18-7_5_19_23-26.pdf.

"Justice Agreement—Highs and Lows." ScotusBlog, accessed June 21, 2022, https://www.scotusblog.com/wp-content/uploads/2019/07/StatPack_OT18-7_5_19_23-26.pdf.

Kagan, Elena. "Confirmation Messes, Old and New." Review of *The Confirmation Mess*, by Stephen L. Carter. *University of Chicago Law Review* 62 (Spring 1995): 919–42.

Kakutani, Michiko. *The Death of Truth*. New York: Tim Duggan Books, 2018.

Kalmbacher, Colin. "Sotomayor Pens 'Brutal' Dissent by Repeatedly Citing Kavanaugh Back at Himself as Conservative Majority 'Guts' Precedent in Juvenile Punishment Case." *Law and Crime*, April 22, 2021, https://lawandcrime.com/supreme-court/sotomayor-pens-brutal-dissent-by-repeatedly-citing-kavanaugh-back-at-himself-as-conservative-majority-guts-precedent-in-juvenile-punishment-case/.

Kanai, Ryota, Tom Feilden, Colin Firth, and Geraint Rees. "Political Orientations Are Correlated with Brain Structure in Young Adults." *Current Biology* 26, no. 8 (2011): 677–80.

Kane, Paul. "Graham: Judicial Confirmation Process Could Get Even More Toxic." *Washington Post*, March 26, 2022, https://www.washingtonpost.com/politics/2022/03/26/lindsey-graham-supreme-court.

Kanter, Rosabeth Moss. "Is Tribalism Inevitable?" *Huffington Post*, July 26, 2013, https://www.huffingtonpost.com/rosabeth-moss-kanter/is-tribalism-inevitable_b_3661436.html.

Kaplan, David A. *The Most Dangerous Branch: Inside the Supreme Court in the Age of Trump*. New York: Broadway Books, 2018.

Kapur, Sahil, and Frank Thorp V. "Is the Supreme Court Confirmation Process Irreparably Broken? Some Senators Say Yes." NBC News, April 2, 2022, https://www.nbcnews.com/politics/supreme-court/supreme-court-confirmation-process-irreparably-broken-senators-say-yes-rcna22608.

Kar, Robin Bradley, and Jason Mazzone. "The Garland Affair: What History and the Constitution Really Say About President Obama's Powers to Appoint a Replacement for Justice Scalia." *New York University Law Review Online* 91 (May 2016): 53–114.

Karol, David. "Abortion Will Remain a National Issue No Matter What the Supreme Court Does." *Washington Post*, December 20, 2021, https://www.washingtonpost.com/outlook/2021/12/20/abortion-will-remain-national-issue-no-matter-what-supreme-court-does/.

Kennedy v. Bremerton School District, 139 S. Ct. 634 (2019).

Kennedy v. Bremerton School District, 4 F.4th 910 (4th Cir. 2021).

Kennedy v. Bremerton School District, 142 S. Ct. 2407 (2022).

Kennedy v. Bremerton School District, 142 S. Ct. 2407 (2022), Brief for Bremerton Community Members as Amici Curiae Supporting Respondents.

Kessen, Ben. "Big Bird's Vaccination Announcement Sparks Backlash from Conservatives, GOP." NBC News, November 7, 2021, https://www.nbcnews.com/news/us-news/big-bird-vaccine-announcement-sparks-backlash-conservatives-gop-n1283425.

"Ketanji Brown Jackson Won't Be Able to Change a Radical Court. Yet." *New York Times*, February 27, 2022, SR8.

Khan, Shamus. "Kavanaugh Is Lying. His Upbringing Explains Why." *Washington Post*, September 28, 2018, https://www.washingtonpost.com/outlook/kavanaugh-is-lying-his-upbringing-explains-why/2018/09/27/2b596314-c270-11e8-b338-a3289f6cb742_story.html.

Kim, Seung Min, and Robert Barnes. "Supreme Court Term Limits Seem to Be Popular and Appear to Be Going Nowhere." *Washington Post*, December 28, 2021, https://www.washingtonpost.com/nation/2021/12/28/supreme-court-term-limits.

Kirschenbaum, Julia, and Michael Li. "Gerrymandering Explained." Brennan Center for Justice, August 12, 2021, https://www.brennancenter.org/our-work/research-reports/gerrymandering-explained.

Klein, Ezra. "David Shor Is Telling Democrats What They Don't Want to Hear." *New York Times*, October 8, 2021, https://www.nytimes.com/2021/10/08/opinion/democrats-david-shor-education-polarization.amp.html.

———. "Dobbs Is Not the Only Reason to Question the Legitimacy of the Supreme Court." *New York Times*, June 30, 2022, https://www.nytimes.com/2022/06/30/opinion/dobbs-mcconnell-supreme-court.html.

———. "What a Reckoning at the Supreme Court Could Look Like." *New York Times*, July 10, 2022, https://www.nytimes.com/2022/07/10/opinion/supreme-court-biden-reform.html.

———. *Why We're Polarized*. New York: Avid Reader Press, 2020.

Kmiec, Keenan D. "The Origin and Current Meanings of 'Judicial Activism.'" *California Law Review* 92 (October 2004): 1441–77.

Kruzel, John. "Solid Majority Believes Supreme Court Rulings Based More on Politics Than Law." *The Hill,* October 20, 2021, https://thehill.com/regulation/court-battles/577444-solid-majority-believes-supreme-court-rulings-based-more-on-politics.

Lambright, Daniel. "Man, Morality, and the United States Constitution." *University of Pennsylvania Journal of Constitutional Law* 17 (May 2015): 1487–514.

Lasch, Christopher. *The Culture of Narcissism: American Life in an Age of Diminishing Expectations.* New York: W.W. Norton & Company, 1979.

Laser, Rachel. "Supreme Court Ruling Is Greatest Loss of Religious Freedom in Decades." Americans United, June 27, 2022, https://www.au.org/the-latest/press/supreme-court-kennedy-bremerton-decision/.

Lemon v. Kurtzman, 403 U.S. 602 (1971).

Lessig, Lawrence. "Fidelity in Translation." *Texas Law Review* 71 (May 1993): 1165–268.

Levi, Edward H. *An Introduction to Legal Reasoning.* Chicago: University of Chicago Press, 1948.

Levinson, Jessica. "A Bombshell Term at the Supreme Court Will Scar America for Decades." MSNBC, July, 8, 2022, https://www.msnbc.com/opinion/msnbc-opinion/how-supreme-court-term-will-scar-america-decades-n1296909.

———. "Conservative Supreme Court's Gerrymandering Flip-Flops Spell Trouble." MSNBC, March 10, 2022, https://www.msnbc.com/opinion/msnbc-opinion/supreme-court-election-hypocrisy-north-carolina-alabama-n1291360.

———. "Justice Elena Kagan Has a Prescription for an Ailing Court." MSNBC, August 2, 2022, https://www.msnbc.com/opinion/msnbc-opinion/kagan-roberts-know-supreme-court-burning-n1297556.

———. "Trump's Supreme Court Is About to Reshape Gun Control." MSNBC, April 27, 2021, https://www.msnbc.com/opinion/trump-s-supreme-court-about-reshape-gun-control-n1265424.

Levitsky, Steven, and Daniel Ziblatt. *How Democracies Die.* New York: Broadway Books, 2018.

Lewis v. United States, 445 U.S. 55 (1980).

Lewis, Anthony. *Make No Law: The Sullivan Case and the First Amendment.* New York: Random House, 1991.

Lidsky, Lyrissa Barnett. "Nobody's Fools: The Rational Audience as First Amendment Ideal." *University of Illinois Law Review* (2010): 799–850.

Lindquist, Stefanie A., Joseph L. Smith, and Frank B. Cross. "The Rehnquist Court in Empirical and Statistical Retrospective: The Rhetoric of Restraint and the Ideology of Activism." *Constitutional Commentary* 24 (Spring 2007): 103–25.

Liptak, Adam. "A Leaky Supreme Court Starts to Resemble Other Branches." *New York Times,* May 11, 2022, https://www.nytimes.com/2022/05/11/us/supreme-court-leak-roe-wade.html.

———. "A Supreme Court in Disarray After an Extraordinary Breach." *New York Times*, May 3, 2022, https://www.nytimes.com/2022/05/03/us/politics/supreme-court-leak-roe-v-wade-abortion.html.

———. "A Supreme Court Term Marked by a Conservative Majority in Flux." *New York Times*, September 30, 2021, https://www-nytimes.com/2021/07/02/us/supreme-court-conservative-voting-rights.amp.html.

———. "Adding Gorsuch, a Polarized Supreme Court Is Likely to Grow Even More So." *New York Times*, April 10, 2017, A9.

————. "Clarence Thomas Is the Court's Most Committed Advocate for Gun Rights." In "Live Updates: Supreme Court and Senate Take Rare, Divergent Steps on Gun Safety," *New York Times*, June 23, 2022, https://www.nytimes.com/live/2022/06/23/us/gun-control-senate-supreme-court#clarence-thomas-gun-rights-supreme-court.

————. "Confirmation Hearings, Once Focused on Law, Are Now Mired in Politics." *New York Times*, March 23, 2022, https://www.nytimes.com/2022/03/23/us/politics/ketanji-brown-jackson-confirmation-hearing.html.

————. "Gridlock in Congress Has Amplified the Power of the Supreme Court." *New York Times*, July 2, 2022, https://www.nytimes.com/2022/07/02/us/supreme-court-congress.html.

————. "June 24, 2022: The Day Chief Justice Roberts Lost His Court." *New York Times*, June 24, 2022, https://www.nytimes.com/2022/06/24/us/abortion-supreme-court-roberts.html.

————. "Justices Are Long on Words, Short on Guidance." *New York Times*, November 17, 2010, A1.

————. "Justices Sotomayor and Barrett Say the Supreme Court Remains Collegial." *New York Times*, July 28, 2022, https://www.nytimes.com/2022/07/28/us/supreme-court-sotomayor-barrett.html.

————. "Supreme Court Allows Court-Imposed Voting Maps in North Carolina and Pennsylvania." *New York Times*, March 7, 2022, https://www.nytimes.com/2022/03/07/us/supreme-court-voting-maps.html.

————. "Supreme Court Backs Catholic Agency in Case on Gay Rights and Foster Care." *New York Times*, June 17, 2021, https://www.nytimes.com/2021/06/17/us/supreme-court-gay-rights-foster-care.html.

————. "Supreme Court Rejects Maine's Ban on Aid to Religious Schools." *New York Times*, June 22, 2022, https://www.nytimes.com/2022/06/21/us/politics/supreme-court-maine-religious-schools.html.

————. "Supreme Court Restores Alabama Voting Map That a Court Said Hurt Black Voters." *New York Times*, February 7, 2022, https://www.nytimes.com/2022/02/07/us/politics/supreme-court-alabama-redistricting-congressional-map.amp.html.

————. "Supreme Court Revives Republican-Drawn Voting Map in Louisiana." *New York Times*, June 30, 2022, https://www.nytimes.com/2022/06/28/us/supreme-court-louisiana-voting-map.html.

————. "Supreme Court to Hear Case of Web Designer Who Objects to Same-Sex Marriage." *New York Times*, February 22, 2022, https://www.nytimes.com/2022/02/22/us/colorado-supreme-court-same-sex-marriage.html.

————. "Supreme Court Sides with Coach Over Prayers at the 50-Yard Line." *New York Times,* June 27, 2022, https://www.nytimes.com/2022/06/27/us/politics/supreme-court-coach-prayers.html.

————. "A Transformative Term at the Most Conservative Supreme Court in Nearly a Century." *New York Times*, July 1, 2022, https://www.nytimes.com/2022/07/01/us/supreme-court-term-roe-guns-epa-decisions.html.

Liptak, Adam, and Alicia Palipiano. "Tracking the Major Supreme Court Decisions This Term." *New York Times*, July 1, 2021, https://www.nytimes.com/interactive /2021/06/01/us/major-supreme-court-cases-2021.html.

Litman, Leah. "COVID at the Court: South Bay United Pentecostal." *Take Care*, February 6, 2021, https://takecareblog.com/blog/covid-at-the-court-south-bay -united-pentecostal.

Little, Rory. "Heller and Constitutional Interpretation: Originalism's Last Gasp." *Hastings Law Journal* 60 (June 2009): 1415–30.

Locke v. Davey, 540 U.S. 712 (2004).

Lopez, Ashley. "The Christian Right Is Winning Cultural Battles While Public Opinion Disagrees." NPR, July 1, 2022, https://www.npr.org/2022/07/01/1109141110/the -christian-right-is-winning-cultural-battles-while-public-opinion-disagrees.

Loving v. Virginia, 388 U.S. 1 (1967).

Luban, David. "What's Pragmatic About Legal Pragmatism?" *Cardozo Law Review* 18 (September 1996): 43–73.

Lukianoff, Greg, and Jonathan Haidt. *The Coddling of the American Mind: How Good Intentions and Bad Ideas Are Setting Up a Generation for Failure*. New York: Penguin Press, 2018.

Madison, James. "The Federalist No. 10." *The Federalist Papers*. Edited by Clinton Rossiter. New York: Penguin Books, 1961, 77–84.

———. "The Federalist No. 37." *The Federalist Papers*. Edited by Clinton Rossiter. New York: Penguin Books, 1961, 224–31.

———. "The Federalist No. 51." *The Federalist Papers*. Edited by Clinton Rossiter. New York: Penguin Books, 1961, 320–25.

———. "Letter to Thomas Jefferson, October 17, 1788." In *Selected Writings of James Madison*, edited by Ralph Ketcham, 160. Indianapolis: Hackett Publishing, 2006.

Mangan, Dan. "Trump: I'll Appoint Supreme Court Justices to Overturn Roe v. Wade Abortion Case." CNBC, October 19, 2016, https://www.cnbc.com/2016/10/19 /trump-ill-appoint-supreme-court-justices-to-overturn-roe-v-wade-abortion-case .html.

Manjoo, Farhad. "What If Humans Just Can't Get Along Anymore? *New York Times*, August 4, 2021, https://www.nytimes.com/2021/08/04/opinion/technology-internet -cooperation.html.

Marbury v. Madison, 5 U.S. (1 Cranch) 137 (1803).

Marcus, Maeva. "Is the Supreme Court a Political Institution? *George Washington Law Review* 72 (December 2003): 95–112.

Marcus, Ruth. "How Low Will the Supreme Court Go on Guns?" *Washington Post*, June 10, 2022, https://www.washingtonpost.com/opinions/2022/06/10/supreme -court-second-amendment-brett-kavanaugh.

———. "The Radical Conservative Majority's Damage to the Supreme Court Cannot Be Undone." *Washington Post*, June 24, 2022, https://www.washingtonpost.com/ opinions/2022/06/24/supreme-court-conservative-majority-rule-of-law.

———. "The Supreme Court Hangs a Gun on the Wall." *Washington Post*, April 27, 2021, https://www.washingtonpost.com/opinions/the-supreme-court-hangs-a-gun -on-the-wall/2021/04/27/352af482-a780-11eb-8c1a-56f0cb4ff3b5_story.html.

———. "The Supreme Court Is Broken. So Is the System That Confirms Its Justices." *Washington Post*, April 8, 2022, https://www.washingtonpost.com/opinions/2022/04/08/supreme-court-broken-jackson-kagan-bork.

Markels, Alex. "Why Miers Withdrew as Supreme Court Nominee." NPR, October 27, 2005, https://www.npr.org/2005/10/27/4976787/why-miers-withdrew-as-supreme-court-nominee.

Masses Publishing Co. v. Patten, 244 F. 535 (S.D.N.Y 1917).

Mathis, Joel. "Ted Cruz Checked His Twitter Mentions and a Little Bit of Our Democracy Died." *Yahoo*, March 24, 2022, https://www.yahoo.com/lifestyle/ted-cruz-checked-twitter-mentions-154452447.html.

Matthews, Dylan, and Byrd Pinkerton. "The Incredible Influence of the Federalist Society, Explained." *Vox,* June 3, 2019, https://www.vox.com/future-perfect/2019/6/3/18632438/federalist-society-leonard-leo-brett-kavanaugh.

Mauro, Tony. "High Court Justices Take Bush v. Gore for a Spin." *Recorder*, February 21, 2001, http://academic.brooklyn.cuny.edu/history/johnson/mauro.htm.

Mazzei, Patricia. "Florida Judge Will Temporarily Block 15-Week Abortion Ban." *New York Times*, June 30, 2022, https://www.nytimes.com/2022/06/30/us/florida-abortion-ban-blocked.html.

McConnell, Michael W. "Accommodation of Religion." *Supreme Court Review* (1985): 1–59.

McCoy, Jennifer, and Benjamin Press. "What Happens When Democracies Become Perniciously Polarized." Carnegie Endowment for International Peace, January 22, 2022, https://carnegieendowment.org/2022/01/18/what-happens-when-democracies-become-perniciously-polarized.

McCulloch v. Maryland, 4 Wheat. 316 (1819).

McDonald v. City of Chicago, 561 U.S. 742 (2010).

McKenzie, Robert Tracy. *We the Fallen People: The Founders and the Future of American Democracy*. Westmont, IL: IVP Press, 2021.

Medina, Jennifer, and Reid J. Epstein. "Republican Celebrations and Democratic Anger Reveal a Widening Political Divide." *New York Times*, November 19, 2021, https://www.nytimes.com/live/2021/11/19/us/kyle-rittenhouse-trial/rittenhouse-verdict-conservatives-liberals.

Merrett, Frank. "Reflections on the Hawthorne Effect." *Educational Psychology* 26, no. 1 (2006): 143–46.

Merrill v. Milligan, 142 S. Ct. 1105 (2022).

Messerly, Laurie. "Reviving Religious Liberty in America." *Nexus: A Journal of Opinion* 8 (2003): 151–64.

Metaxas, Eric. *If You Can Keep It: The Forgotten Promise of American Liberty*. New York: Penguin Books, 2017.

Mill, John Stuart. *On Liberty and Other Writings*. Edited by Stefan Collini. Cambridge: Cambridge University Press, 1859, 1989.

———. "On Liberty." In *The Basic Writings of John Stuart Mill*. New York: The Modern Library, 1859, 2002, 3–122.

———. *On Liberty, Utilitarianism and Other Essays*. Edited by Mark Philip and Frederick Rosen. Oxford: Oxford University Press, 1859, 2015.

Millhiser, Ian. "Chief Justice Roberts's Lifelong Crusade Against Voting Rights, Explained." *Vox*, September 18, 2020, https://www.vox.com/21211880/supreme -court-chief-justice-john-roberts-voting-rights-act-election-2020.

———. "A Grand Supreme Court Showdown Over Gerrymandering Ends in a Whimper." *Vox*, March 7, 2022, https://www.vox.com/platform/amp/22966311 /supreme-court-gerrymandering-toth-moore-harper-chapman-north-carolina -pennsylvania-redistricting.

———. "The Nihilism of Neil Gorsuch." *Vox*, October 2, 2021, https://www.vox .com/22431044/neil-gorsuch-nihilism-supreme-court-voting-rights-lgbt-housing -obamacare-constitution#content.

———. "Originalism, Amy Coney Barrett's Approach to the Constitution, Explained." *Vox,* October 12, 2020, https://www.vox.com/21497317/originalism-amy-coney -barrett-constitution-supreme-court.

———. "Why Democrats Can't Get a Fair Shake in the Supreme Court, In One Chart." *Vox*, February 14, 2022, https://www.vox.com/2022/2/14/22925457/supreme-court -senate-confirmation-ketanji-brown-jackson-leondra-kruger-michelle-childs.

Miranda v. Arizona, 384 U.S. 436 (1966).

Mooney, Chris. *The Republican Brain: The Science of Why They Deny Science—and Reality*. Hoboken, NJ: John Wiley & Sons, Inc., 2012.

———. "Scientists Are Beginning to Figure Out Why Conservatives Are . . . Conservative." *Mother Jones*, July 15, 2014, https://www.motherjones.com/ politics/2014/07/biology-ideology-john-hibbing-negativity-bias/.

"Motivated Reasoning." *Psychology Today*, accessed June 21, 2022, https://www .psychologytoday.com/us/basics/motivated-reasoning.

Mounk, Yascha. *The People vs. Democracy: Why Our Freedom Is in Danger & How to Save It*. Cambridge: Harvard University Press, 2018.

N.Y. State Rifle & Pistol Ass'n v. City of New York, 140 S. Ct. 1525 (2020).

N.Y. State Rifle & Pistol Ass'n v. Bruen, 142 S. Ct. 2111 (2022).

New York Times v. Sullivan, 376 U.S. 254 (1964).

Newkirk II, Vann R. "How Shelby County v. Holder Broke America." *Atlantic*, July 10, 2018, https://www.theatlantic.com/politics/archive/2018/07/how-shelby -county-broke-america/564707.

Newport, Frank. "Religion Big Factor for Americans Against Same-Sex Marriage." Gallup Research, December 5, 2012, https://news.gallup.com/poll/159089/religion -major-factor-americans-opposed-sex-marriage.aspx.

Nichols, Tom. *The Death of Expertise: The Campaign Against Established Knowledge and Why It Matters*. New York: Oxford University Press, 2017.

Noonan, John. "The Purposes of Advocacy and the Limits of Confidentiality." *Michigan Law Review* 64, no. 8 (1966): 1485–92.

Obergefell v. Hodges, 576 U.S. 644 (2015).

O'Brien, David M. "Judicial Roulette: Report of the Twentieth Century Fund Task Force on Judicial Selection." Twentieth Century Task Fund. New York: Priority Press Publications, 1988.

O'Connell, Samantha. "Supreme Court 'Shadow Docket' Under Review by U.S. House of Representatives." American Bar Association, April 14, 2021, https://www

.americanbar.org/groups/committees/death_penalty_representation/publications/
project_blog/scotus-shadow-docket-under-review-by-house-reps/.

O'Connor, Sandra Day. "Remarks at the Inaugural Sandra Day O'Connor Distinguished Lecture Series: Lubbock, Texas, November 16, 2007." *Texas Tech Law Review* 41 (Summer 2009): 1169–72.

Olken, Samuel R. "Justice George Sutherland and Economic Liberty: Constitutional Conservatism and the Problem of Factions." *William and Mary Bill of Rights Journal* 6 (Winter 1997): 1–88.

Olson, Henry. "Republicans Are Right to Oppose Ketanji Brown Jackson." *Washington Post*, March 21, 2022, https://www.washingtonpost.com/opinions/2022/03/21/republicans-are-right-to-oppose-ketanji-brown-jackson-supreme-court-nominee-confirmation-hearings/.

Orentlicher, David. "Politics and the Supreme Court: The Need for Ideological Balance." *University of Pittsburgh Law Review* 79 (Spring 2018): 411–35.

Oreskes, Naomi. "The Reason Some Republicans Mistrust Science: Their Leaders Tell Them To." *Scientific American*, June 1, 2021, https://www.scientificamerican.com/article/the-reason-some-republicans-mistrust-science-their-leaders-tell-them-to/.

Ossoff, Jon. "Sen. Ossoff's Opening Statement in Supreme Court Nomination Hearing." March 21, 2022, https://www.ossoff.senate.gov/press-releases/watch-sen-ossoffs-opening-statement-in-supreme-court-nomination-hearing/.

Ostberg, C. L., and Matthew E. Wetstein. "Strategic Behaviour and Leadership Patterns of Modern Chief Justices." *Osgoode Hall Law Journal* 55 (Spring 2018): 478–514.

Oxner, Reese. "Uvalde Gunman Legally Bought AR Rifles Days Before Shooting, Law Enforcement Says." *Texas Tribune*, May 25, 2022, https://www.texastribune.org/2022/05/25/uvalde-shooter-bought-gun-legally/.

Packer, George. "How America Fractured into Four Parts." *Atlantic*, July/August 2021, https://www.theatlantic.com/magazine/archive/2021/07/george-packer-four-americas/619012/.

Patel, Kavita. "Republicans Losing Faith in Their Doctors Makes the Covid Pandemic Worse." MSNBC, December 27, 2021, https://www.msnbc.com/opinion/republicans-losing-faith-their-doctors-makes-covid-pandemic-worse-n1286560.

*Patterson v. Color*ado, 205 U.S. 454 (1907).

Paul, Pamela. "In the Face of Fact, the Supreme Court Chose Faith." *New York Times*, July 17, 2022, https://www.nytimes.com/2022/07/17/opinion/kennedy-bremerton-supreme-court.html.

Payne v. Tennessee, 501 U.S. 808 (1991).

Pelosi, Nancy, and Chuck Schumer. "Pelosi, Schumer Joint Statement on Reported Draft Supreme Court Decision to Overturn Roe v. Wade." Office of the Speaker of the House, May 2, 2022, https://www.speaker.gov/newsroom/5222-2.

Pengelly, Martin. "Clarence Thomas: Supreme Court Could Be 'Compromised' By Politics." *The Guardian*, March 12, 2022, https://www.theguardian.com/us-news/2022/mar/12/clarence-thomas-supreme-court-conservative-politics.

Peppers, Todd C. *Courtiers of the Marble Palace: The Rise and Influence of the Supreme Court Law Clerk.* Stanford, CA: Stanford University Press, 2006.

Perlman, Merrill. "How Is Skepticism Different Than Cynicism? Find the Answer in Ancient Greece." *Columbia Journalism Review,* October 15, 2015, https://www.cjr .org/language_corner/skepticism-cynicism.php.

Peruta v. California, 137 S. Ct. 1995 (2017).

Pfeffer, Stephen T. "Hostile Takeover: The New Right Insurgent Movement, Ronald Reagan, and the Republican Party, 1977–1984." PhD diss., Ohio University (2012), http://rave.ohiolink.edu/etdc/view?acc_num=ohiou1345147645.

Piazza, James A. "Politician Hate Speech and Domestic Terrorism." *International Interactions* 46, no. 3 (2020): 431–53.

Pilkington, Ed. "Report Shows the Extent of Republican Efforts to Sabotage Democracy." *Guardian,* December 24, 2021, https://www.theguardian.com/us -news/2021/dec/23/voter-suppression-election-interference-republicans.

Pinker, Steven. *Enlightenment Now: The Case for Reason, Science, Humanism, and Progress.* New York: Viking, 2018.

Pisani, Joseph. "Mr. Potato Head Drops the Mister—Sort Of." Associated Press, February 25, 2021, https://apnews.com/article/mr-potato-head-goes-gender-neutral -d3c178f2b9b0c424ed814657be41a9d8.

Pittman, Ashton. "Southern 'Defiance': The Fight for Roe Rages in Mississippi." *Jackson* (MS) *Free Press,* May 29, 2019, https://www.jacksonfreepress.com/news /2019/may/29/southern-defiance-fight-roe-rages-mississippi.

Pitzl, Mary Jo. "Brnovich: 1864 Ban on Abortions in AZ is Law." *Arizona Republic,* Jun 30, 2022, A1.

Planned Parenthood v. Casey, 505 U.S. 833 (1992).

Posner, Ricard A. "A Tribute to Justice William J. Brennan, Jr." *Harvard Law Review* 104, no. 1 (1990): 13–15.

———. "Reasoning by Analogy." Review of *Legal Reason: The Use of Analogy in Legal Argument,* by Lloyd L. Weinreb. *Cornell Law Review* 91 (March 2006): 761–74.

———. "The Supreme Court, 2004 Term–Foreword: A Political Court." *Harvard Law Review* 119 (November 2005): 32–102.

Post, Robert. "The Rehnquist Court and Beyond: Revolution, Counter-Revolution, or Mere Chastening of Constitutional Aspirations? Originalism As a Political Practice: 'The Right's Living Constitution.'" *Fordham Law Review* 75 (November 2006): 545–74.

Post, Robert, and Reva Siegel. "Questioning Justice: Law and Politics in Judicial Confirmation Hearings." *Yale Law Journal Pocket Part* 115 (January 2006): 38–51.

Presidential Commission on the Supreme Court of the United States. Final Report. December 7, 2021, https://www.whitehouse.gov/wp-content/uploads/2021/12/ SCOTUS-Report-Final-12.8.21-1.pdf.

Pruitt, Sarah. "How Robert Bork's Failed Nomination Led to a Changed Supreme Court." History.com, September 21, 2018, https://www.history.com/news/robert -bork-ronald-reagan-supreme-court-nominations.

"Public's Views of Supreme Court Turned More Negative Before News of Breyer's Retirement." Pew Research Center, February 2, 2022, https://www.pewresearch.org/politics/2022/02/02/publics-views-of-supreme-court-turned-more-negative-before-news-of-breyers-retirement.

Rabban, David M. *Free Speech in Its Forgotten Years.* Cambridge: Cambridge University Press, 1997.

Rabin, Roni Caryn. "Gun Deaths Surged During the Pandemic's First Year, the C.D.C. Reports." *New York Times*, May 10, 2022, https://www.nytimes.com/2022/05/10/health/cdc-gun-violence-pandemic.html.

Radin, Max. "The Theory of Judicial Decision: Or How Judges Think." *American Bar Association Journal* 11 (June 1925): 357–62.

Ramirez, Marc. "Conservatives Spent Decades Pushing to Upend Roe v. Wade. And 'It's Only the Beginning.'" *USA Today,* May 4, 2022, https://www.usatoday.com/story/news/nation/2022/05/04/supreme-court-ruling-could-victory-anti-abortion-rights-groups/.

Rebe, Ryan J. *The Partisan Court: The Era of Political Partisanship on the U.S. Supreme Court.* Lanham, MD: Lexington Books, 2021.

Reich, Robert. "The New Tribalism and the Decline of the Nation State." *Huffington Post*, March 24, 2014, https://www.huffingtonpost.com/robert-reich/the-new-tribalism-and-the_b_5020469.html.

Remnick, David. "Is a Civil War Ahead?" *New Yorker*, January 5, 2022, https://www.newyorker.com/news/daily-comment/is-a-civil-war-ahead.

"The Republican Party's Supreme Court." October 26, 2020, *New York Times*, https://www.nytimes.com/2020/10/26/opinion/amy-coney-barrett-supreme-court.html.

Rhodes, Charles W. "Rocky." "Navigating the Path of the Supreme Court Appointment." *Florida State University Law Review* 38 (Spring 2011): 537–95.

Ringhand, Lori A. "In Defense of Ideology: A Principled Approach to the Supreme Court Confirmation Process." *William and Mary Bill of Rights Journal* 18 (October 2009): 131–71.

Roe v. Wade, 410 U.S. 113 (1973).

Ropeik, David. "How Tribalism Overrules Reason, and Makes Risky Times More Dangerous." BigThink.com, May 14, 2012, https://bigthink.com/risk-reason-and-reality/how-tribalism-overrules-reason-and-makes-risky-times-more-dangerous.

Rosen, Jeffrey. "Court Approval." *The New Republic*, July 23, 2007.

Rosenberg, Gerald N. "The Road Taken: Robert A. Dahl's Decision-Making in a Democracy: The Supreme Court as a National Policy-Maker." *Emory Law Journal* 50 (Spring 2001): 613–30.

Rosenfeld, Sam. *The Polarizers.* Chicago: University of Chicago Press, 2018.

Rozenblit, Bruce. *Us Against Them: How Tribalism Affects the Way We Think.* Kansas City: Transcendent Publications, 2008.

Rubin, Jennifer. "The Supreme Court's Religion-Driven Mission Sets Off a Firestorm." *Washington Post*, May 3, 2022, https://www.washingtonpost.com/opinions/2022/05/03/supreme-court-alito-roe-wade-ruling/.

Russomanno, Joseph. "Cause and Effect: The Free Speech Transformation as Scientific Revolution." *Communication Law and Policy* 20 (Summer 2015): 213–59.

S. Bay United Pentecostal Church v. Newsom, 140 S. Ct. 1613 (2020).

S. Bay United Pentecostal Church v. Newsom, 141 S. Ct. 716 (2021).

S. Bay United Pentecostal Church v. Newsom, 140 S. Ct. 1613 (2020), Petition of Writ of Certiorari.

Saad, Lydia. "What Percentage of Americans Own Guns?" Gallup, November 13, 2020, https://news.gallup.com/poll/264932/percentage-americans-own-guns.aspx.

Sandel, Michael J. *The Tyranny of Merit: What's Become of the Common Good?* New York: Farrar Strauss Giroux, 2020.

Santa Fe Independent School District v. Doe, 530 U.S. 290 (2000).

Sargentich, Thomas O. "Is the Supreme Court Undoing the New Deal: The Impact of the Rehnquist Court's New Federalism: The Rehnquist Court and State Sovereignty: Limitations of the New Federalism." *Widener Law Journal* 12 (2003): 459–536.

"Sasse Cites 'Jackassery' in Warning Against Cameras in Supreme Court." *Wall Street Journal,* March 23, 2022, https://www.wsj.com/livecoverage/supreme-court-confirmation-hearings-ketanji-brown-jackson-2022-03-23/card/sasse-cites-jackassery-in-warning-against-cameras-in-supreme-court-sviheOZfF674JOwo1dLc.

Savage, Charlie. "Abortion Ruling Poses New Questions About How Far Supreme Court Will Go." *New York Times,* June 24, 2022, https://www.nytimes.com/2022/06/25/us/supreme-court-abortion-contraception-same-sex-marriage.html.

———. "Decades Ago, Alito Laid Out Methodical Strategy to Eventually Overrule Roe." *New York Times*, June 25, 2022, https://www.nytimes.com/2022/06/25/us/politics/samuel-alito-abortion.html.

Sawyer, Logan E., III. "Principle and Politics in the New History of Originalism." *American Journal of Legal History* 57, no. 2 (2017): 198–222.

Scalia, Antonin. "Morality, Pragmatism and the Legal Order." *Harvard Journal of Law and Public Policy* 9, no. 1 (1986): 123–24.

———. "Originalism: The Lesser Evil." *University of Cincinnati Law Review* 57 (1989): 849–65.

Scalia, Antonin, and Bryan A. Garner. *Reading the Law: The Interpretation of Legal Texts.* Eagan, MN: Thomson/West, 2012.

Schauer, Frederick. "Is There a Psychology of Judging?" John F. Kennedy School of Government/Harvard University, KSG Faculty Research Working Paper Series RWP07–049, October 2007, http://ksgnotes1.harvard.edu/Research/wpaper.nsf/rwp/RWP07-049.

———. *Playing by the Rules: A Philosophical Examination of Rule-Based Decision-Making in Law and in Life.* Oxford: Clarendon Press, 1991.

Scherer, Michael. "Supreme Court Goes Against Public Opinion in Rulings on Abortion, Guns." *Washington Post,* June 24, 2022, https://www.washingtonpost.com/politics/2022/06/24/supreme-court-goes-against-public-opinion-rulings-abortion-guns/.

Scherer, Michael, Josh Dawsey, Caroline Kitchener, and Rachel Roubein. "A 49-Year Crusade: Inside the Movement to Overturn Roe v. Wade." *Washington Post*, May 7, 2022, https://www.washingtonpost.com/politics/2022/05/07/abortion-movement-roe-wade/.

Sedgwick, Philip. "The Hawthorne Effect." *British Medical Journal* 344 (2011): 1468.

Segal, Jeffrey. "Why We Have the Most Polarized Supreme Court in History." *Conversation*, March 14, 2016, https://perma.cc/QCJ5-4SY8.

"Senate Judiciary Committee Holds Hearing on the Nomination of Ketanji Brown Jackson to be an Associate Justice on the Supreme Court of the United States, Day 1." Committee on the Judiciary, March 21, 2022, https://www.judiciary.senate.gov/meetings/the-nomination-of-ketanji-brown-jackson-to-be-an-associate-justice-of-the-supreme-court-of-the-united-states.

Semnani, Khosrow. "Trump's Fear-Mongering Threatens GOP." *Deseret News*, December 15, 2015, http://www.deseretnews.com/article/865643874/Trump7s-fear-mongering-threatens-Republican-Party.html.

Serwer, Adam. "The Constitution Is Whatever the Right Wing Says It Is." *Atlantic*, June 25, 2022, https://www.theatlantic.com/ideas/archive/2022/06/roe-overturned-supreme-court-samuel-alito-opinion/661386/.

———. "The Lie About the Supreme Court Everyone Pretends to Believe." *Atlantic*, September 28, 2021, https://www.theatlantic.com/ideas/archive/2021/09/lie-about-supreme-court-everyone-pretends-believe/620198/.

Shaman, Jeffrey M. "The End of Originalism." *San Diego Law Review* 47, no. 1 (2010): 83–108.

Shapiro, Ilya. "The Politics of Supreme Court Confirmations and Recommendations for Reform." Cato Institute, July 20, 2021, https://www.cato.org/testimony/perspectives-supreme-court-practitioners-views-confirmation-process.

Shaw, Kate, and John Bash. "We Clerked for Justices Scalia and Stevens. America Is Getting Heller Wrong." *New York Times*, May 31, 2022, https://www.nytimes.com/2022/05/31/opinion/supreme-court-heller-guns.html.

Sheehan, Colleen A. "The Measure and Elegance of Freedom: James Madison and the Bill of Rights." *Georgetown Journal of Law and Public Policy* 15 (Summer 2017): 513–26.

Shelby County v. Holder, 570 U.S. 529 (2013).

Shelby County v. Holder, 570 U.S. 529 (2013) (No. 12–96), Transcript of Oral Argument, February 27, 2013, 1–84.

Sherman, Mark, and Gary D. Robertson. "Justices Seem Poised to Hear Election Cases Pressed by GOP." Associated Press, June, 19, 2022, https://apnews.com/article/2022-midterm-elections-us-supreme-court-pennsylvania-constitutions-north-carolina-b1aaaf54cda0deada714a4eb57643d94.

Shermer, Michael. *The Believing Brain: From Ghosts and Gods to Politics and Conspiracies—How We Construct Beliefs and Reinforce Them as Truths*. New York: Times Books, 2011.

———. "What Skepticism Reveals About Science." *Scientific American*, July 1, 2009, https://www.scientificamerican.com/article/what-skepticism-reveals/.

Shesol, Jeff. "The Willful Naïveté of Stephen Breyer." *New York Times,* January 27, 2022, https://www.nytimes.com/2022/01/27/opinion/breyer-supreme-court.html.

"Should Supreme Court Justices Have Term Limits? Pro/Con." *Philadelphia Enquirer,* September 24, 2020, https://www.inquirer.com/opinion/commentary /supreme-court-term-limits-lifetime-appointment-ruth-bader-ginsburg-20200924 .html.

Siegel, Reva B. "Constitutional Culture, Social Movement Conflict and Constitutional Change: The Case of the de facto ERA; 2005–06 Brennan Center Symposium Lecture." *California Law Review* 94 (October 2006): 1323–419.

———. "Dead or Alive: Originalism as Popular Constitutionalism in Heller." *Harvard Law Review* 122 (November 2008): 191–245.

———. "Symposium: The Second Amendment and the Right to Bear Arms After D.C. v. Heller: Heller & Originalism's Dead Hand—In Theory and Practice." *UCLA Law Review* 56 (June 2009): 1399–424.

Silverman, Ellie. "Outside of Kavanaugh's Home, a Neighbor Rallies for Abortion Rights." *Washington Post*, May 7, 2022, https://www.washingtonpost.com/dc-md -va/2022/05/07/wooten-holway-protest-justice-kavanaugh-neighbor/.

Silvester v. Becerra, 138 S. Ct. 945 (2018).

Slack, Charles. *Liberty's First Crisis: Adams, Jefferson, and the Misfits Who Saved Free Speech*. New York: Atlantic Monthly Press, 2015.

Smith, Aaron. "Eight Years After Sandy Hook, Mass Shootings Are Up, But Federal Gun Control Remains the Same." *Forbes*, December 11, 2020, https://www.forbes .com/sites/aaronsmith/2020/12/11/eight-years-after-sandy-hook-mass-shootings -are-up-but-federal-gun-control-remains-the-same.

Snyder, Timothy. *On Tyranny: Twenty Lessons from the Twentieth Century*. New York: Crown, 2017.

Sollinger, Rickie, ed. *Abortion Wars: A Half-Century of Struggle, 1950–2000*. Berkeley: University of California Press, 1998.

Solnit, Rebecca. "An Assault on the Truth." *New York Times*, January 9, 2022, SR4.

Solum, Lawrence B. "Original Ideas on Originalism: District of Columbia v. Heller and Originalism." *Northwestern University Law Review* 103 (Spring 2009): 923–81.

Sosa, David. "The Unintentional Fallacy." Review of *A Matter of Interpretation*, by Antonin Scalia." *California Law Review* 86 (July 1998): 919–38.

Sotomayor, Sonia. *My Beloved World*. New York: Vintage Books, 2014.

Sprunt, Barbara. "Judge Ketanji Brown Jackson Confirmation Hearings: What Happened Tuesday." NPR, March 22, 2022, https://www.npr.org/2022/03/22 /1087967982/judge-ketanji-brown-jackson-confirmation-hearings-what-happened -on-tuesday.

Stern, Mark Joseph. "Republicans Don't Need to Win Elections. They Already Won the Supreme Court." *Slate*, January 24, 2022, https://slate.com/news-and-politics /2022/01/supreme-court-affirmative-action-republican-policy.amp.

———. "Sotomayor Calls Out Kavanaugh for Breaking His Promise to Death Row Inmates." *Slate*, May 24, 2021, https://slate.com/news-and-politics/2021/05/ sotomayor-kavanaugh-supreme-court-death-penalty.html.

Stevenson, Jonathan, and Steven Simon. "We Need to Think the Unthinkable About Our Country. *New York Times*, January 13, 2022, https://www.nytimes.com/2022/01/13/opinion/january-6-civil-war.

Stewart, Katherine. "Eighty-One Percent of White Evangelicals Voted for Donald Trump. Why?" *Nation*, November 17, 2016, https://www.thenation.com/article/archive/eighty-one-percent-of-white-evangelicals-voted-for-donald-trump-why/.

Stone, Geoffrey R. "Our Politically Polarized Supreme Court?" *Huffington Post*, November 25, 2014, http://www.huffingtonpost.com/geoffrey-r-stone/our-politically-polarized_b_5879346.html.

Stone, Geoffrey R., and David A. Strauss. *Democracy and Equality: The Enduring Constitutional Vision of the Warren Court*. New York: Oxford University Press, 2020.

Stracqualursi, Veronica. "'Pro-Mom, Pro-Baby, Pro-Life': People at Anti-Abortion Convention Celebrate Roe's Downfall and Focus on 'Long Battle Ahead.'" CNN, June 24, 2022, https://www.cnn.com/2022/06/24/politics/national-right-to-life-supreme-court-dobbs-decision/index.html.

"Statistics." ScotusBlog, July 2, 2021, https://www.scotusblog.com/statistics/.

Strauss, David A. "The Living Constitution." University of Chicago School of Law, September 27, 2010, https://www.law.uchicago.edu/news/living-constitution.

Strum, Philippa. *Brandeis: Beyond Progressivism*. Lawrence: University of Kansas Press, 1993.

Sullivan, Andrew. "America Wasn't Built for Humans." *New York Magazine*, September 18, 2017, http://nymag.com/daily/intelligencer/2017/09/can-democracy-survive-tribalism.html.

Sullivan, Becky. "What Conservative Justices Said—and Didn't Say—About Roe at Their Confirmations." NPR, May 3, 2022, https://www.npr.org/2022/05/03/1096108319/roe-v-wade-alito-conservative-justices-confirmation-hearings.

Sunstein, Cass R. "Interest Groups in American Public Law." *Stanford Law Review* 38 (November 1985): 29–87.

———. "Second Amendment Minimalism: Heller as Griswold." *Harvard Law Review* 122 (November 2008): 246–74.

Sunstein, Cass R., and Edna Ullman-Margalit. "Second-Order Decisions." *Ethics* 110, no. 1 (1999): 5–31.

"The Supreme Court Might Never Recover from Overturning Roe v. Wade." *Washington Post*, May 3, 2022, https://www.washingtonpost.com/opinions/2022/05/03/supreme-court-might-never-recover-overturning-roe-v-wade/.

"Supreme Court Nominations (1789-present)." United States Senate, accessed June 30, 2022, https://www.senate.gov/legislative/nominations/SupremeCourtNominations1789present.htm.

Talbot, Margaret. "Amy Coney Barrett's Long Game." *New Yorker*, February 7, 2022, https://www.newyorker.com/magazine/2022/02/14/amy-coney-barretts-long-game/amp.

Tavernise, Sabrina. "First They Fought About Masks. Then Over the Soul of the City." *New York Times*, December 26, 2021, https://www.nytimes.com/2021/12/26/us/oklahoma-masks.html.

Teles, Stephen M. *The Rise of the Conservative Legal Movement: The Battle for Control of the Law*. Princeton, NJ: Princeton University Press, 2010.

Ten Cate, Irene M. Speech. "Truth, and Freedom: An Examination of John Stuart Mill's and Justice Oliver Wendell Holmes's Free Speech Defenses." *Yale Journal of Law and the Humanities* 22 (Winter 2010): 35–81.

TerBeek, Calvin. "'Clocks Must Always Be Turned Back': Brown v. Board of Education and the Racial Origins of Constitutional Originalism." *American Political Science Review* 115, no. 3 (2021): 821–34.

———. "The Search for an Anchor: Living Constitutionalism from the Progressives to Trump." *Law and Social Inquiry* 46 (August 2021): 860–89.

Thompson, Derek. "Millions Are Saying No to the Vaccines. What Are They Thinking?" *Atlantic*, May 3, 2021, https://www.theatlantic.com/ideas/archive/2021/05/the-people-who-wont-get-the-vaccine/618765.

Thompson, Michael J., and Gregory R. Smulewicz-Zucker, eds. *Anti-Science and the Assault on Democracy*. Amherst, NY: Prometheus Books, 2018.

Thrush, Glenn. "As Republicans Prepare to Grill Jackson, They Are Re-Litigating Kavanaugh's Confirmation Battle." *New York Times*, March 21, 2022, https://www.nytimes.com/2022/03/21/us/politics/ketanji-brown-jackson-kavanaugh.html.

Tierney, Sneed, and Lauren Fox. "Takeaways From Ketanji Brown Jackson's First Day of Supreme Court Confirmation Hearings." CNN, March 21, 2022, https://www.cnn.com/2022/03/21/politics/ketanji-brown-jackson-hearing-monday-takeaways/index.html.

Tillis, Thom. "Tillis Delivers Opening Remarks in SCOTUS Confirmation Hearings." March 21, 2022, https://www.tillis.senate.gov/2022/3/tillis-delivers-opening-remarks-in-scotus-confirmation-hearings.

Tinker v. Des Moines Independent School District, 393 U.S. 503 (1969).

Tocqueville, Alexis de. *Democracy in America*. Translated by Harvey C. Mansfield and Delba Winthrop. Chicago: University of Chicago Press, 2000.

Todres, Jonathan. "A Healthier Legal Profession Starts with Law Schools." *Bloomberg Law,* March 15, 2022, https://news.bloomberglaw.com/us-law-week/a-healthier-legal-profession-starts-with-law-schools.

Toft, Monica Duffy. "How Civil Wars Start." *Foreign Policy*, February 18, 2021, https://foreignpolicy.com/2021/02/18/how-civil-wars-start.

Toobin, Jeffrey. "Activism v. Restraint." *New Yorker*, May 24, 2010, 19.

Torchinsky, Rina. "After the Leaked Roe Opinion, Justice Thomas Says the Supreme Court Can't Be Bullied." NPR, May 7, 2022, ttps://www.npr.org/2022/05/07/1097382507/supreme-court-abortion-clarence-thomas-bullied-roe-v-wade.

Totenberg, Nina. "Robert Bork's Supreme Court Nomination 'Changed Everything, Maybe Forever.'" NPR, December 19, 2012, https://www.npr.org/sections/itsallpolitics/2012/12/19/167645600/robert-borks-supreme-court-nomination-changed-everything-maybe-forever.

———. "Supreme Court Justices Aren't 'Scorpions,' But Not Happy Campers Either." NPR, January 18, 2022, https://www.npr.org/2022/01/18/1073428376/supreme-court-justices-arent-scorpions-but-not-happy-campers-either.

Townley, Justin. "The Great Recession and the Politics of Economics: Is the Color of the Economic Crisis the Color of Presidential Fear?" *Berkeley La Raza Law Journal* 22 (2012): 51–66.

Tracy, Abigail. "Donald Trump Made Justice Kennedy an Offer He Couldn't Refuse." *Vanity Fair*, June 29, 2018, https://www.vanityfair.com/news/2018/06/donald -trump-justice-anthony-kennedy-retirement.

Treisman, Rachel. "Big Bird Got 'Vaccinated' Against COVID-19, Drawing Outrage from Republicans." NPR, November 8, 2021, https://www.npr.org/2021/11/08 /1053548074/big-bird-covid-19-vaccine-conservative-backlash-ted-cruz.

Tyler, Tom R. "Viewing CSI and the Threshold of Guilt: Managing Truth and Justice in Reality and Fiction." *Yale Law Journal* 115 (March 2006): 1050–85.

U.S. Const., Amend. I.

U.S. Const., Amend. II.

U.S. Const., Amend. X.

U.S. Const., Amend. XIV,§ 1.

U.S. Const., Amend. XV.

U.S. Const., Amend. XXVII.

U.S. Const., art. I, § 4.

U.S. Const., art II.

U.S. Const., art. III.

"US Supreme Court to Hear Case of Artist Threatened Under 'Orwellian' Colorado Law." Alliance Defending Freedom, February 22, 2022, https://adflegal.org/press -release/us-supreme-court-hear-case-artist-threatened-under-orwellian-colorado -law?sourcecode=10020697_r200.

United States v. Miller, 307 U.S. 174 (1939).

Vaglica, Paul E. "Step Aside, Mr. Senator: A Request for Members of the Senate Judiciary Committee to Give Up Their Mics." *Indiana Law Journal* 87 (Fall 2012): 1791–824.

Vandevelde, Kenneth J. *Thinking Like a Lawyer: An Introduction to Legal Reasoning.* Boulder, CO: Westview Press, 1996.

Varol, Ozan O. "The Origins and Limits of Originalism: A Comparative Study." *Vanderbilt Journal of Transnational Law* 44 (November 2011): 1239–97.

Vermeule, Adrian. "Beyond Originalism." *Atlantic*, March 31, 2020, https://www .theatlantic.com/ideas/archive/2020/03/common-good-constitutionalism/609037/.

———. "Supreme Court Justices Have Forgotten What the Law Is For." *New York Times*, February 3, 2022, https://www.nytimes.com/2022/02/03/opinion/us -supreme-court-nomonation.html.

Vitiello, Michael. "How Imperial Is the Supreme Court? An Analysis of Supreme Court Abortion Doctrine and Popular Will." *University of San Francisco Law Review* 34 (Fall 1999): 49–98.

Vladeck, Stephen I. "Roberts Has Lost Control of the Supreme Court." *New York Times*, April 13, 2022, https://www.nytimes.com/2022/04/13/opinion/john-roberts -supreme-court.html.

———. "The Solicitor General and the Shadow Docket." *Harvard Law Review* 133 (November 2019): 123–63.

"Voting Laws Roundup: December 2021." Brennan Center for Justice, December 21, 2021, https://www.brennancenter.org/our-work/research-reports/voting-laws -roundup-december-2021.

"Voting Laws Roundup: February 2022." Brennan Center for Justice, February 9, 2022, https://www.brennancenter.org/issues/ensure-every-american-can-vote/ voting-reform/state-voting-laws.

Waldman, Michael. "How the NRA Rewrote the Second Amendment." *Politico*, May 19, 2014, https://www.politico.com/magazine/story/2014/05/nra-guns-second -amendment-106856/.

Waldman, Paul. "The Supreme Court's EPA Ruling Says: We'll Do Whatever We Want." *Washington Post*, June 30, 2022, https://www.washingtonpost.com /opinions/2022/06/30/supreme-court-epa-climate-change-conservative-message/.

Walter, Barbara. *How Civil Wars Start*. New York: Crown, 2022.

Ward, Myah. "Trump, in Return to D.C., Hints at 2024 While Rehashing 2020." *Politico*, July 26, 2022, https://www.politico.com/news/2022/07/26/trump-dc-2024 -capitol-riot-00048052.

Warren, Elizabeth. "Expand the Supreme Court." *Boston Globe*, December 15, 2021, https://www.bostonglobe.com/2021/12/15/opinion/expand-supreme-court/.

Warren, LaShawn. "Voting Discrimination is Getting Worse, Not Better." ScotusBlog, February 18, 2021, https://www.scotusblog.com/2021/02/voting-discrimination-is -getting-worse-not-better/.

Warren, Samuel, and Louis Brandeis. "The Right to Privacy." *Harvard Law Review* 4, no. 5 (December 1890): 193–220.

Washington, George. "Farewell Address." National Archives, September 17, 1796, https://founders.archives.gov/documents/Washington/05-20-02-0440-0002.

Wegman, Jesse. "Gerrymander, U.S.A." *New York Times*, July 12, 2022, https://www .nytimes.com/2022/07/12/opinion/texas-redistricting-maps-gerrymandering.html.

———. "Ginni and Clarence Thomas Have Done Enough Damage." *New York Times*, March 25, 2022, https://www.nytimes.com/2022/03/25/opinion/ginni-clarence -thomas-trump.html.

———. "Justice Thomas Should Take a Long Look in the Mirror." *New York Times,* May 15, 2022, https://www.nytimes.com/2022/05/15/opinion/clarence-thomas -supreme-court.html.

———. "The Supreme Court Is Out of Step with Most Americans." *New York Times*, May 3, 2022, https://www.nytimes.com/2022/05/03/opinion/supreme-court-roe -wade.html.

Wehner, Peter. "The End of Trump Can Be the Beginning of America." *New York Times*, January 22, 2021, https://www.nytimes.com/2021/01/22/opinion/trump -legacy.html.

Weisman, Jonathan. "Spurred by the Supreme Court, a Nation Divides Along a Red-Blue Axis." *New York Times*, July 2, 2022, https://www.nytimes.com/2022/07 /02/us/politics/us-divided-political-party.html.

West Virginia v. Environmental Protection Agency, 142 S. Ct. 2587 (2022).

Westneat, Danny. "The Myth at the Heart of the Praying Bremerton Coach Case." *Seattle Times*, June 29, 2022, https://www.seattletimes.com/seattle-news/politics/the-myth-at-the-heart-of-the-praying-bremerton-coach-case.

Whitehouse, Sheldon. "Sen. Whitehouse: Three New Supreme Court Justices Being Told What to Do by Donor Front Groups." Interview by Joy Reid, *The Reidout*, MSNBC, March 23, 2022. Audio, 2:05. https://www.msnbc.com/the-reidout/watch/sen-whitehouse-speaks-about-dark-money-at-ketanji-brown-jackson-s-supreme-court-hearing-136040005543.

Whitney v. California, 274 U.S. 357 (1927).

Whittington, Keith E. "The New Originalism." *Georgetown Journal of Law and Public Policy* 2 (Summer 2004): 599–613.

Whole Woman's Health v. Jackson, 642 S.W.3d 569 (Tex. 2022).

Whole Woman's Health v. Jackson, 141 S. Ct. 2494 (2021).

Whole Woman's Health v. Jackson II, 142 S. Ct. 522 (2021).

Wiesman, Steven R. "Introduction to Daniel Patrick Moynihan." In *Daniel Patrick Moynihan: A Portrait in Letters of an American Visionary*, edited by Steven R. Wiesman, 1–25. New York: Public Affairs, 2010.

Wilkinson, J. Harvie III. "Of Guns, Abortions, and the Unraveling Rule of Law." *Virginia Law Review* 95 (April 2009): 253–323.

———. "Subjective Art; Objective Law." *Notre Dame Law Review* 85 (June 2010): 1663–86.

Williams, Pete. "Supreme Court Chief Justice Roberts Stresses Need for Judicial Independence," NBC News, December 31, 2021, https://www.nbcnews.com/politics/supreme-court/supreme-court-chief-justice-roberts-stresses-need-judicial-independence-n1286813.

Williamson, Elizabeth, and Emily Steel. "Conspiracy Theories Made Alex Jones Very Rich. They May Bring Him Down." *New York Times*, September 7, 2018, https://www.nytimes.com/2018/09/07/us/politics/alex-jones-business-infowars-conspiracy.amp.html.

Willis, Jay. "A Brief Guide to Supreme Court Confirmation Hearings, the Silliest Ritual in Washington." *Balls and Strikes*, March 15, 2022, https://ballsandstrikes.org/nominations/supreme-court-confirmation-hearings-brief-guide.

Wisconsin Legislature v. Wisconsin Elections Commission, 142 S. Ct. 1245 (2022).

Wolf, Richard. "Supreme Court Sidesteps Major Second Amendment Case, a Setback for NRA." *USA Today*, April 27, 2020, https://www.usatoday.com/story/news/politics/2020/04/27/guns-supreme-court-setback-national-rifle-association/2634492001/.

Wolsey, Roger. "Progressive Christianity Isn't Progressive Politics." Huffington Post, February 10, 2012, https://www.huffpost.com/entry/progressive-christianity-isnt-progressive-politics_b_1897381.

Woodward, Bob, and Robert Costa. "Virginia Thomas Urged White House Chief to Pursue Unrelenting Efforts to Overturn the 2020 Election, Texts Show." *Washington Post,* March 24, 2022, https://www.washingtonpost.com/politics/2022/03/24/virginia-thomas-mark-meadows-texts/.

Woodward, Calvin, and Hannah Fingerhut. "Supreme Court Leak Further Erodes Trust in Government." Associated Press, May 8, 2022, https://www.pbs.org/newshour/amp/nation/supreme-court-leak-further-erodes-public-trust-in-government.

Zeitlin, David J. "Revisiting *Richardson v. Ramirez*: The Constitutional Bounds of Ex-Felon Disenfranchisement." *Alabama Law Review* 70, no. 1 (2018): 259–92.

Zelman, Elizabeth Crouch. *Our Beleaguered Species: Beyond Tribalism.* Scotts Valley, CA: CreateSpace Publishing, 2015.

Zernike, Kate, and Adam Liptak. "Texas Supreme Court Shuts Down Final Challenge to Abortion Law." *New York Times*, March 11, 2022, https://www.nytimes.com/2022/03/11/us/texas-abortion-law.html.

Zhou, Li. "Republicans Made Ketanji Brown Jackson's Confirmation Hearing About Brett Kavanaugh." *Vox*, March 21, 2022, https://www.vox.com/22990018/ketanji-brown-jackson-confirmation-hearing-brett-kavanaugh.

Ziegler, Mary. *Abortion and the Law in America: Roe v. Wade to the Present.* Cambridge: Cambridge University Press, 2020.

———. "The Conservatives Aren't Just Ending Roe—They're Delighting in It." *Atlantic*, May 3, 2022, https://www.theatlantic.com/ideas/archive/2022/05/supreme-court-leak-overturn-roe-polarization/629743/.

———. "The End of Roe Is Coming, and It Is Coming Soon." *New York Times*, December 1, 2021, https://www.nytimes.com/2021/12/01/opinion/supreme-court-abortion-mississippi-law.html.

———. "Grassroots Originalism: Judicial Activism Arguments, the Abortion Debate, and the Politics of Judicial Philosophy." *University of Louisville Law Review* 51 (2013): 201–38.

———. "Roe's Death Will Change American Democracy." *New York Times*, June 24, 2022, https://www.nytimes.com/2022/06/24/opinion/roe-v-wade-dobbs-democracy.html.

Zietlow, Rebecca E. "The Judicial Restraint of the Warren Court (and Why it Matters)." *Ohio State Law Journal* 69 (2008): 255–98.

Zilis, Michael. "The Political Consequences of Supreme Court Consensus: Media Coverage, Public Opinion, and Unanimity as a Public-Facing Strategy." *Washington University Journal of Law and Policy* 54 (2017): 229–43.

Acknowledgments

A project like this typically is not completed without the help of several people. This one is no exception. First, there are the good people at Lexington Books who saw the promise that the book held from its humble beginnings. I especially want to thank both Sara Noakes and Carter Moran for their quick, professional, and insightful answers to my many questions throughout the process.

Second, my thanks to Arizona State University and my colleagues at the Cronkite School of Journalism and Mass Communication for their support on multiple levels. This project is especially a testament to the value of sabbatical leave and the opportunities it provides for focused research, analysis, and writing.

Third, my appreciation to friends and family who offered encouragement. This especially includes my wife, Julie, who, though she often questioned whether devoting my days, weeks, and months at the computer was the wisest way to spend my sabbatical leave, never wavered in her loving support. The jury remains out on her question.

Lastly, a special thanks to the special people who agreed to review all or parts of this book's manuscript drafts: Wat Hopkins, Elliot Rothenberg, Case Smith, Rod Smolla, Bob Trager (aka "Trager"), and Kyu Youm. Not only did each of them make this book better in his own way, but their inspiration over the years surfaces in these pages.

As this project neared completion, I was especially mindful of the progression from Trager—a Stanford Law graduate, my mentor, one-time professor, and dissertation director more than a few years ago—to Case—a former student of mine whose senior honors thesis I directed, and who is studying at Harvard Law as of this writing. The torch is passed, and the fire burns.

Index

Index

Due Process Clause. *See*
	Fourteenth Amendment
Dworkin, Ronald, 70n57

economic gaps, 18, 33n20
Effectiviology, 66n29
"Eighty-One Percent" (Stewart), 135n9,
	136n24, 137n26, 168n38
Eisler, Kim Isaac, 69n48, 73n80
election law. *See* voting rights
Emmerich, Charles J., 118n4
"Ending *Roe* Is Institutional
	Suicide" (Feldman), 139n61,
	140n66, 177n131
Enlightenment Now (Pinker),
	35n33, 42n130
Epstein, Lee:
	on death of Ginsburg, 119n11;
	party and nominee ideology, 110;
	religious liberty and, 109,
		119n14, 120n16
Equal Justice Under Law, lack
	of, 162–63
Establishment Clause, 114–15. *See also*
	religious liberty
Everson v. Board of Education, 118n3
exclusionary nationalism, 20
Executive Order No. 14,023. *See*
	Presidential Commission on the
	Supreme Court of the United States
"Expand the Court" (Warren),
	165n14, 176n111
expert advice, ignoring if not liking,
	40n112, 41n116

factionalism, 154–55, 173n82
facts, beliefs versus, 29. *See*
	also science
false realities, 29, 34n22
Fandos, Nicholas, 42n129
"Farewell Address"
	(Washington), 32n13
Farias, Christian, 72n71, 90n7, 129,
	142n98, 163n1
fear and safety:

confirmation process and, 150;
gun laws and, 39n95, 95–96;
opponents as menace, 20, 36n43,
	45n162, 121n38;
populism and, 17–18,
	32n16, 33n19;
predictability easing, 40n103;
worldview and, 18, 22–24, 95–96,
	103nn10–11
Federal Justice Center, 176n113
"The Federalist No. 10" (Madison),
	172n74, 173n82
"The Federalist No. 37"
	(Madison), 70n57
"The Federalist No. 78" (Hamilton),
	70n57, 156, 173n90
Federalist Society, 170n52, 170n56
Feilden, Tom, 38n85
Feldman, Noah:
	calling *Dobbs* a
		catastrophe, 174n93;
	females excluded
		from constitutional
		ratification, 139n61;
	focus on past by originalists, 130;
	on living
		constitutionalism, 140n66;
	on tyranny of the majority,
		156, 177n131
Feldman, Stephen M., 76n110
Festinger, Leon, 44n151
"Fidelity in Translation" (Lessig), 70n57
Fifteenth Amendment, 91n24
Fillingane, Joey, 138n44
Finley, Bruce, 36n47
firearms. *See* gun rights
First Amendment, 60–61, 77nn122–126,
	118. *See also* religious liberty
Firth, Colin, 38n85
Fisher, Louis, 53
fixed worldview:
	overview of, 20–22;
	abortion rights, 130–31;
	belief confirmation sought by, 27;

sexual orientation discrimination,
xiv, 169n46;
on textualism, 106n39
Gosar, Paul, 18–19
Graber, Mark, 69n52
Graglia, Lino A., 77n118
Graham, Ruth, 124n91
"Graham: Judicial Confirmation
Process" (Kane), 174n99
Grant, Adam, 25–26, 28, 42n127
Grassley, Chuck, 61
"Grassroots Originalism" (Ziegler),
72nn76–77, 73n79, 136n18
"The Great Recession"
(Townley), 32n16
Greene, Jamal:
abortion rights, 126;
expansion of Supreme
Court, 160–61;
on *Heller*, 96–97;
on moral issues, 81;
nuance and flexibility and, 56, 58
Greenhouse, Linda:
on abortion rights, 127, 141n77;
on *Brnovich v. Democratic
National Committee*, 86;
on case selection, 90n8, 104n25;
on *Dobbs*, 129, 138n48,
139n57, 143n113;
on *Heller*, 105n34;
Justice on the Brink, 49–50,
104n25, 105n34, 119n9,
143n113, 169n48;
on *New York State Rifle & Pistol
Ass'n v. Bruen*, 107n52;
on party and nominee ideology,
49–50, 125;
on racial discrimination in
redistricting, 87–88;
on religious liberty, 110, 111;
"Requiem for the Supreme
Court," 139n57, 141n77;
"Stephen Breyer Was the Right
Justice," 73n83;

"The Supreme Court,
Weaponized," 78n134,
90n8, 138n48;
"This Is What Judicial Activism
Looks Like," 67n37
Griswold v. Connecticut, 75n99, 76n112
"The Growing Religious Fervor" (Dias
& Graham), 124n91
gun ownership and death rates, 95, 100,
103n4, 103n6, 103n9, 107n58
gun rights:
expansion of, xii, 78n135;
extended by *New York State
Rifle & Pistol Ass'n v.
Bruen*, 99–102;
in *Heller*, xi, 96–98;
safety associated with guns, 24;
viewed as second class rights, 98,
99, 106n40;
worldview and, 95–96

Haidt, Jonathan, 20, 39n86, 173n81
Hakim, Danny, 164nn8–9, 171n61
Hamilton, Alexander, 70n57,
156, 173n90
The Handmaid's Tale (Atwood), 125
Hartig, Hannah, 141n92
Hasen, Richard L., 94n69
"The Hawthorne Effect"
(Sedgwick), 175n109
"A Healthier Legal Profession"
(Todres), 64n12
Healy, Melissa, 43n139
"Heller and Constitutional
Interpretation" (Little), 104n17
Heller case. See *District of
Columbia v. Heller*
Hendrickson, Mark, 59
"A Heritage of Religious Liberty"
(Adams & Emmerich), 118n4
Herron, Andrew R., 47n183
Hetherington, Marc J. See *Prius or
Pickup?* (Hetherington & Weiler)
higher education, 29, 46nn171–72
historical tradition, focus on, xi–xii

About the Author

Joseph Russomanno is a professor in the Walter Cronkite School of Journalism and Mass Communication at Arizona State University. As a teacher, researcher, and writer, his career has focused on First Amendment law, particularly speech and press freedom, including an emphasis on the role and rulings of the Supreme Court of the United States.

Prior to entering the academy, he was a broadcast journalist in local news, working in both radio and television.

This is his fifth book. He received his PhD from the University of Colorado-Boulder and MA from the University of Missouri.